DG
9/12/06

Beyond The Bridges

Beyond The Bridges

By

Jerry M. Hay

J. R. Simpson & Associates
Florissant, Missouri 63033-1227

Beyond The Bridges

Jerry M. Hay
Floyds Knobs, IN 47119

Published by:
J. R. Simpson & Associates, Inc.
Florissant, Mo. 63033-1227

Printed in the United States of America

Library of Congress Control Number: 2006923829

ISBN 987-0-9703086-6-5

Dedication

To Debbie Goodale, my Sweetie

Table of Contents

Table of Contents Cont.

Illustrations

Illustrations—Cont.

Introduction

Most people cross our river bridges en route to a destination without realizing what is below them. They may glance over the guardrail and see water, but have no idea that they are above a waterway that connects to the rest of the world. A water highway that can be traveled with no traffic jams; a scenic route that offers beauty and peace, a byway that provides adventure and discovery. Many other people cross these bridges with their boats in tow, on their way to a favorite lake. They look down at that river and admire its presence and may even be inspired to experience it, but are hesitant to risk their safety and their boat in those mysterious waters. They travel on to the seemingly safer environment of a lake, missing the opportunity to explore the mysteries and romance of the river.

River boating is different than lake boating and one is wise to be dubious about attempting it with no knowledge of those differences. River boating isn't for everyone. It requires a constant awareness of the surroundings, respect for the river's power, an effort to learn as much as possible about a river, and common sense. These elements, along with proper gear, will allow a boater to do something that few lakes provide. Most lakes are contained, and most boaters on lakes have a very limited range. River boating provides the opportunity to actually travel someplace. Whether it is a short trip to the next town down the river or an extensive trip of days or weeks, the journey will take boaters along a constantly changing shoreline with an established goal to reach. The trip back is just as interesting because rivers appear mysteriously different when going the other direction. Most rivers undergo constant change, so regardless of how many times a section of river is traveled there are new sights to see and challenges to overcome.

River travel offers a unique experience that seldom can be found in this modern world. Most rivers are tree-lined with relatively high banks. This provides the same sense of remoteness and natural beauty that the early explorers encountered. There are fewer indications of civilization along our rivers than anywhere else. Even floating past farm fields and suburban areas, the shoreline corridor of trees serves as a natural barrier, giving us the sense of being at one with nature, with little awareness of what is beyond the riverbanks. Floating past cities and towns is also a pleasant experience. It gives us a different perspective of the city that few people who live there ever see.

To understand the magic of rivers it is important to not only provide specific information about them but to share stories that are interesting, humorous and sometimes unbelievable. My own mistakes are also featured, not only because they are often entertaining, but also so that others will learn from them. The spirit of the river includes its power, its people, and all the fascinating stories that it has created by its whim or the err of man.

Beyond the Bridges offers a blend of river adventure stories with emphasis on lessons learned, interesting features about river towns, and stories of people along the rivers. It provides valuable information for boaters seeking the challenges, beauty, and mysteries of our waterways. Aspects of safe and enjoyable river boating, from canoes to cruisers, are featured. Some of this book is written from aboard my own paddlewheel houseboat, while on voyages of the nation's rivers. Others are written as I work aboard steamboats as Riverlorian. Many are written from a campsite along a riverbank. Experienced river boaters agree that the challenges of traveling rivers and streams require the basic knowledge of navigation, hazards, boat handling, and safety that this book offers. River travel can be a rewarding experience, whether by canoe or the comfort of a steamboat. It allows us to see a part of our world that few people experience. It is my hope that anyone reading this book will never look at the river the same way again, while crossing that bridge. You will be among those of us who appreciate the mysterious world "Beyond the Bridges".

Beyond The Bridges

Chapter 1

A Boy and a Jonboat

Back in the 1960s there was a boy who had spent countless hours throughout his youth hanging around the river. He loved nothing better than to watch the river and talk to the rivermen putting in or taking out their boats. He also lived near an elderly man name Charlie, a retired riverman who enjoyed talking about his days on the river and all his adventures. The boy would sit on Charlie's porch and never tire of hearing his river stories, even if he had heard them before. By the time the boy was fifteen, he had saved enough money to buy an old ten-foot jonboat. It was dented and had no motor but did have a set of oars, complete with oarlocks. The boat wasn't much but it was the boy's pride and joy. He spent many days paddling up and down the river, often pretending that he was on a great journey. He wanted to take trips on the river but his parents were afraid to let the youth go off on his own, on the dangerous river. The boy would argue that paddling in one direction all day posed no more danger than paddling back and forth all day on a section of the river. He also added that if he drowned, did it make any difference if he was two miles down the river or two hundred? His logic had merit but made no difference to his parents.

While on the river one day he met some men with canoes. They were practicing for a long canoe trip that their canoe club members were planning to take on the river. They told him that they were going to put their canoes in one hundred miles up the river and paddle to a point two hundred miles downstream from their starting point. The boy's interest was intense. A two hundred-mile canoe trip would be awesome. He asked the men if the trip was for members only, and they said yes. He asked if a person really had to have a canoe to join the club or would a jonboat do, and they said canoes only. Not yet discouraged, the boy stated that it was a free river and someone could put a boat in at the same place they do. He added that this person could just happen to travel in the same vicinity as them. He went on to propose that this person might even, by chance, be taking his boat out at the same place as the group. The men could not disagree with him but one of them mentioned that there would be no way that a jonboat could keep up with the sleek, fast canoes. The boy continued to ask questions about the date and time of the launching. The men were friendly enough but did not take the boy seriously.

The boy knew how his parents felt about traveling the river alone, so this could be an opportunity to go with adult supervision, or so his story would be. He cleverly insinuated that he had been invited to go with the group on their two hundred-mile trip, and would be looked after by responsible, experienced adults. He did not actually lie, since the men did acknowledge his plan and gave him all the information about the trip. He felt no need to be in the company of the canoe club on the trip, but it provided the opportunity to get his parent's blessing. All he needed was a ride to the put-in spot and a ride home from the take-out spot. After much debate and reassurance by the boy, his father agreed to take him and pick him up.

In the next few weeks the boy was making his plans and gathering supplies for the seven-day trip. He didn't see any reason why he couldn't paddle downstream, thirty miles a day. He had the boat and gear loaded in his father's truck the night before launching day. The next morning they were on their way. Upon arriving at the launching site, the boy asked his dad to stop short of the ramp so that he could fill his water container at the nearby faucet. He was actually trying to keep his father some distance from the canoe club members, who were already at the launching ramp. He needed to keep his Dad from engaging in a conversation with these fellows to discover that the boy wasn't invited on the expedition. As he pulled his boat from the truck bed he said he would just drag it to the river from there. He waved at some of the canoeists, who waved back, then encouraged his dad to leave. After all, he didn't want to look like a daddy's boy. Dad went along with that and pulled away. The boy felt a little guilty for the deception, but the fact was that he would be close to these fellows in case of emergency. Not that he would need them.

He dragged the boat to the water's edge and recognized one of the men in the group as one whom he had spoken to weeks before. The man walked up to him and said, "What the hell?" The boy stated that he was setting off on a paddle trip down the river and figured to go about two hundred miles. The man smiled and wished him luck. The canoeists were not leaving for about two hours but the boy had no use for them at this point. They had served their purpose by just being there, so he pushed off and began paddling down the river. The weather was good and the river was swift. He paddled for nearly half the day before being overtaken by the canoeists. They waved and smiled as they passed him. The boy was surprised to see how much faster the canoes were. They were gliding as though on ice, and each of them had two people paddling. The lone boy in his clumsy boat was left behind. He really didn't expect to keep up with the canoes but seeing them gliding away inspired him to try. He didn't care how long he paddled; he would catch up with them when they camped. He paddled on and on. It was still daylight when he spotted the canoes and tents set up on a beach. It was a long beach so he decided to use the same one for his camp, but a few hundred feet from theirs. He set up his camp, made a little fire, ate hot dogs cooked on a stick, and settled in for his first overnight camp on the river, alone. Well, sort of alone!

The next morning the boy arose before daylight and pushed off while the canoeists slept. He now had a quest. It was to keep up with the canoe club. He would no longer pull over to eat, but let the boat drift and continue moving. He paddled hard but was surprised to see the canoeists pass him at only 9am. They would have a lot more hours to get ahead of him. Regardless of his lack of speed, the boy was thoroughly enjoying his adventure. He was one with the river and felt right at home. He was strong and could paddle tirelessly. Since he was in a jonboat with oarlocks, he paddled with his back facing the direction he was going. When his arms needed a rest he would keep them stiff and use his legs, sliding on the flat surface of the seat. That night it was well after dark when he saw the campfires of the canoeists. Being on the river at night was a new and awesome experience. It was more dangerous and required being very alert. The river looked and sounded much different, and was scary. He could not see approaching snags and other obstacles, so he listened carefully for the movement of water rushing around them. He tried to steer clear of the sounds but sometimes would come to a sudden halt, or the boat would spin around as it hit something. Running into a sawyer or drift pile could capsize the little boat. He paddled on past the canoe camp and found a suitable campsite a couple of miles downriver.

The boy pushed off early again the next day and, as the day before, the canoeists overtook him by mid-morning. This time several of them stopped to see how he was doing. They were surprised to still see the youth and impressed that he had gotten so far in such a vessel. They invited him to camp with them that night if he got that far. The boy thanked them and assured them that he would get that far, wherever it was. He did get there well into the evening. They sat around the fire and chatted for a while, but the boy needed sleep. The weather was so nice that evening that he didn't bother with his tent and used only his blankets under the stars.

Morning came and the boy was startled awake by one of the canoeists. The man told the boy that it was getting on in the day and he might want to get moving if he intended to get a head start again. He quickly gathered his gear and pushed off, eating cold snacks for breakfast as he paddled. Once again the canoeists passed him, right on schedule. The boy was happy that they had treated him so well and was now even more determined to stay with them. He paddled past his hometown and familiar section of river. He felt like an explorer returning from unknown territory, then as he went on he was leaving for the unknown. There was no reason to stop there unless he was to give up after one hundred miles. That thought had not even occurred to him. It was Independence Day and he thought this was about as independent as he had ever been in his life, and it felt good. That night he again caught up with the canoe club at their camp. He thought about going on by and getting a few more miles on the river, but the men spotted him and invited him to come ashore. They had some fireworks to celebrate the fourth of July and was waiting for the boy before shooting them off. They also saved a couple of hamburgers for him, which was greatly appreciated.

After another beautiful night on the river, morning came quickly and the boy slipped away to continue his journey. He figured that he must paddle about two hours for every hour the canoeists paddled. He gouged a large **THANK YOU** message in the sand with a stick for the men to find. This day would turn out to be as nice as previous ones, but the boy was beginning to experience muscle cramps. By early evening he was hurting and exhausted and could go no farther. He considered drifting into the night to gain a few more miles but was afraid he might fall asleep. Sleeping on a drifting boat could prove disastrous. He could be drawn into a logjam, or hit a bridge and capsize the boat. He pulled over at a sandy beach, rolled up in a blanket and slept, short of catching up with his new friends.

The morning found the boy with sore muscles, chapped lips, bug bites, and sunburn. He pushed off very early, hoping to catch up with the canoe club at their camp. He only went about three miles before passing them, still sleeping. The wind had changed direction, whipping into a head wind, that made the little boat more difficult to keep straight and harder to paddle. He wasn't making very good time. He did find that he could do better close to shore in the windbreak created by the trees, but then had less current to help propel the boat. When the canoeists passed him later in the morning they expressed relief at seeing him, having been worried that he may have gotten into trouble. Even the sleek and fast canoes were having trouble against the strong wind. The struggle continued all day and he knew that he must be falling farther behind the group. It wasn't necessary that he stay with them, but it was something he had set out to do since the first day. Toward evening the wind calmed down and the boy began to look for the canoe camp. He paddled on and on into the night with no sighting. It was getting very late, and he was again exhausted and hurting. He decided that he would just lay back and rest a while and drift. Just a short break might ease the pain in his back.

The boat pivoted in the current and caused the rising sun to hit the boy's face, waking him up in a confused state of shock. He had fallen asleep and apparently had drifted all night. The boat was still moving and he had no idea how far he had drifted or where he was. When he realized what had happened he was thankful to even be alive. He had drifted past the canoe camp without being seen and again the men were worried about him. By now they had come to admire this spunky kid and considered him part of the group. The boy paddled on, hoping to see something that might be recognizable on his map. He paddled for about three hours, and then after going around a large bend he saw a water tower. As he got closer, he saw that the sign on the tower had the name of the town where the canoe club was taking their boats out. Could this be? He paddled to the shore and there was the boat ramp as described. This was the town. Where were the canoeists? He finally had it figured out. He had drifted all night, passed their camp, and continued downriver to within a few hours of the destination. He had not only kept up with the canoe club, but had arrived at the destination before them.

After pulling the boat from the water and getting his gear ready to transport, he decided to wait a while before calling his father from a pay phone to pick him up. He just didn't feel right leaving without seeing the canoeists come in, for two reasons. They had waited for him that night to do fireworks. He also wanted to see their faces when they found him already there. A factor that the boy had not considered was that the men had planned to call the police to search for him as soon as they landed. Just after noon he could see a dozen canoes coming around the bend. As might be expected, the men were shocked, amazed and delighted to see the young man waving to them from the landing. As each canoe pulled up there was whooping and congratulations to each other for completing the trip. The boy was included in the celebration. Some of them walked into town to call for their rides. One man told the boy that there would be room in his truck for his boat and gear if he wanted to ride. He accepted and was delivered home.

After arriving home and telling of his adventure, the boy's father walked outside with him and began quizzing him about the canoe club and how he had become a member. He was asking tough questions that the boy was having trouble answering, without lying. His father smiled and admitted to knowing about the boy's manipulation of the truth from early on. Upon the first mention of the trip he had contacted one of the fellows he knew in the canoe club and found out that his son was not a member, nor had he made any plans with the club to be with them on the trip. But his father knew how much the boy wanted to make the trip and asked the man if he would mind keeping an eye on him. His dad knew the whole scam the boy had planned, even as he took him to the put-in spot where the boy had tried to keep his father from talking to anyone there. What surprised the boy's father and everyone in the club was that he not only finished the trip, but beat them to the take-out. They all assumed that a couple of days would be all the kid could take, then they would get to a phone to call for his father to pick him up. A few weeks later, the canoe club had a party to celebrate the successful journey. The boy was invited and was given one of the official medals they all received for completing the trip. He was also given membership to the canoe club, the only member they ever had with no canoe.

Note from author: That medal, given so many years ago, is highly valued by its owner to this day. I know because I am the owner...... I was that boy.

A few years later I had acquired more than oar power for that jonboat, having advanced to the use of an outboard motor. I worked part-time jobs and saved enough to buy a used ten-horsepower motor. This considerably increased the range that could be traveled and provided an easier way to go upriver. If I had gas and oil, I was happy. The boat had some additional improvements, like a pad for the aluminum seat, fishing rod holders, a store-bought anchor (no more concrete blocks for me), and other gear that made cruising nicer. Sometimes I would travel upriver until the fuel ran out, then drift or paddle back to the landing. Each journey became a bit farther and required increasing the number of gas cans. It did not take long to begin understanding that hitting shoals and logs with an outboard was much more costly than banging the obstruction with oars, and so began the fine art of reading the river more carefully.

I was very happy on the Wabash River with my little boat and had visions of what it must have been like in the days when steamboats traveled that river. There was one steamboat still operating called the *Delta Queen,* but she would never be able to come up the Wabash with her great height and deep draft. I had planned to see that legendary boat someday and maybe even take a ride on her. What an incredible river trip that would be. Then I began to hear some bad news about the *Delta Queen*. A tragedy on another boat would cause the government to take actions that would shut the *Delta Queen* down.

In the 1960s an offshore passenger ship named *Yarmouth Castle* burned with a tragic loss of life. The ship had a steel hull, but a wooden superstructure. It was an American-registered vessel and the reaction of Congress was to pass a new law with very broad terms. In simple terminology, the law stated that no vessel would be allowed to carry fifty or more overnight passengers if it was made of wood. This law was written with ocean-going vessels in mind, but Congress had not considered the only overnight passenger boat at the time on the inland waterways. The *Delta Queen* also has a steel hull and wooden superstructure, but does not travel offshore. She is always close to a riverbank and can be evacuated easily to shore, without causing passengers to endure the sea. Regardless of that, the *Delta Queen* was included in the law and would have to shut down. A great effort by many loyal fans and supporters was begun to save the boat. They were successful in getting a two-year exemption from the law. The exemption provided that the boat must be made fireproof, which is impossible without rebuilding the entire boat down to the hull. The owners did make many improvements, including fire-resistant paint and a sprinkler system, but there was resistance to allowing another extension. It appeared that the *Delta Queen* was doomed.

In 1970 the *Delta Queen* was making her last run on the rivers. As she made her way down the Ohio River, many people came to the

riverfront to get a last look at her. Some schools were dismissed so
that children could see the last steamboat in history. At some towns
where she landed, taps were played as she pulled away. I was keeping up on this and just had to be one of those who would get a last
look at the *Delta Queen*. I decided that I would do it, and what better way than by boat? I began making plans to take my little jonboat with my ten-horsepower motor and set out to see the *Delta
Queen* as she came down the Ohio River. The trip would mean going
about 150 miles down the Wabash River to the Ohio River, then 89
miles to Paducah for a total of 239 miles. Having no real good idea
about how much fuel the journey would take, I bought and bor-
rowed as many gas cans as I could carry. The *Delta Queen's* final
journey was published in newspapers, so I knew what day she was
scheduled to be at Paducah.

I left early one morning, allowing three days to get there.
Squatting on the bench seat, with my body twisted sideways, operating a tiller outboard was never a problem for a few hours of intermittent cruising. I will admit that even as a teenager that position
became very uncomfortable, but I figured out a way to make it more
bearable. I would lock the motor pointed straight and steered by
using an oar along the side of the boat at the water's surface, like a
rudder. I also piled some of my gear on top of the gas tank and tied it
down for a backrest. This worked fine until the motor would hit a
sandbar and send the little boat careening out of control until I could
grab the tiller handle. I was coming onto New Harmony, Indiana,
when I decided to get more fuel, as I had no idea where fuel could be
found on the Ohio River. I carried two empty five-gallon cans nearly
two miles to a gas station and filled them up. As I started to walk
back with eighty pounds of gas, a nice fellow in a pickup truck pulled
over and offered to give me a lift, which I gratefully accepted. Hoosier
hospitality was alive and well. After heading on down the river, I
camped overnight near the mouth of the Wabash and Ohio rivers and
spent the evening watching the enormous towboats go by. I had never
seen such monster-size boats and wondered how well my little boat
would handle the wake from those beasts. The Ohio River was so
wide that I could barely see the other side. I knew that this would be
a different river world than I was used to.

Upon turning onto the Ohio River I was scared and with good
reason. I had only about ninety miles to go, which was plenty of
time. It was fortunate that I had the time because of the high winds
on that big river, creating large waves. Jonboats have a flat bottom
and are not designed for choppy waters. To try to get up any speed

caused terrible jolts as the bottom slapped against the waves. I had to zigzag to maintain an angle to the chop and the wakes from towboats in order to keep the water from washing over the bow and into the boat, and to prevent being rocked from side to side. Progress was very slow. I found that I could stay close to the bank and on the inside of bends to get out of some of the wind and wakes in the main channel. Later in the afternoon it clouded up and cooled off, causing the winds to die down. I had thought it would be very cool to catch up with and overtake the *Delta Queen* on her way to Paducah, but at the speed I was making she would more likely overtake me. After arriving at Paducah, I set up camp on the point of a large island across from the mouth of the Tennessee River and went a few hundred yards up the Tennessee to be able to add another river to my list of rivers traveled. I continue to keep this list, that has grown considerably over the years. Downtown Paducah and the boat landing were within sight, so it made an ideal place to watch for the *Delta Queen*. I didn't know what time she would be coming in the next day, but hoped to see her come by my camp to make her landing at Paducah. Another evening was spent watching towboats and the busy harbor along the Tennessee River.

The next morning I woke up later than I had expected. It was 8am, but that was not a concern. Being a light sleeper, a 275-foot steamboat going by would wake me up, with the channel so close. I climbed out of the tent and looked upriver on the chance that the *Delta Queen* may be coming in. I saw nothing. Then I turned to go back into the tent and there she was. The *Delta Queen* was landed at the riverfront. How did she get past me without waking me up? Oh well, it wasn't that important, and I didn't even think about that until later because I was so awed by the sight of her. What an absolutely beautiful boat. She looked much larger than I had imagined. I didn't know how long she would be at Paducah, so I hurried to break camp and get across the river for a closer look. After landing and tying off my boat I walked to the stage where people were getting on and off. Porters were carrying supplies onboard. It was a very busy place. I stood watching and walked the length of the boat several times. A man in uniform was near the stage, so I started asking him questions. After I told him about my trip to see the *Delta Queen,* he invited me to go aboard and look abound. I couldn't believe it! I was going aboard the legendary *Delta Queen* steamboat. I walked up the main stairs and into a large lounge area. It was like stepping back into time, when steamboats ruled the rivers. I saw the famous grand staircase leading to a bar. I walked every floor of the boat, taking it all in. The engine room was fascinating to me and the engineer showed me how it all worked. The man in uniform, who let me on the boat, was the first mate, and upon seeing me again offered to take me to the pilothouse. On entering the pilothouse I expected to see a ship's wheel, but it had levers for steering. He said that was changed in 1953 for a safer steering system with hydraulics instead of cables. I couldn't believe that I was in the pilothouse of the famous boat. All the crew who I met was great and I felt bad that they were going to lose their jobs, particularly when I saw the pride they had in their work and the *Delta Queen*.

The boat was scheduled to leave Paducah at noon, so I stayed on until the last call was made by the captain for all visitors to go ashore. I wished I could go with them. I would have cared about nothing else, including leaving my boat unattended, for a ride on that boat. I stood at the landing as the boat backed off, and into the channel. Steam was released from the capstan as she turned downriver. I watched and listened as the calliope played and onlookers chanted, "Save the *Delta Queen*". As I watched the beautiful steamboat fade away down the Ohio River, I was very happy to have gotten to know her, but sad that I would probably never see her again. Little did I know that the *Delta Queen* would be saved and continue to ply the rivers. Little did I know that some thirty years later, I would be one of the proud crew of that magnificent boat.

Photo by Author

The Steamboat Delta Queen

Chapter 2

The Wabash 500

I have done many exciting and adventurous things in my life, including cross-country motorcycling, sky diving, scuba diving, caving and more. I even got close to an erupting volcano in Hawaii, but I can say without hesitation that I like nothing better than a cruise on a river. Most of my journeys have had some level of adventure, beauty, friendship, and many lessons learned.

One of my most memorable and well-publicized trips came about when my friend, Dennis came to me with a unique idea. There was no record of anyone ever traveling the entire length of the Wabash River in a powerboat. The reason is because the Wabash begins as a tiny stream and gains size on its five hundred-mile course to the Ohio River. The first one hundred or so miles are rocky, shallow, and narrow and are difficult to navigate, even in a canoe. An important piece of equipment for a journey would be the right boat. Dennis had already purchased a 17-foot flat-bottom aluminum bass boat, with an inboard jet drive. This would allow operation in very shallow waters. He then had a canvas cabin built on the boat for weather protection. We began serious planning of what we came to call the "Wabash 500."

Dennis would be the pilot, and turned out to be very skillful at it. He had a knack for handling tricky maneuvers and had quick reflexes. Our next crewman was to be a fellow name Percy, our engineer. Percy is a Kentucky-born mountain man who once hiked the entire Appalachian Trail. Being mechanically inclined, he was responsible for upkeep of the vessel and as it turned out, clever at figuring out how to solve other problems. Another member of the team was Rod. He was to follow our route in a truck and provide us with fuel and other necessities. He would camp with us each night (when he could find us), and we would keep in radio contact with him, when within range. My job was to be navigator. My responsibilities included using my own maps, along with highway maps, keep a journal, and generally I was supposed to know where we were. I was also to read the river ahead of the boat, watching for hazards, and to select rendezvous points to meet Rod.

The Wabash is a very remote river with no marinas. In some stretches it is 40 miles between bridges and many of those are in remote locations with nothing to offer in supplies. It was necessary to plan well for fuel, supplies, and locations to meet our chaser truck. Once the boat was completely outfitted we decided to make an overnight test run. We put her in the river and headed upstream, (always test upstream so you can float back in a breakdown). We loaded the boat with as much gear as we would take on the longer journey. The canvas cabin was small for three men, but sufficient. A local TV station heard about our plans and interviewed us before embarking on our test run. The boat handled remarkably well considering the load, but I could see that we were drawing somewhat more water than the few inches that we expected. At full throttle it would get up on plane and run much shallower. In shallow water the choice is to run slow and deep, with a greater chance of hitting submerged rocks, or to run fast and shallow with less chance of striking rocks. But if the latter happens the damage could be extensive. All seemed well after about 30 miles, then we made a mistake. How a boat with three experienced rivermen failed to see a gravel bar at the mouth of a tributary is a mystery, but it happened. The boat bottom scraped over the rocks, the engine seized up, and we came to an abrupt halt.

It was easy enough to free the boat since we were able to stand in the shallow water and push. When Dennis attempted to restart the engine he found it to be locked up. Not being sure what happened, our only choice was to drift downstream to the town of Montezuma. Dennis called a friend to bring the trailer there, where we took the boat out and went home. Our shakedown cruise ended short of our expectations. We later discovered that rocks had shattered the jet drive intake shield located in the hull. A piece of the shield lodged in the impeller, which seized up the entire drive train. Knowing that on the Wabash 500 trip we would likely hit more gravel bars and rocks, some alterations were needed. The solution was to have a stronger intake shield. A few days later Dennis installed a custom-made stainless steel shield. With that being the only serious problem we encountered, the boat was now ready for the trip. All we needed now was higher water.

Prior to the trip I had scouted the river by automobile. This mission was to determine where supplies could be found and to look for other difficulties. I found some serious log jams but that could be solved with an onboard chain saw. I also needed to find out about bridge clearances on the upper river. For the trip to be successful we needed enough water to float the boat but not too much, as we could not get under some of the low bridges. I met a man name Ernie in the little town of New Corydon, Indiana. The town is located in east-central Indiana near the Ohio border. Ernie lived near one of the low bridges and agreed to call me when the river level was just right. How would he know? I took measurements of the clearance and painted two marks on the bridge support. A water level between those marks would provide the right level to float the boat while enabling us to get under the bridge. Upon completing this mission we began the wait, as the beginning of our journey was now in Ernie's hands.

A few weeks later there had been quite a lot of rain in the northern part of the state and I was expecting a call from Ernie at any time. We finalized our plans and the call finally came. Ernie was out of town but indicated that the river had been much higher and was now going down, with the level right between the marks. Since the river was now dropping we left the next morning for Fort Recovery, Ohio, which is near the headwaters of the Wabash. We wanted to get beyond the low bridges as soon as possible. At Fort Recovery there is no launching ramp so we backed the trailer down a little dirt road and into the river on some fairly solid ground. Upon having a short ceremony and placing a sign on the boat, "Ohio River or Bust", we set off in what appeared to be deep water but it was only deep for about one hundred yards around the first bend. There the river widened, then split into ribbon-like creeks meandering around sandbars. We ground to a halt in the low water. We could see deeper water ahead but had to get the 2,000-pound boat past the shallows. This required pulling, pushing, and winching from trees. That first obstacle took about two hours. We were happy to get back aboard the boat and go on. We made a few hundred feet then the same thing happened again. This went on all day. The river had drained off much faster than we expected and was still falling. At the end of the first day I calculated our progress. We had made six miles that day. I figured at this rate that it would take eighty-three days to complete this trip, so it just had to get better. Most of the day had been spent walking and we were tired. We could not make it to a bridge where Rod was to meet us, so he went to a motel in Ft. Recovery while we camped.

Early the next morn-ing I checked a stick that I had placed at the water's edge and found that the river had not dropped much and was nearly stationary. That was good news! We shoved off again and the

water depth kept getting better. We celebrated as we went under the state line bridge into Indiana. As we approached New Corydon I could see my marks on the bridge. The level was nearly two feet below the bottom line. There would be no problem with clearance under the

Photo by Author

Stuck in the shallows

bridges. We continued to run aground and were never able to go faster than an idle. Just past New Corydon a huge log jam became our next obstacle. We broke out the chain saw and went to work, taking about three hours to cut a narrow path through it. The temperature had dropped that day and we spent most of it in the cold water. In this section the river has changed its course many times creating oxbows, or false rivers. The maze of waterways is confusing and several times we had to turn back and find the active channel, after running into a dead end. Approaching Bluffton, Indiana, things began to look better. The river was still shallow in many places and had a rocky bottom, but we were making much better time. We got a treat at Bluffton as a fast food restaurant was located right at the river's edge. We considered staying there but wanted to push on with a few hours of daylight left. I knew a big obstacle was ahead and wanted to get close to the town of Markle so we would encounter it in morning hours in case of trouble. That turned out to be a good decision. We made it to Markle and set up camp in the dark, having gained 60 miles that day.

The Army Corps of Engineers built a large levee at Markle, with a control gate. The gate would allow water to continue to flow past the town in controlled amounts. The overflow around the levy was a new channel that had been cut into the bedrock. This channel is the only way to get past Markle. At the point where the old river channel and new channel meet is a falls. This causes some serious rapids upstream and an extreme navigational challenge at the falls. I had been through these rapids before in a canoe but never in a heavy boat like we had. At the falls one could choose to take a chute or the cascading drop of about fifteen feet. The chute is the safest bet, assuming one can maneuver into that position. We set out thinking we would pull over to the bank near the chute before reaching the falls, and then plan our descent.

Photo by Author

Markle Rapids

Percy advised Dennis that if he began to lose control, he should turn the boat around against the current, since jet drives do not have good steering in reverse. Anticipation was mounting as the water began to run faster. We could see many rocks ahead that must be steered around. Passing under the Highway Three Bridge was pretty much the point of no return. Dennis increased the throttle to stay faster than the current, which is a must if you want to steer. Suddenly the boat hit a submerged rock and careened sideways. Dennis tried to right the boat but the current was too strong and we were at its mercy. With no way to get to the chute our only option was the falls, but we needed get the boat turned into the falls. Going through sideways would mean certain capsizing. We all struggled with the oars, attempting to turn the boat, but it slammed into an immovable wall of rocks on the starboard side, coming to a stop. The water swelled up on the port side, nearly swamping the boat. We struggled to keep the boat from flipping over, and then noticed that it had stabilized and was no longer bobbing like a cork. In fact it became motionless and we could walk about on it with no tipping. Then we discovered why. The rocks had knocked a hole in the bottom of the boat and it had sunk in the shallow waters. Sinking was probably the only thing that kept if from capsizing. The water had filled the hull under the sub-floor decking and the engine compartment. There we were sitting in the middle of rapids, against some rocks, with a hole in the boat...then it started raining. How were we going to get out of this mess? Being an optimist, I mentioned that those rocks and that hole in the boat may have saved our lives by keeping us from being swept into the falls broadside. Now all we had to do was come up with a way to get

the boat out of the water. How hard could it be? Very hard!

First we had to get a line to shore, with was very difficult. Struggling against the current I slowly worked my way to shore with a rope attached to the boat. It was raining and the water was

Photo by Author
Dragging lines to shore

numbing cold. After getting a line to shore we attached a hand winch to a tree, hoping to drag the boat to shore and perhaps get the truck to that location. At the same time we were in radio contact with Rod, trying to tell him how to find us. All three of us were in the water, pulling and drawing the winch tighter. The tension was too much for the line and it snapped, hit me across my chest and knocked me down. It really hurt but I was apparently not injured. We had plenty of rope but even after doubling the line we stripped the gears on the winch, making it useless. The boat was stuck tight. We were all cold and exhausted. Dennis looked at me and said, "Are we going to get this boat out of here?" I said, "Sure Dennis, you are a smart guy and will think of something." I guess that must have inspired him because he came up with another plan. Rod finally located us by driving on the levee. He had some steel cables and chains in the truck. Knowing that the boat kevels would not be strong enough for the tension of dragging the boat with the truck, we wrapped a tow line around the hull and hooked that to the cable and chains attached to the truck on the levee. With the strong currents, the only safe way we could make the crossings back and forth was to hang onto a rope still attached from the boat to a tree. With the rigging in place Rod moved the truck forward and down the other side of the levee, causing a huge amount of tension on the cable. We stood back! The powerful truck in four-wheel drive struggled, but the boat began to move toward shore, with the aluminum hull grinding on the rocks. There was a deep channel near the shore which was where we needed to take the boat. Finally it was sitting next to the bank. The boat was swamped, but the built-in floatation kept it from sinking further.

The next phase of the plan was to get the boat onto the trailer. The levee bank was too steep to back the truck and trailer down, much less pull a boat back up. Then Dennis had an idea. Drive the truck into the river so that we could push the boat onto the trailer. The water was only a couple of feet deep and had a rock bottom. Rod was apprehensive to try that but since the truck belonged to Dennis it was his call. We plugged up the hole as best we could and began bailing water out, to get it to float as much as possible. The truck traveled along the levee to a slope that would allow it to get into and out of the river. In a short while we saw the Chevy and trailer plowing down the river toward us. Rod turned a circle, yelling to hurry up while he kept the engine running fast to avoid flooding. As soon as he backed up, we pushed the boat onto the trailer and quickly tied it down. Off he went back up the river with the boat in tow. We stood there so happy to see the boat being taken out of the rapids that we had forgotten to say where to meet, and the radio was in the boat. We started to walk upstream along the levee, then spotted the truck and trailer waiting for us. Now it was time for another plan. Do we quit and go home? Not yet! We discovered later that some onlookers had reported our dilemma and we were featured on the Fort Wayne evening news. The reporter had tried to catch up with us for an interview, but we wasted no time looking for a place to repair the boat.

The city of Huntington was not far away, so after finding that the hole in the hull wasn't all that bad we went in search of a welding shop. We found one in Huntington and they had our hull patched in just a few minutes. According to my maps there was a dirt road leading to the river just below the falls. We drove there and were pleased to find that the bank slope looked like it would permit a launching. We eased the boat back into the river and celebrated our victory. The journey wasn't over yet, nor was the challenges. I knew of a spillway dam in the city of Huntington, which should have enough water flowing over and very little drop. If all went well the boat would clear the dam and drop down to the lower water level, but I was now getting concerned. Before that we would have to portage the boat around a large reservoir dam.

We went on as the water widened into the only reservoir on the river. Knowing we must take out, Rod met us at a launching ramp on the lake just above the dam. We pulled the boat out and put in at another ramp just below the dam. The lake gave us a false sense of security, being so deep and easy to navigate. Even with all the rain we had, the river below the dam was shallow and the Army Corp of Engineers was not letting much water through the dam. Again, I was thinking about that spillway (low head) dam at Huntington. Just above that dam is a diagonal shoal that runs across the river. We passed over it with no problem. As we approached the dam, it was difficult to determine how much the level dropped off below it. We pulled the boat over and walked to the dam wall and found a drop of about three feet. There was about eight inches of water flowing over the dam. We knew that the boat would draft about six inches on plane (full speed). This meant that if we ran too slowly, we were likely to hit the dam. We also knew that the boat must be going fast enough so as not to nose-dive into the lower level. There was no place nearby to take the boat out and around the dam without losing many miles of the river, which was something we were reluctant to do. After all, the point of this journey was to travel the entire river. Dennis' boat, so Dennis' decision!

A decision was made. We would lighten the boat as much as possible. Percy and I would stay ashore while Dennis shot the dam. Percy and I would have lines and station ourselves on each side of the dam in case a rescue was needed. The moment arrived. Dennis headed upstream to get a good run, and then punched the throttle wide open. I was below the dam and could only hear the sound of the boat coming until it got within a few yards of the dam. The boat sailed gracefully into the air an incredible distance before making touchdown on the water below. It was a hard but perfect landing, with all of us whooping it up. Dennis took a couple of victory laps on the river then headed for shore to pick us up, nearly crashing into a revetment in his excitement. Another obstacle was now behind us. We camped for the night just below Huntington. We had plenty to talk about that night. It stopped raining, at least for a while.

The river was getting noticeably wider as we continued the next morning. Large tributaries flow in from the many drainage basins. We were making much better time, but dared not become complacent. The river still had surprises in store for us. More shallows, rocks, and snags caused us keep a vigilant eye on the river ahead. Percy developed a good eye for reading the river and would often take the point position for me. We developed hand signals for the pilot to watch for and respond to. Each of us began to rotate positions and all took part in every aspect of the journey. Sometimes the jet drive intake would become clogged with corn stalks or other floating debris, so one of us would have to get under the boat to pull the material out. Since Percy was the smallest, we could hang him from the side of the boat upside down where he could reach the intake. It was nice to finally be able to ride in the boat without having to wade in cold water and push through the shallows. The sky looked threatening that morning and we expected to endure some storms by afternoon. But at least the boat was floating and we were getting some river miles behind us. After what we had been through, why worry about a little storm?

We passed Wabash, Indiana, namesake of the river and the first city in the world to have electric lights. There were no serious problems but the sky was looking pretty nasty and cold winds were pushing from the Northwest. Just past Peru, Indiana, the storm hit, and not at the best place. The river splits into several islands and there was a place between two bridges called "the gauntlet" by the locals. The boat was fairly stable in the wind but the heavy rain made it very difficult to see which channel was best to take. It is hard to read the river when you can't see more than thirty feet in front of the boat. We looked for a place to hold up, but with all the lightning it wasn't safe to land along the tree-lined shore. We pushed on until the boat came to a sudden stop on a sandbar. We had run aground. I said, "This looks like a good place to sit out this storm." So we sat and watched the lightning, trees swaying, and debris flowing down the river. I can't say that it was a relaxing break, but it was as safe a place as any. Lightning is scary stuff but I would rather be in a metal boat than standing in the water trying to push it off. The chances of a hit are the same, but at least a metal boat would send the worst of the charge into the water and not through my body. When the worst of the storm had passed we got out and pushed the boat off the sandbar. At Logansport the river split again creating a large island in the middle of town. Picking the channel side was difficult and our choice was wrong. We hit a large rock hiding just below the surface and immediately watched

Photo by Author
Percy, Jerry, and Dennis (left to right)

for water to come into the boat. This time it just made a dent and we continued. We camped for the night at George-town.

The landing at George-town has a small ramp and picnic park. There was a sign that said no overnight camping. We were tired, hungry and another storm was com-ing in, so we set up camp. A highway runs right next to the landing soon a fellow stopped by

to see our curious- looking boat. He told us that the sheriff would run us off if he came by, pointing at the sign. We ignored the warn-ing and that damn sign. About the time we got everything set and were in the tent, a patrol car pulled in. I told the guys to let me han-dle this and walked toward the car. The deputy got out and said howdy as I returned the friendly greeting. He said "Hey, ain't you the guys I've been hearing about on the news, trying to run this whole river?" I admitted that we were the guilty party. He then said, "Well we are sure happy you stopped in Carroll County. Anything I can do fer yah?" I thanked him and said no, but as it turned out I should have asked him for shelter for the night. I went back to the tent and announced that it was OK, and that I had used my charm and diplomacy to get us out of this mess. My friends were impressed. To top off our evening another storm passed through. We slept through the storm fairly well until the large tent collapsed on us. The water was pouring from the road through the collapsed tent but it was still providing some shelter. When positioned just right we could locate a dry spot under the canvas and so that is how we spent the rest of the night. An alarmed motorist stopped the next morning to see what was going on. Four lumps shaped like bodies under a canvas would get someone's attention, I suppose.

After being awakened by the concerned citizen we discovered blue skies, warm sun, and a rising river. There were a lot of logs and other debris flowing down the river, but the higher water would help us get past the shallows below Georgetown. We packed up and headed out, finding the rapids very mild and deep with an occasional rock to dodge. Just downriver there was a public camp but we did not want to go through the rapids in the evening to get there the night before.

Most of our journey had been to the West, but approaching Delphi, Indiana, the river turns to the Southwest. As we passed Delphi I noted that we had traveled 176 miles. Just below Delphi is a remaining section of the old Wabash-Erie Canal, so we decided to take a little side trip up the canal as far as we could go. Just past the town of Americus we passed the mouth of the Tippecanoe River. This confluence is the site of the well-known Indian battle that made William Henry Harrison famous and become known as Old Tippy. "Tippecanoe and Tyler Too" became his presidential campaign slogan in 1840. Chief Tecumseh's village was located at this junction and named for his brother The Prophet. Prophetstown is no longer there, but a new state park is being constructed at the site. The Tippecanoe is a beautiful waterway and great for canoeing, but too shallow for most powerboats. We had gotten to the place where the Wabash is a big river, and we could run at cruising speed most of the time, which was about 25 miles per hour.

Another landmark city we came to is Lafayette. The city has a very nice riverfront, lined with parks. West Lafayette is home to Purdue University and rowing teams can often be seen on the river. Large islands are commonplace on the river as it widens. We stopped at Attica, Indiana, for supplies then went on down to Covington, where the river turns its course south toward the Ohio River. Covington is located at mile 241. On past Perrysville and Cayuga, we were thoroughly enjoying the pace and nice weather. We spotted several eagles in this section of river. Percy had told me that he had friends who had a cabin on the river near Newport and they might have a surprise for us. It was beginning to get late when we saw a huge blue tarp hanging between two trees along the riverbank. Written on the tarp was "Percy stop here", with an arrow. We pulled over to follow several signs to a nice cabin. On the door a sign said, "The place is yours for the night. Frig is full." What a treat! Hot showers, food, beer, and all the creature comforts were to be enjoyed. After the previous nights of mud, storms, cold, and general discomforts, this was heaven.

The next morning we were all charged up and ready to put some miles under the hull. We soon passed the mouth of Sugar Creek. This is another popular and beautiful creek for canoeists. This was also the place where we hit the gravel bar on our test run, and chose to pass the mouth on the other side of the river. On past Montezuma and Clinton, we arrived at Terre Haute. We did not intend to stay long but had been advised that local television stations would be at the dock at noon to interview us. We were a little early so we stayed upriver for a while so that we could make our grand entrance for the cameras and spectators. I was surprised at how many turned out, being unaware of just how much publicity this trip had generated along the river towns. Terre Haute is the largest city on the Wabash River and my hometown. It has a very nice riverfront park, along with an excellent dock. There is a launching ramp and nice pier. I am always appreciative of river towns that have not forgotten their river heritage and make efforts to keep their riverfronts useful and well kept.

Still fairly refreshed from our night in the cabin, we had no need to go home for anything, so after visiting with friends and doing interviews, we shoved off for the final 200 miles of our journey. Neither low water nor high was to be a problem now. The river stage was just right. We still had to dodge a lot of floating trees and snags, but the river and weather were finally cooperating with our plans. The Wabash has no buoys, charts, or other navigational aides so it is prudent to always be alert for hazards, even in good water. Steamboats used to travel the Wabash up to Terre Haute before if became non-navigable, due primarily to agricultural runoff and bank erosion. These factors have silted up the river, making it too shallow in many places. There are still swing bridges that no longer operate. These are railroad bridges that would swing open to allow steamboats to pass.

At mile 316 the river becomes the border between Indiana and Illinois. Originally the line was drawn in the center of the river but over the years the river has changed course by making cutoffs across bends. Where this has happened, the river may be entirely in Indiana or Illinois but the general accepted dividing line is still the center of the river. At Darwin, Illinois, we saw the Darwin Ferry. This is the last operating ferry on the Wabash. It is cooperatively owned and operated by farmers who use it to take trucks and equipment across the river. It is propelled by an attached jonboat with a diesel inboard drive and steered by overhead steel cables crossing the river. Below Darwin we stopped at Hutsonville, Illinois, to take on fuel. Hutsonville reminds me of a small western town, with one street and storefronts. Then we traveled a few miles further to Merom. Merom is located on a 200-foot bluff on a large bend and offers a great view of the river for many miles. Sightings of other boaters become more common on the lower river. The farther downriver we went the more difficult it was to imagine that this is the same tiny river we were on a few days earlier. Huge islands and long beaches are constant. The riverbank is so remote that there is no sign of human intervention. How refreshing it is to view a river that probably looks the same as it did to explorers over two hundred years ago. We stopped at one of the beaches for a break. Dennis is a city boy and one of the challenges he had been facing was going to the bathroom (number two specifically). He would either use the porta-potty or wait until we stopped at a town. Percy and I had no problem running into the woods to take care of our business. It was at this island that Dennis made a big step toward becoming a wilderness man. He headed off into the woods determined to overcome his phobia. He was gone for a long time and we were beginning to wonder what happened to him, but then finally saw him return to the boat with a big grin on his face. We asked him to tell us all about it but he refused. We could see he was proud though and he did bring it up several times during the day. He had finally gone in the woods and become one with nature. I'm just happy that I was there to share in his triumphant moment.

We passed historic Vincennes, Indiana, and under the beautiful Jefferson Memorial Bridge. I have friends at the Vincennes Boat Club who had offered to let me spend the night there, but decided to get a few more miles in, so we continued on down the river. The weather appeared to be changing again with threatening clouds moving in from the west. We arrived at St. Francisville, Illinois. There is a dock and the park has a shelter with a tin roof. We decided to set up our tent in the shelter, hoping it wouldn't be blown down this time. There is a shallow cave in the bluff behind the shelter, which got my interest. Rod had not found us yet, even though we described exactly where we were. He claimed to be just south of the same bridge we were by. We finally discovered that he was three river miles from us at another bridge, but only a half-mile by car. He eventually found us and we settled in. Rod spotted the cave and thought it would be fun to sleep in it, instead of the tent with the rest of us. He gathered his sleeping bag and went off to the cave.

Later, the storm hit hard. I enjoyed listening to the rain hitting the tin roof of the shelter and we were staying nice and dry with upturned picnic tables shielding the wind. Then we remembered Rod in the cave and wondered how he was doing. After a brief discussion we came to the conclusion that if he wanted to come back to the tent he would do so. Morning came and the sky was clear again. I walked to the cave to see how Rod had done in the storm. He was curled up in fetal position in a very wet sleeping bag. The water coming down the bluff flowed into the cave roof to the wall, and then proceeded to flow across the floor to the outside, passing right under Rod's sleeping bag. He was just too stubborn to admit defeat and come into the dry tent. He never did admit that he had anything but a pleasant night's sleep, but must have been pretty miserable.

The next morning we passed the mouth of the White River. The White is the largest tributary of the Wabash and increases its size considerably. Just above the mouth are rapids in low water, due to the remains of an 1831 lock and dam that washed out during flooding. Its ruins can still be seen and large chunks of rock and concrete create a serious hazard. However, the water was high enough to not cause a problem. The river develops sharp bends from this area to the Ohio, creating a much greater distance to travel than as the crow flies. At Grayville, Illinois, we passed the former channel of the river. Grayville used to be on the river until 1985. During flooding that year, the river cut across the bend and now the town is two miles from the river. The town has asked the Corp of Engineers to put the river back but have had no luck. The little café next to the river has changed its name to the Hard Times Café. The water was high enough that we could have taken the old backwater channel to the town but had no reason to go there.

The next town is the historic village of New Harmony, Indiana. At one time New Harmony was a socialistic society. It is a beautiful place and was our final stopover on the trip. A television station from Evansville had requested we stop there for an interview. The news lady asked each of us a similar question, "What has been the high point of the journey for you?" Percy and I gave the standard answers about team effort, natural beauty, and such things. When the interviewer asked Dennis the question I interrupted and said, "Dennis, aren't you going to tell about your trip to the woods on that Island? Remember how proud you were?" Dennis refused but turned red and the interviewer insisted on knowing the secret. Since she was so persistent I just had to tell her. Even though the lady thought that was very impressive, she chose not to share the accomplishment with her viewers.

We moved on and entered the Grand Chain of Rocks at mile 460. This required some zigzagging and running a chute between islands, but we had no problem. We expected to see the beautiful Ohio River in a couple of hours. We became more quiet in thought while gliding along this huge river, knowing that the end of our journey was near. We rounded the huge bends, passed the beautiful sandy beaches and miles-long islands full of trees. We shut off the engine and drifted for a while just to listen to the sound of silence. At mile 491 we saw the point along the left bank. That point is the end of the Wabash River, where it pours into the Ohio. We could see the John T. Myers Lock in the distant east. We had a little ceremony as we left the brown waters of the Wabash and entered the green waters of the Ohio. This is still a very remote location with no place to take the boat out, so we had to go ten miles down the Ohio to Shawneetown, Illinois, to a launching ramp to meet Rod.

We soon discovered that this flat-bottom boat was in the wrong waters on the Ohio. The western wind was bearing down the river creating massive chop. Towboats were tossing us around like a floating can. Memories came back to me of another journey I took down

Photo by Author
Wabash River enters Ohio River

this river many years before, in a flat-bottom jonboat. Those ten miles took nearly two hours and we were happy to see the ramp at Shawneetown. We also saw lots of people there and wondered what was going on. Maybe some special event? In a way, I guess it was. The people of Shawneetown were there to greet us, having heard about the trip all the way down the Wabash via newspapers, radio, and TV. Rod had also arrived early and alerted folks at one of the local taverns of our ETA. We pulled up to the sight of cameras and an invitation to come to the Cabin for dinner. The Cabin is the nicest tavern in New Shawneetown. We were also offered rooms for the night at the Shawnee Chief Motel, which we accepted. That night at the Cabin we celebrated and partied with the locals who viewed us as celebrity river rats. We had a great time. What a great way to end the journey.

The next morning we all climbed into the truck and headed home. The trip was a success. The boat performed well but was left with a few scars. After taking that trip and discovering just how challenging it was to navigate the Wabash in a powerboat, I was inspired to write a guide book of the Wabash River, noting landmarks, hazard locations, supply locations, detailed maps, and other information. Two years later, the Wabash River Guide Book was published and has been a huge success. At the time of this writing it is in the third edition. I remain grateful to my friend, Dennis Meng, for making that trip possible. We have taken many river trips since then and some of our other adventures are included in this book.

The Wabash River is one of Indiana's best-kept secrets. Most people only notice it when it floods. Other times it is something that passes under bridges without being appreciated for the beauty and challenges this mighty river has to offer. The Indians named it Wah-Bah-Shik-Ka, meaning "water over white stones", for the clear riverbed of limestone in its upper reaches. The French pronounced it Ouabache, which led to the modern-day name of Wabash. It was created during the runoff from melting glaciers at the end of the

Photo by Author
The crew partying at journey's end

last ice age. It is rich in history and was a major transportation route for Indians, explorers, canal barges, and riverboats. The landscape along the river can change suddenly from forest to urban, then from urban to farmland, them from farmland to hills and bluffs. The water can become calm, choppy, slow, swift, deep, or shallow at the turn of the next bend. It is an unpredictable river and at times dangerous. I have traveled many rivers but my heart will always be with the Wabash.

Chapter 3

The Wabash Queen

Paddlewheel boats had always held my fascination and interest. Seeing the legendary *Delta Queen* had left an imprint that fostered my imagination of owning a sternwheeler some day. I had forgotten just how long that had been part of me until I was going through some papers one day that had been packed away for years. I found a folded sheet with a drawing that I had made in my spare time while serving in the U.S. Air Force. The drawing was my dreamboat of the future, which I hoped to build some day. It was a paddlewheel riverboat. While gazing at the drawing I realized that even though I had forgotten about the drawing, my 30-year dream had never dimmed. Over the years I had collected things that could be useful on my future riverboat. One item in particular is a large wooden ship's wheel that was for sale at a nautical shop I visited while vacationing. I just had to have it, knowing that someday I would have the rest of the boat to go with it. Now when most folks build a boat, the steering wheel may be one of the last things they acquire, but that wheel hung on my wall for twenty years just waiting for a boat to be built under it, keeping my vision alive.

A few years ago I was traveling in northern Indiana and spotted a houseboat on a trailer. Upon closer inspection I discovered that it was a classic Yukon Delta. I immediately visualized this as the boat of my dreams. I could see the potential for building a true paddlewheel-powered vessel that I could travel the rivers with in style. It would have an upper bridge with the ship's wheel that could finally come off the wall. The boat was for sale and I made the owner an offer that he accepted. We hooked the old boat up to my truck and I headed home with this wonderful project. When my friends saw it, all they saw was a beat-up old boat. But I saw the future *Wabash Queen* and knew exactly what she would look like when completed.

Starting with the cabin, my first priority was to make it weather-proof by sealing up all the obvious leaks. The streaked walls indi-

cated several leaks in the roof. After caulking known trouble spots on the roof, I coated the entire top with aluminum coating. This material is commonly used on mobile homes. Since I planned to build a fly bridge it was important to seal everything while it could be accessed. I did not want to have to tear it all out later to find a leak. The next

Photo by Author

The "before" photo

decision was what to do with the exterior walls. The existing walls were finished with vertical strips of aluminum siding, similar to a camper. It had many dents, torn places, and was just plain ugly. I could not imagine why a previous owner had painted flowers on the exterior of such a noble vessel, but I did know that they had to go. My first thought was to tear it off and replace it with a similar siding, but I could not find this material. Then I considered using plastic sheeting that is commonly used in bathroom walls. It would be water resistant and low maintenance, but it is thin and would require plywood backing, which is heavy. I decided on 4-inch vinyl house siding. This could be installed right over the existing material. It is waterproof, lightweight, easy to find, and looks good. In fact, I remembered that the *Delta Queen* had similar siding made of wood. If it was good enough for the *Delta Queen* it would be good enough for the *Wabash Queen*.

Before putting siding on, it was important to build the upper helm first so that the siding could continue right up onto the extended walls of the helm console, so it would not have a built-on look. The upper helm was to provide a console for instruments, seating for three, and of course house the ship's wheel for steering. The front of the existing roof was rounded and too weak to support much weight. I built a wooden frame, supported by the stronger sidewalls. After covering the frame with plywood and installing a strong brace to support the wheel, I was ready to put siding on the entire boat. This part was great fun as I could stand back and look at progress quite often. The siding made a huge difference in her looks.

The Wabash Queen was beginning to take shape. Between major steps of the project I spent countless hours on refinements and repairs. The obvious big thing that was still missing was a method of propulsion. Some folks suggested that I should put a paddlewheel on for show but use a more efficient method of moving the boat. I had already decided that if this was to be a paddlewheeler, then it would be the real thing with no hidden screws. I had researched using steam power with the vision of traveling the rivers with only water and wood needed for fuel. A steam engine and boiler system would be hard to find, very heavy, and take up a great amount of space. I looked into small diesel engines, car engines, and even electric golf cart motors. All methods had their advantages and drawbacks. Having put that on the back burner I decided to go ahead with the paddlewheel assembly, being certain that I would be able to rig some type of drive system to it. I used two antique farm planter wheels, a steel axle, and 1"x4" boards. Next I had an aluminum frame built at a local fabricating shop and bolted it to the transom to mount bearings to and carry the paddlewheel.

With the big red paddlewheel now installed, it was irresistible to walk past the stern without giving it a spin. Now the boat had a paddlewheel but still had no power to turn it. But having it on inspired me to reach that goal. The simplest way to transfer power from the

Photo by Author
Paddlewheel is the only propulsion.

engine to the wheel, and provide a single-lever action for forward and reverse, was to use a hydrostatic transmission. Having seen that type of transmission in garden tractors, I began shopping and located an old Wheel Horse tractor with no engine. I knew that there would be a lot of stress on the unit and needed a strong motor mount for the transmission, which had to be mounted higher than the transom. The engine would supply power to the transmission by pulley, and then a chain drive would run the paddlewheel from the transmission. I built the mount with 2"x12" boards, framed in steel. The wood could be shaped easily and absorb vibration while the frame would provide strength and hopefully prevent any twisting. Now I had a boat, a paddlewheel, and a transmission to the wheel, but still no means to power it all.

I needed a test engine to see how the system would work. I am not an engineer and so the size of the pulleys and gears would be guesswork. I purchased an old 16-horsepower, single-cylinder, cast-iron engine from the back lot of a lawn shop. This would at least spin the wheel and give me an idea of how the system would function. Since I considered the engine to be temporary, I built a wooden motor mount and used lag bolts to mount it to the floor, in line with the transmission above it. The boat was not in the water and I had been spinning the paddlewheel for weeks just to see it turn, so when the time came to see it turn under its own power, it was an exciting moment. I fired up the engine and slightly engaged the lever forward. The wheel began to move. I slowly moved the lever back and the wheel reversed. Cool! I again moved the lever forward, this time fully engaged. The entire boat surged as the paddlewheel spun so fast that it became a red blur. I thought, "Hmmm, maybe a gear ratio problem here." Even though it was fun to see it spinning that fast I knew that it was geared way too high and would not have enough low-end torque when in the water. The solution was pretty simple. I kept changing the size of the sprockets and pulleys to lower the paddlewheel rpm until I felt it was about the right speed with the lever fully engaged and the engine about mid-throttle. Now I could not walk past the boat without starting the engine and watching the paddlewheel turning. No more spinning by hand.

The next phase was to devise a method of steering the boat, an important feature not to be overlooked. I located a large stainless steel box at a scrap junkyard and cut two rudder-shaped pieces from it. Each rudder measured 24"x12". I had no idea what size rudders would be best but that was the largest size that I could cut from the box. I mounted the rudders on two pivoting posts on the paddlewheel mount, behind the wheel. I then needed to hook both the upper helm ship's wheel and the lower helm steering wheel to the rudders. Using a standard boat cable steering box in the upper helm, I tied the cable into the existing lower helm cable, then hooked them to the pivoting rudder assembly. Then I discovered a little problem. If I turned the wheel left, the rudders would turn left, causing, the boat to turn right. This was not something that I felt I could get used to. I then built a box with a pivoting arm and tied the steering cable to one side of the arm, then hooked the rudder cable to the other side of the arm. This reversed the action of the rudders and solved the problem.

I had built an extended bow deck that would provide a mount for the swiveling gangway or stage, which would be used to board the boat and take on supplies. Even though I wanted to maintain the sternwheeler integrity of the boat from the exterior, I chose to utilize high-tech and modern conveniences inside. I equipped her with the standard navigation equipment like marine radio, GPS, depth finder, and safety gear, and also installed a lap-top computer, generator, air conditioning, and of course a color TV. The *Wabash Queen* was to be as self-contained as possible so that I could enjoy long journeys to remote places. This meant installing a forty-gallon water supply and six batteries. With inverters and converters built in to my electric box, I could switch to the use of AC and DC items from all means of electric power source. Nearly everything could run off shore power, generator, or battery.

The first time she was to be put afloat for testing I assembled a launch crew of about a dozen friends and two other boats. I didn't want to draw a crowd on the first launch, especially if things went wrong, so I selected a remote ramp on the Wabash River. I backed the tow vehicle down the ramp and she was cast off. Phase one was successful,

Photo by Author
Preparing to launch

being that she floated. She was listing to the port side, which was not a big problem, and solved simply by shifting some weight. I fired her up and slowly engaged the transmission and to most of my friends' surprise, the paddle began to turn and the *Wabash Queen* was moving under her own power. That is until I increased the throttle for a little more speed. That is when the boat began to vibrate badly and the drive chain began slipping on the sprocket teeth, creating a terrible jerking that broke loose the entire transmission mount. We towed her back to the ramp. I considered the test successful because she did the two basic things that would be necessary for a functioning boat. She floated and moved under her own power. Everything else could be worked out. I strengthened the transmission mount and added idle gears with turnbuckles to

help keep the chain tighter and prevent the slippage of the chain on the sprockets. A few days later we re-launched the boat and proceeded downriver to my dock with no serious problems. Steering needed to be improved as it was very sluggish, but I could

Photo by Author
Being towed out of the trees

work on that at the dock.

With the *Wabash Queen* back in the river and at my dock, it was time to test the new rudders that I built. I decided to tie a 100-foot line from the boat to the dock, just in case I had trouble, so that I could pull her back to the dock. The current was very strong and I didn't want to be swept downstream. As it turned out, the rudders worked great but the chain drive broke and caused the boat to lurch to the port side so hard that the rope snapped. So there I was drifting without power in a 6,000-pound boat toward a bridge in fast current. A collision with the bridge would surely wreck the boat. I had no time to think this problem through, but only to act. I pulled in the broken line, put the end in my teeth and jumped in the river toward shore. I swam as hard as I could so I would get to shore before I ran out of slack in the rope. Fortunately, I made it just in time to loop the rope around a tree, just short of the bridge. With the boat now stopped I laid on the muddy bank for a while, recovering from a feat that would have made Crocodile Dundee proud. After resting for a while and pondering whether I might be getting too old for this stuff, I hiked back to my dock and got my other boat, which I used to tow the *Wabash Queen* back. Upon inspecting the rope I discovered that it had apparently gotten burned almost through when it lodged against the muffler pipe during a previous use. Lesson learned: Always check a line before using it. Also, I should have had an anchor onboard and ready to pay out to stop the runaway boat. My motto is that I never make the same mistake twice. I'm too busy making new ones.

With the tests behind me, I had a good idea of what needed to be done and set out to make the necessary changes. After a few more tests I finally had all the bugs worked out, or at least I thought so. One day while cruising downriver with strong current and cross-winds the steering cable fouled going into a tight bend. Before I had a chance to drop anchor the boat swung broadside into the trees. The river was over the bank so there was no shore to bump into, only trees. I tied off to one of them to secure the boat and made repairs to the rudder cables. The next problem was to get out of the trees. I could not move forward or reverse the way the boat was wedged. Fortunately a friend happened by and saw my precarious position. He tied off a line to his boat and was able to tow the *Wabash Queen* back out into the open river so that I could proceed. The boat took a few scratches, one broken window, and one busted stack light, but that's all in a day on the river. The *Wabash Queen* is not a fast boat, but who is in a hurry to get anywhere with this kind of scenery? She makes up for her lack of speed in comfort and efficiency; she runs all day on a few gallons of fuel. And that sound...that mild puckity-puck and water thrashing over the paddles is incredible. The *Wabash Queen* was now ready for a few day's trial run.

I had also made a few recent changes to increase performance. Having observed that the paddles turned at a fairly fast speed without actually grabbing much water, I decided to replace the four-inch-wide paddles with eight-inch ones, doubling the displacement. This made a significant difference in the thrust and allowed the engine to run at a lower rpm. The new problem this change created was increased vibration and strain on the drive train. After looking closely at photos of other sternwheelers I noticed that the entire paddlewheel assembly might be too deep in the water, causing the paddleboards to enter and exit the waterline at too much angle, causing a lift and drag-down thrust at the same time, wasting horsepower. Before making such a difficult change as would be necessary to lift the paddles higher, I wanted to test the theory by weighing down the bow of the boat, which would cause the stern to lift higher in the water. I placed several containers on the bow deck and filled them with water until the paddles lifted about four inches higher. I knew that the boat would not steer as well with the bow down but was delighted to find that the raised stern not only decreased vibration, but also increased the boat's speed. The existing framework allowed me to re-install the paddlewheel assembly about four inches higher, and then I adjusted the linkages and chain. I discovered that the old 16-horsepower engine was sufficient and built a more permanent motor mount.

One of the things that I had discovered in this entire project is that I could locate most of what I needed locally. I could also alter or completely build components to suit my needs. I'm certain that the Wheel Horse Company never had my use in mind for their hydrostatic transmission. From using screen print frame posts for rudder arms to converting planter wheels to paddlewheels, I found ways to make use of what was available. Between hardware stores, lumberyards, junkyards, and a camper store, I have pretty well equipped the boat. Even my dinghy is half of a broken canoe that I cut off and built a transom for mounting a trolling motor. When a visitor was admiring the gangway that I was operating with a series of lines and pulleys, he was surprised to find that it was actually an aluminum ladder with a deck built on it. It was lightweight and strong. The sense of accomplishment with this project has been great. The challenges have been both frustrating and exciting.

Enough improvements had been made to take the *Wabash Queen* out for a shakedown cruise. The Wabash River had been very low. The entire month of September had passed with no rainfall in the valley. It was mid-October and the fall foliage was beginning to take on color. The weather was warm and the nights were clear. The low water would make the upriver part of the journey faster due to slow currents, but navigation would be more challenging with the number of sandbars and snags. I was prepared to deal with that, and then it rained for three days prior to departure and the river rose nearly six feet. I was now wondering how the *Wabash Queen* would handle the strong currents. I figured that if she could go upriver in the swift currents, whirlpools, and other challenges the Wabash unleashes, then she would do fine in navigable rivers. I invited a friend and her dog, Babe, to join me on this test cruise. She loves the river and had been such an inspiration during the building of the *Wabash Queen* that I drafted her for the First Mate position on this cruise. Her dog didn't have any river experience but I was sure that this new world of smells would keep her ever-searching nose quite busy. We decided to head upriver from Terre

Haute with no particular destination in mind. After double-check-ing the list to make sure we had everything we needed, I fired up the engine and pulled away.

The current was very strong so upriver travel was quite slow. I figured we were only gaining about two miles per hour against the current. The weather was good and the river was beautiful, and we were in no hurry. We had not shoved off until late afternoon, so it was dark by the time we passed the small town of Tecumseh. Even in the dark on the far side of the river, the *Wabash Queen* was attracting attention. Some folks at Tecumseh were calling to us and even used their hand-cranked siren as we passed by. I called back a greeting on my loud speaker that we might be able to accept their invitation to stop by on the return trip. A fog was moving in and I wanted to find a spot to beach the boat for the night. I would normally have dropped anchor for the night, but my canine guest was in serious need of relief that could only be enjoyed on land. The night air was cool and the warm river continued to create a dense fog. Scanning the shoreline became difficult. I have a one-million candlepower searchlight, but that much light only reflects back in the fog. It was hard to tell the shoreline from the low-hanging fog. When I spotted a sandy beach I decided to go for it. Allowing for the current I steered the boat upriver for the selected landing spot and she bumped the shoreline right where I expected her to, however, the riverbed was shallower than I expected and we grounded before getting close enough to get off the boat and go ashore.

I decided that another spot would have to be found. We would need to get close enough to shore to at least reach the beach with the gangway. I put the transmission lever in reverse to pull away from the sandbar, but she didn't move. I increased the throttle to get more thrust. The water was thrashing hard, the engine was laboring, and the boat was vibrating, then she finally broke loose. During this time, my attention was on the bow of the boat to see if she was pulling away, so I was not aware of what was happening in the stern. I was preparing to make landfall at another spot when I noticed that the boat was not handling the same. She seemed sluggish and strained. I got out of my seat to check the stern and was shocked to discover about four inches of water in the cabin floor. I didn't know why, but it appeared that the *Wabash Queen* could be sinking. Not knowing where the water was coming from or how fast it was com-ing in, my first priority was to get the boat out of the channel and into shallow water. If she was sinking, I needed to get her to as shal-low of water as possible, for our safety and for the boat's recovery.

I had a bilge bump on board, but it was not wired in yet and would take a few minutes to hook up, and then it might not be enough. I couldn't spare a few minutes anyway; I had to run the boat aground hard! I went back to the helm, restarted the engine, and slammed the transmission in reverse so that I could position the bow toward the beach and run aground. As soon as the paddles churned in reverse I immediately saw what had happened. In hard reverse the paddles were shoveling huge amounts of water over the transom and into the boat. What a relief! Now I knew where the water was coming from and could stop the flow by simply shutting down.

Knowing now that the boat was not sinking, there was no need to run aground, so the next step was to get the boat anchored so that we could begin pumping and cleaning. After I finally got the anchor paid out the boat came to a stop. We now had plenty of time to hook up the pump, move wet items to dry, and clean up the mud and sand that had been shoveled in with the water. By the time we completed our clean-up operation it was late and we were very tired, so I decided to cancel the plan to go ashore and get some sleep. Babe would just have to do her business on the outer deck. My first mate turned out to be a great help during this emergency by keeping a cool head and instantly recognizing ways she could assist. The dog found her relief on the forward deck, which was easily washed off with a bucket. We enjoyed our evening meal and reflected on what we had just been through. I double-checked the anchorage, and then we turned in for the night.

The fog that moved in the night before burned off, with the heat of the morning sun. It was a beautiful morning and it would be much easier to approach the shoreline to check out the boat and take a walk. Still uncertain of what damages there may be to the hull or drive train, I weighed anchor and eased the boat up to a beach that had a steep bank to prevent running aground. After dropping the gangway to exit the boat and securing it with sand anchors and lines, my companions went for a long overdue walk while I checked out the *Wabash Queen*. No serious damage was apparent. The paddles had a few nicks and the chain needed to be adjusted tighter. The stress of powering off the sandbar had slightly bent the transmission mount, creating a little slack in the chain. The beach was a treasure trove of fossils, so I was busy looking for some keepers when I spotted my friend walking along the beach toward me with a leash in her hand and no dog attached. As she approached, I could see that she was upset. She thought the dog would stay close to her in this strange place so she unleashed her. We were not certain whether Babe went to explore or decided to go home, but she ran off along the shore then disappeared into the woods. Each time she approached the dog it would run again. After many attempts, then finally losing track of the dog, she came back to the boat without her. She was afraid that she would never see her dog again. In most cases, I would have been pretty sure that we could just wait and let the dog find her way back to the boat, but being a city dog, and her owner being so upset, I asked her to stay with the boat and I went searching for it.

The long beach was on an inside bend so I was hoping to walk it to the end and come across the dog, but at the north end of the beach there was no sign of her. I then began a zigzag search pattern into the woods to look for her while working my way back toward the boat. I hadn't gone more than one-hundred yards into the woods when I spotted a levee that was quite steep. I guessed it to be too steep for the overweight dog to care to climb. This was good because now I had a perimeter from the beach to the levee that she would be confined within. As I hiked the zigzag pattern I finally spotted her busily absorbing her surroundings with that powerful nose. I was afraid

Author walking his passenger

she might run if I approached her so I squatted down and talked to her from a distance. She eventually came to me and I snapped on the leash. As we walked along the beach toward the boat, I could see my friend looking our way. When she saw that I was returning in the company of her beloved pooch, she began running toward us, arms open, reminding me of those old movie scenes where the couple is running to each other to embrace. The dog was happy to see her and may have run to greet her, but I was not letting go of that leash for any reason. It was not a difficult decision to keep the dog on a leash for all future shore excursions.

We continued our journey upriver. The *Wabash Queen* was running well, the weather was great, and the scenery was magnificent. There were a few places where the river narrowed and caused the current to increase significantly. It became apparent to me that some changes would be needed on the boat to give her even more thrust in faster currents. On one narrow bend the boat could go no faster than the speed of the current and we were not gaining, so I had to hug the shoreline to get out of the channel and benefit from the eddies. Since the *Wabash Queen* has a draft of only eight inches, I was able to run in the shallow, slower moving water there. The stacks are twelve feet above the waterline, so I had to be careful about tree limbs hanging over the water along the shore. We approached a large island, known to as Staff Island. The island is about _-mile long and one hundred yards wide. One side of the island has a deep, narrow channel and the inside chute is very shallow. The channel side is, of course, the boater's choice when passing by the island, but again the current was very strong and I decided to try the shallow side. We had only gone about one-hundred feet past the point before we ran aground hard on a submerged sandbar. Remembering what happened the night before when I tried to power off a sandbar, I looked at other options. First we could shift some weight by going to the stern, causing the bow to rise and possibly float free. If that didn't work the next step would be to push the boat off with poles. If those attempts failed I would get off the boat and try to push her off, wiggling the bow sideways to break the suction that is created between the hull and sand. If I did this I would attach a line from myself to the boat so that the boat couldn't float off without me. Sometimes a pole can be cut to use as a pry bar to wedge under the hull. I equipped the *Wabash Queen* with a power winch, so the final option would be to pull her off. Hooking the winch cable to a conveniently located tree or other solid object could do this, or I could set the anchor behind the boat and hedge her off with the winch. Running aground while going upriver is not as difficult to dislodge as a downriver grounding, so we only had to go to option two and push the boat off with oars. I eased her back to the island point and passed through the difficult channel by shore hugging and shifting from side to side. This method is similar to tacking a sailboat against the wind.

As we approached the head of the island, the beautiful beach was too inviting to pass by. I had planned to go several more hours before anchoring or beaching for the night, but this remote island with its huge beachhead of nearly white sand leading up to a forest was calling my name. The beachhead is two-hundred yards from the tree line to its point and about six-hundred yards around the point. There were no human footprints and few signs that people ever visited it. The last high water had cleaned and reclaimed the island to its natural state, although it had also deposited plenty of driftwood. This would provide plenty of firewood for our night on the beach. I don't believe that we could have gone to any place on earth and found a more peaceful, tranquil, and beautiful place than we had before us that day on the Wabash River in Indiana. The approach to the beach was shallow, but after a couple of tries, I found a place that I could land the boat close enough to swing down the gangway and go ashore. The current was still strong so to secure the boat I ran a line from the bow and another from the stern to augers in the sand, then secured the gangway with two steel rods through eyelets into the sand. To keep the current from pushing the stern into shore, I wedged a pole from a bracket on the transom into the riverbed. This four-point system would prevent the boat from moving in any direction regardless of current, waves, and wind. With the hull of the boat floating, instead of grounded, I felt a little more comfortable about staying overnight without worrying about a sudden drop in the river stage. On free-flowing rivers like the Wabash, a boat that is nudged against the shore could be grounded by morning.

We spent the rest of the day enjoying the beach and exploring the island. The weather was uncommonly mild for October in Indiana. The pooch was adapting well to this sandy world and even took a little wade in the river. While my friend went ashore for a walk I decided to play with some of the gadgets aboard the *Wabash Queen*. I got a location fix on the GPS, fired up the laptop computer to take notes and view a river mapping program, and tested other things we might need. The place was such a paradise that we decided that there was no reason to go further, so we would spend another night there. When evening came the stars were so bright that they actually provided light on the beach. After making a campfire, I stood back and was in awe of this-long-dreamed of sight before me. The *Wabash Queen* with the warm light glowing from the cabin, the water, sand, camp fire, and sky was a scene that will forever be with me. I decided to take a photograph of this night scene so I turned on all the DC lights on the boat then started the generator and switched on all the AC lights, including the stack lights on the upper helm. The Wabash Queen lit up in glory. The glow could probably have been seen from aircraft. Even the water reflected her beauty. To celebrate this voyage we indulged in champagne and shrimp cocktail by the fire. The rest of the evening was spent chatting and soaking in all that this wonderful place *beyond the bridges* had to offer.

Photo by Author
Morning fog

The next morning we were greeted with another heavy fog. Standing on the beach, looking back at the *Wabash Queen*, she appeared to be floating in the air, with the fog surrounding her. Nothing could be seen but the boat and fog. We were in no hurry to leave this little paradise, so we spent the day and another night there and began our trip back at about 4pm the fourth day. This time we were going downriver and it was necessary to power the boat away from the beach into the current to avoid being swept toward a shallow section and drift pile just downriver from the spot we had beached. Upon getting sufficient distance from the beach I turned the boat around and with the current. The strength of the current was now even more apparent. The rudder steering was less responsive with the current pushing us, so the avoidance of objects had to begin sooner. It was also easy to over-steer, but it didn't take long to catch on to the formula. However far I turned the wheel, I needed to turn it back about halfway as soon as the bow began to shift direction. We did a lot of zigzagging and I came to the conclusion that the boat may need yet larger, rudders or more of them. For most of the trip back we steered from the upper bridge. Going from the cabin helm to the upper helm is like getting on a different boat. Everything is different. Besides the elevation, the steering, the sound, and the overall feel you have for the boat changes. The biggest difference on the return trip was time. It took eight running hours to reach the island against the strong currents. The trip back only took an hour and a half. I calculated the current to be about six mph, so in terms of distance over water, we traveled forty-eight miles farther than the actual distance going to the island. In any event, my conclusion was that the *Wabash Queen* was running too slow upriver, steering was too sluggish downriver, and adjustments would be needed.

The Wabash is a remote river with little traffic. In four days we had only seen four other boaters. One of these was my son, Darin. He had taken my deck boat upriver to see how our shakedown cruise was going. I felt like this trip had not only been a successful test of the *Wabash Queen*, but I also witnessed another river convert. I believe that the domestic housedog, who was very apprehensive about this boat ride, had become very comfortable with it and was now a river dog. We arrived at the dock but waited until later to unload. It was time to reflect again on the beauty, adventure, and fun of this little trip and take stock of things that needed to be done to the boat before her next journey. Even though this was only a four-day cruise, I learned a lot about the boat and as always I learned a few more lessons.

Lessons Learned: It's safer to beach or anchor a boat before dark. The river is much more deceptive at night. Distance is more difficult to judge. Shallows are better hidden, and in general the river is harder to read in the dark. The shoreline is also more difficult to judge, especially during poor weather conditions. I still prefer to get the boat secured to a bank before dark and will proceed more carefully if it is dark and/or foggy. Setting anchor is usually something that is done at a leisurely pace, when preparing for a stopover but I found that dropping anchor in a hurry is sometimes necessary. When we needed to stop the boat the night she took on water, I had to fiddle around with lines that held the anchor to the bow, and then had difficulty getting the chain through the holding bracket. By the time I finally lowered the anchor and paid out the line, we had drifted quite a distance downriver. I realized that I must refit the anchor system to allow for a quick release in emergencies. That night, the *Wabash Queen* drifted harmlessly in the channel and I could have powered up and held her steady, but under different circumstances when the engine is down, drifting could be dangerous. I have also come to the conclusion that the best possible mooring system is a good solid tree along the shore. Upon my return, I made changes that would allow me to drop the anchor with the pull of a pin and made a larger opening for the chain to slip through more easily.

Another lesson from this trip had to do with preparation. My use for a bilge pump had been to remove rainwater from the bow and stern. I should have known better than to go out without having the pump ready to switch on quickly. The *Wabash Queen* now

Photo by Author

Rollin' on the river

has three pumps installed. Two of them are wired to switches and one will kick on when water activates a built-in float. This boat has no flotation, so pumping water out is very important, which I can now do at the rate of thirty gallons a minute. I had tested the boat quite often while tied to my dock. I had run it hard forward to see if water would be thrown over the transom, which it didn't. I had not ran her hard in reverse. If I had done that, I would have seen the problem and built a splashguard. The message here is, test thoroughly and consider every possible condition. I assumed that reverse would always be at slow rpm, so I had not even tried it at high speeds. Finding out that water could be shoveled into the stern of the boat would have been much safer at my dock than out on the river at night. The paddlewheel now has a splashguard and hard reverse is no problem. As I take more trips on the *Wabash Queen* I continue to learn more lessons.

Chapter 4

Reading the River

When we are in our cars we can usually see upcoming hazards. If we are paying attention we will steer around an object in the road. The same thing applies to most methods of transportation, from walking to flying an airplane. The surrounding element is air and the bottom is earth, so any object is usually visible to us and can be avoided. The difference in boating is that our vehicle is traveling through two elements at the same time; Air and water. Even though a portion of our vehicle is submerged in water, we can usually only see above the surface. So that seemingly smooth waterway we are traveling can and does have unseen objects that we can collide with. River boating is different than lake boating. Rivers have more floating objects, submerged obstacles and sandbars. An advantage to boating rivers is that moving water provides many more signs of these things than does still water.

Piloting a boat safely requires constant awareness of one's surroundings, and particularly of what is ahead. If you wait too long to react to an object, you may have to do some dangerous maneuvers to avoid it, then while your attention is on that you could run aground or hit something else. So the best policy when sighting an object is to make a gradual maneuver well in advance of it. Remember boats don't have brakes. If an object is suddenly spotted the safest procedure is to throttle back and veer off at the same time. Keep in mind that boats do not steer like cars. When you steer a boat it is the stern of boat that actually changes direction and tends to swing out. If a boater gets too close to an object to steer off, the back of the boat and possibly the prop can still collide with it.

There are several less obvious signs that can warn a boater of a submerged object. Look for "V"-shaped patterns in the river. This indicates that there may be a hazard ahead. The current is passing by or over a stationary object and creating a wake on the water's surface. This is often a snag extending from a sunken log, but could be any object that is near or at the waterline, yet grounded on the riverbed. One of the worst objects to hit is a vertical steel pipe just below the waterline. Hitting one of those can turn a great day of boating into a disaster (the author knows this one from experience). Many times a "V" pattern will be caused by a small swimming animal, which we also want to avoid for their sake. It is not important to analyze what might be creating the wake. It is important to begin maneuvers away from them as soon as they are spotted. Don't wait until it's too late to make a decision about it! All stationary objects in moving water create turbulence, some less noticeable than others. Large rocks, discarded appliances (sad but true), and other large objects do not slice the water as do small objects and so do not always have the defined "V" pattern at the surface. The current passes over them in the form of a swell. A swell can be created by an object several feet below the surface, depending on its size and the current's speed. A boat hull may pass easily over the object, but the prop may not. Many props and lower units have been ruined this way. Don't take the risk!

Avoid any disturbance to the natural flow of the river. In some rivers there are sections that are shallow and rocky with swells and boils from bank to bank. In this case a wise boater will slow down, steer toward the least active swells, and if possible, elevate the prop. It is best to keep the boat under power for steering. Drifting into a section like this can allow the boat to become stuck broadside against a rock, which in faster waters could lift one side of the boat high enough to swamp it. Swells in the river are more difficult to spot when traveling downstream. This is because the slight rise of water will hide its trailing wake from a distance. The combination of this and the boat being pushed by the current dictates that we should take extra care in watching for the warning signs and take evasive action sooner. Steering is not as responsive downstream as it is upstream.

Sand and gravel bars are the most deceptive of submerged objects. The huge amounts of agricultural runoff and bank erosion create an on-going challenge to river boaters in the form of sandbars, which can form and change very quickly during periods of high water. Running into a sandbar can result in a minor inconvenience or become a life-threatening situation. A few years ago, a family was enjoying a cruise down the Wabash River in Indiana in an old pontoon boat. The current was very fast and they were heading downriver at full throttle. Not noticing a submerged sandbar that could have been avoided, the port side pontoon ran aground with such force that it spun the boat sideways and ripped loose from the deck. Two people fell overboard and were able to get to the sandbar. The rest of the boat with only one pontoon when down the river until the deck grounded in shallow water with three other people hanging onto it. A passing fisherman came to their rescue, and then picked the two people up that were still standing in knee-deep water on the sandbar. This story is an extreme example of what can happen when we are not reading the river.

The best known and usually accurate rule for staying in the deepest part of the river or channel is to steer to the outside of bends and in the middle of the river in straight sections. As we are cruising on a river we can actually look well ahead of our position and visualize the course of least resistance as the water is flowing downriver. That path of least resistance is where the channel will generally flow. As water rounds a bend it tends to flow faster, scouring out a channel. Where the flow comes out of a bend and into a straight section or an opposite bend, it will make a cross-over to the middle or opposite side. There are exceptions to this and the river can surprise us when we least expect it. Whether traveling on straight or winding rivers, caution should be taken when approaching tributaries. Streams carry silt, gravel and rocks that will often build up just below the mouth of the tributary. It is wise to steer away from these outlets. Bridges and other man-made obstacles can create a dam effect as the collection point for sand, silt, and gravel. Caution is advised even when approaching areas that show signs of a bridge that

Photo by Author
Abandoned bridge piers

has been removed. Care is not always taken when bridges are demolished, and there is often material dropped in the riverbed that can not only create a sandbar but can damage a boat in low water.

In addition to these obvious signs of possible shallow water, there are also surface water reactions that can act as a warning. Always look for a break in the continuity of the water. If the water is choppy, take notice of a smoother spot. If the water is smooth, beware of choppy spots. These conditions can be the result of wind or shifting channels, but can also be the effect of shallow water passing over a sandbar. Shallow waters also have an affect on the prop wash of powerboats. If you notice any difference in the feel of the boat or the prop wash changing, you should be aware of possible water-depth change. Another indication of a sandbar is the movement of floating objects. Eddies are often formed just down-river from a sandbar that floating objects can get caught in. If an object is not moving with the current it may be in an eddy near a sandbar, or may be in shallow water and not floating at all. Either case is a good reason to avoid the area. Depth finders are also very helpful when running at slower speeds. You can usually see a gradual decrease in the depth reading and become aware of approaching shallows. If you are running fast, it is best to rely on reading the river, as you will already be grounded by the time the depth finder sends its signal and you can react to it.

While boating on navigable rivers and following the sail lines and buoys, sandbars are not of great concern. But when diverting from the buoy markers and on other waterways, sandbars are something that a boater should be on constant alert for. Getting a small craft free from being grounded is usually fairly easy, but in some cases can be quite difficult, dangerous, and damaging to the boat. Piloting a boat at night makes spotting signs of submerged sandbars and other objects more difficult and requires slow speed and vigilant watch. It also requires listening for turbulent water. Some friends of mine were cruising the White River in Indiana at night. They were traveling upriver when they ran aground hard with their 21-foot cabin cruiser. It was late so they decided to secure the boat where they were stuck, get some sleep, and take care of it in the morning. What they didn't anticipate was the river falling rapidly overnight. The next morning they discovered that the boat was no longer in the water, and it took an entire day of digging a canal under the hull to finally float the boat off. The lesson learned here may be to address the problem when it occurs and sleep later. Many rivers have an unpredictable rise and fall rate which should always be kept in mind when a situation like this arises. This factor should also be considered when beaching a boat for the night.

Color can also be a factor while reading the river. The sky color usually determines the reflected color of the water; however, the actual color that you see at close range can tell you something about what may be below the surface. First, any sudden change in water color could be a sign of depth change. Even murky waters will have a lighter appearance in shallow areas because more light is reflected off the riverbed. Shallow water also tends to have submerged vegetation that will affect the color. Judging water color for navigation is more difficult on sunny days, due to the intensity of reflections. A common reason for a sudden change in water color can also be the confluence of a tributary, where the water pouring in is clearer or murkier than the river, which is also a sign to be careful of a sandbar.

Reading the river can also include the riverbank. As a rule the slope of the bank will continue into the water at about the same angle as you see it, so a high steep bank is more likely to have deeper water along it than a gradual sloping bank. Riverbanks with large amounts of erosion are more likely to have sandbars just downriver, usually on inside bends. The shape of the shoreline can also be a factor in water depth. Whether the river is wide or narrow, it is still carrying about the same volume of water, so as a river narrows the current runs faster and scours a deeper channel. The shoreline can also provide warning signs of possible hazards in the river. Any shoreline that has a road leading to it has a greater possibility of having dumped material in the river. I have seen cars, appliances, bathtubs, and many other discarded objects that can damage a boat. One might think that urban areas would have more of this than rural areas, but people will usually go to a remote place to do their dirty work, with less chance of getting caught. Areas with riverside factories, utilities, and other development should alert a boater to the possibility of submerged pipes, concrete, and other materials to watch for and avoid.

Another valuable sense we can use in reading the river is sound. Upcoming hazards can often be detected by sound, before they are sighted, especially on smaller winding rivers. The sound of rushing water should not be ignored. Those sounds could be a harmless brook flowing into the river, a drain pipe, or low hanging tree limbs. It could also be upcoming rapids or dangerous obstacles in the water. During the night an increase in the sound of water can be a signal that it is rising. The sound of an approaching boat and even car or train sounds alert a boater to upcoming conditions. Sounds are especially important when boating after sunset. A spotlight beam has limited range and coverage, so the sound of water passing over a submerged object may be the first alert to it. Depth finders rely on bouncing a sound wave off the riverbed and back to the sending unit. It is also wise to pay attention to sounds above the water for safe navigation.

It is important to determine whether the river is rising, stationary, or falling. There are signs to look for that will help determine which condition is present. Larger than normal amounts of floating debris is the most obvious indicator of a rising river. Debris collects along the bank and is washed away as the water rises. Some debris will also be present after heavy rains with no significant rise. As a general rule debris will tend to float near the center of the river when it is rising and move closer to the shore as it becomes stationary and falls. Observing an eroded mud bank will give clues that the water level is dropping rapidly. The mud will stay wet and appear darker well above the normal splash line. Some debris will also cling to tree trunks and shoreline for a time, further indicating a falling river. A stationary river stage is the most difficult to determine and can usually be noticed by the absence of conditions present during rise and fall. Navigable rivers with dams are usually kept at a determined pool stage with little fluctuation. Free-flowing rivers can change suddenly by upriver weather conditions, thawing, or dam release on tributaries. The most surprising sign that the river stage has changed is to discover water flowing into a tent during the night, or wake up to find

Photo by Author

Reading the river

one's boat sitting high and dry in the same spot it was floating the night before. These are good reasons to be aware of changing river levels. While landed on a beach or camping it is always a good idea to poke a stick at the water's edge and check it now and then, to see if there are any changes.

While reading this information, it may be observed that references made to reading the river includes words like "could", "may", "usually", and "possibly". The reason is that this is not an exact science. All of the things discussed provide a guide to go by and in "most" cases will be accurate, but rivers are unpredictable and when we let our guard down or least expect it, the river will surprise us. We should take nothing for granted. Reading the river is a skill that will develop over time and become second nature. A slight deviation in the flow or an object unnoticed by many people will be detected by an observant boater. Being observant and alert is of paramount importance and indulging in anything that could dull the senses is dangerous. I will not go into the hazards of boating and drinking alcohol but will make this short statement. "Drinking while operating a boat is not illegal in some states, but it is stupid in all of them."

Chapter 5

River Guide Books

Over the years I have produced guide books for non-navigable rivers. The books provide detailed information for boaters, river enthusiasts, and various agencies. Navigable rivers have charts, channel markers, navigation lights and a maintained channel. With a guide book, boaters can travel the rivers with information helpful for safe navigation and supply locations. My first guide book evolved without intent. Having kept journals and sketched maps of the Wabash River on my journeys, people were coming to me to get copies of them. It was often suggested that I should put the information in book form, feeling that it would be in high demand. I wasn't sure just how high the demand would be but the project intrigued me. It would require a great deal of scouting, in addition to the river travels I had done. I had already canoed the entire 500 miles of the Wabash. I had also cruised the length of the river in a powerboat, but this would not be enough. If the guide book was to be complete and comprehensive, much more information would be needed.

Having purchased the most recent U.S. Geological Survey maps for the area, I began to compare them to my maps and make necessary corrections. My maps were more accurate in some aspects and the U.S.G.S. maps were more accurate in other features. Using a computer, I redrew my maps, breaking the river down into 35 sections. I wanted no more than ten to fifteen miles on each section page so that close-up details could be illustrated. The best way to get a real good look at the river, its tributaries, and surrounding terrain, would be to fly over it. This would also provide aerial photos of places that are best shown from above. At some places in the upper reaches of a river there are old oxbows, left when the river changed course. Those oxbows can be confusing during high water, leaving a boater uncertain as to which stream is the main channel.

Aerials with over-lays explaining the old and new channels are a tremendous help when navigating through these areas of false rivers.

Normal river flow (cut-off)

Oxbow flows in high water

Photo by Author

Old river channel

A friend of mine owned an airplane and he agreed to take me on a flight of the entire river. We planned to fly all day, starting at the mouth of the river and follow it to the source near Fort Recovery, Ohio. It was a beautiful day and all was going well. The Wabash is very winding and we flew low-level, following the river. I do not have any problems flying and seldom have those sick feelings one can get from zigzagging and tight-banking in a small plane. After a few hours the motion was beginning to get to me, but I said nothing. We continued and I found myself dreading the next river bend and banking of the plane. I continued to make notes and take photographs. I had to write quickly because each time I looked away from the window and at the writing pad, a wave of sickness erupted in my stomach. Still, I said nothing! There was no way I was going to wimp out on this mission and admit that I was getting motion sickness. I did suggest that we fly a little higher for some wider range photographs, knowing the plane might fly in a straighter line for a while. We continued and I remained silent about my dilemma, but looked around for a receptacle in the event of a full-scale eruption. At about the time we approached Huntington, Indiana, my pilot friend said, "You know, I'm beginning feel kind of sick, so I think we should set down for a while at the Huntington airfield". I grinned and said, "Well, if you must it's OK with me." We landed and I was never so happy to get my feet on the ground. We drank a soda, and then walked around until both of us felt much better. He was impressed that I had not gotten motion sickness, since he did. We took off again and I noticed that he stopped banking so hard and was less interested in low-level flight.

We completed our mission before dark and headed back. I had taken many photographs that would be of much value to the guide book. I had also made several observations of landmarks and things that I had not noted from traveling the river.

Photo by Author
Author goes scouting

The next step was to scout the entire river by land. I wanted to cross every bridge to get an idea of what is there. It is usually difficult to tell what is at the bridges from the river, so it would be helpful to know where supplies and fuel could be purchased. In addition, I wanted to get to know the river communities better and provide information about them. It was also important to know what river roads could lead to places in the event of an emergency. I set out on this mission on my motorcycle with camping gear. I drove to Fort Recovery, where the first possible put-in site for a boat would be. Upon scouting the area along the river, I noticed the train station at Fort Recovery along the river and decided to go in and get any information they may have that could be helpful. The men at the station were very helpful, advising me that folks could launch their canoes there and leave their cars at the station. They were very interested in my project. It happened that they were having a town meeting that evening at the train station and invited me to join them and talk about the upcoming guide book. They also invited me to camp on the lawn by the train station, which I accepted. That evening I explained what I was doing and had a nice time. The next morning I began to zigzag the river at every bridge crossing. I stopped often to talk to local river folks and gather information. When boating the river, I had not paid special attention to boat-launching ramp locations, so I would also gather that information on this drive.

Some of the challenges encountered on this trip were the roads. They would often dead end, causing me to turn back. Other roads would go from pavement to gravel. Gravel roads are no fun on a motorcycle, nor are muddy roads. Several bridges that were shown on highway maps had long been abandoned. Some bridges were no longer even there. Other places had new bridges and were not yet on maps. Discovering all this and making the changes would cause my guide book to have the most updated information. Near Wabash, Indiana, I was told that there were remnants of an old washed-out railroad bridge that is hazardous in low water. I had not noticed it on my trips but wanted to include the location in the guide book. The water was low so I set out walking along the river toward the indicated area, with camera in hand to photograph what I could of it. The riverbank was dry and in some places sandy. In other places it was weedy and mosquito- ridden. I pushed through some difficult growth to discover that I had moved a limb out of my way that was occupied by a colony of hornets. As soon as I saw the hornet's nest I decided that it was a good time to step up the pace. The hornets did not appreciate the disturbance and the pursuit began. I had no place to go but along the riverbank so I ran, jumping over logs and large rocks, but the hornets were closing in. My next option was to jump into the river, but I thought about my camera. I pulled the camera strap from my neck preparing to drop it on shore before diving into the river. At just about the time I dropped the camera and looked back before going in, I saw them turning back. They had apparently chased me far enough from their territory to satisfy themselves. After catching my breath and being thankful that the pursuit had ended short of my taking an unscheduled dip in the river, I continued to search for the bridge ruins. I never found it and assume that if it is there at all, it cannot be much of a hazard. I chose to take a different path back to my motorcycle, for fear of stirring up those hornets again. I made my way through the woods in a circle around the area. A big circle!

While on this scouting mission I discovered a very interesting similarity in the river towns. It seemed that every town having a railroad bridge had a story about the day that a train went off the bridge and into the river. Most of the stories claim that the train engine was still down there somewhere. I realize that bridges did fall down and trains did sometimes derail, however, I just could not imagine that their luck was that bad. I went to one of the bridges that had a story about how the train derailed while crossing the bridge, went flying off, and crashed into the river below. The engine, of course, was never recovered. I looked at the steel truss bridge and noticed that it was built with overhead trusses across the entire length of the bridge. How did the train come off that bridge? There were no open parts of the bridge. Below the bridge is a shallow river with rock bottom. Where did the engine go? Of all the bridge mishap stories I heard, there was only one bridge that I could verify that a train actually did go off of, and that the engine is still in the bottom of the river. Photos from a 1910 newspaper clipping verified this. I also sounded the river just below the bridge to find a very deep hole, which could be formed from undertows created by a large object. The bridge trusses also ended at the main span, leaving an open beam bridge, and space enough that the train could have passed through the

Photo by Author
Biddle Island at Logansport

gap and into the river. Legends and lore do abound on the rivers, but I had found one story that was proven to be true.

Logansport, Indiana, has the only developed island on the Wabash River. Biddle Island is between a large split in the river in the middle of town. It has a highway and railroad bridge crossing it. While scouting the island I met a young man who lives in one of the houses on the island. I mentioned how unique it is to live on the only developed island on the river. He had a puzzled look on his face and asked what I was talking about. He didn't realize that he lived on an island. He knew that there was a river on each side, plus the Eel River runs into the Wabash there, but he just didn't realize that it was an island. He had never heard anyone call it that before. I happened to have my aerial photos with me and showed him a bird's-eye view of where he lived. He was amazed and I left him with a different perspective of his habitat. I left amazed that he didn't know he lived on an island. I found that, except for fishermen, people along the river knew very little about it. Even the fisherman knew only their short section of the river and little about the waters beyond or the river's history. Everyone I met thought a guide book was a great idea. Being a realist, I do know there could be a difference between folks thinking it is a good idea and actually buying it. This scouting mission was accomplishing another thing that I had not anticipated. I met a lot of nice people and made some new friends.

Some of the people, particularly those who live along the river, encouraged me to list them as a place of help or refuge for anyone traveling the river.

On my visit to one of the river towns, I was very disappointed to find the poor condition of the riverfront. The riverbank was nearly destroyed by ATVs, dirt bikes, and 4x4s. Access to the river was nearly impossible. There was no boat launching ramp. Trash and abandoned vehicles lined the riverbank. The town was historically significant with regard to the river but had turned its back on the very river that was responsible for its being founded. A historic building that once housed a bridge toll station sat in ruins. The city of Peru, Indiana, got bad marks in the guide book and was also mentioned in a future article I wrote about river communities. There were supplies and fuel available in Peru but no safe way to get to it. This story has a happy ending. The publicity had apparently created a call for action by the citizens of Peru. Within a few years after the completion of the guide book, the riverfront was cleaned up. Off-road vehicles were no longer permitted to destroy the bank. A boat-launching ramp was installed. The historic tollhouse was being restored. When the Wabash River Guide book was revised in 2002, the information about the city of Peru was updated and it was recommended as a good stopover for river travelers. The process of creating the guide book and developments occurring after the publication inspired several good things that I had not anticipated.

As I traveled the roads along the lower river it became more difficult to stay close to the river. It becomes much more remote with vast areas of bottomlands and greater distances between bridges. I was gathering valuable information with each stop and doing a lot of hiking to verify landmarks and other things that may have been missed on boat trips. There were times when I did not feel comfortable leaving my motorcycle and gear along remote roads, but fortunately nothing was ever bothered. I met many self- proclaimed "River Rats", and heard many river stories. Along with the railroad bridge stories there were also other similar stories. One was about the scuba divers in the river who saw a catfish bigger than a man, which frightened them so much that they would not go back. That story flourished in many communities. There were stories of the bottomless riverbed where no one has ever found how deep it is. There was also a unique story about the UFOs hiding below the muddy waters.

Indian legends abound and there are several bluffs with the same story about the Indian maiden who jumped off the rock because she could not be with her lover from another tribe. This story was sometimes told that both the maiden and her suitor jumped together so they could be with each other for eternity. All are named Lovers Leap. I particularly enjoyed hearing about those dangerous water moccasins lurking in the waters of the Wabash; there are no water moccasins in Indiana. There are, of course, the stories of legendary characters that traveled the river and had stopped at the story-teller's hometown: People like Abraham Lincoln, Daniel Boone, and Davy Crocket, to name a few. It is true that some of these men did travel, or at least cross the Wabash River, but one cannot help but wonder if all those names and dates carved on the bluffs are legitimate. I was also told of the monster in the Wabash. Some call it Ouabache, the French pronunciation for Wabash. Its description is very similar to the Loch Ness monster. Well, I suppose that if Scotland can have their monster there is no reason why we can't have ours.

My scouting mission was complete, but I still had much to do. It took months to compile the information and coordinate it with my charts of each section. There was so much information that I decided to dedicate an entire page, opposite each map section, for the descriptions. I also decided to include "river travel tips" where space was available. It was my goal to make the most complete guide to the river ever produced. Actually a comprehensive guide to the Wabash had never been produced, but I still wanted it to be complete. I didn't really expect it to be of any more interest than for folks and communities along the river. After publication I was pleasantly surprised to discover that the book was in much greater demand than anticipated. Within five years the book had been reprinted several times, and then a revised edition was published in 2002 with updates. The success of the Wabash River Guide book led to my authoring a similar book for the White River in Indiana.

The White River has the East Fork, West Fork, and main river, totally nearly 500 miles. The process of gathering information and scouting the river was similar. The White River has several spillway (lowhead) dams, which limit power-boat use and must be portaged with canoes. After canoeing the river and gathering the best portage information, I studied a canoe guide published by the state. While studying it, I notice   dam and portage instructions at a location near Bedford, Indiana, that did not look familiar. I did not have that site marked with a dam, nor did I remember one being there. How could I have canoed through there and not noticed a dam? Maybe in the high water it became inundated and I just passed over it. No, I would have seen the guide walls and certainly been aware of the turbulence. Some state maps showed a dam at that location. I got on the Internet and searched for a satellite image of the loction. I found it and could see no sign of a dam. I did see an unnaturally

Photo by Author

Lowhead Dam on White River

widened river at that point. I had scouted that section of river by car and had seen no sign of the dam, but I wasn't looking for one.

The next morning I was on my way back to Bedford to take a closer look. I drove up and down the river as close as I could get on both sides. No sign of a dam. I walked in areas that were accessible. Still no dam! Where is the damn thing? After going home from that unsuccessful mission, I had an idea. I should have stopped at the local library. Librarians are wonderful and just love to share information. They are also very good at research. I called the Bedford Library and asked for the reference desk. I was transferred to a nice lady and asked her if she knew anything about a dam a few miles above Bedford. She didn't know of any but said she would check it out and call me back. She called back an hour later with her findings. There is no dam at that site, but there used to be one. It was built in 1893 to operate a grist mill. During the great flood of 1913 the dam was blown up with dynamite to relieve pressure and prevent additional upriver flooding. I said "1913? The dam has not been there for 89 years?" She confirmed that it was true. I was amazed that some recent edition maps still show the dam, and even more astonished that the state canoeing guide shows it with portage instructions. I got it right in my book.

The White River Guide book is also a success and I plan to do guide books for other non-navigable rivers. When one is traveling rivers, he or she will learn a great deal about them. I already knew a lot about these rivers on my various boat trips. Writing guide books has caused me to learn much, much more. The research of its history, towns, landmarks, channels, and other particulars caused me to learn the rivers in ways that can never be done simply by traveling them. When traveling rivers, many things go unnoticed that may be important to some folks. Compiling information on every aspect of a river is hard work, fun, and rewarding. I feel very good about knowing people rely on my guide books to more safely travel the rivers.

Chapter 6

Gilligan Goose

Man meets goose....

My house is located on the banks of the Wabash River and I have my own dock that I call the landing, so it is convenient to jump in the boat and go for a little cruise. Sometimes when the river has been high, then drops quickly, I head out early to the various beaches where I know the fresh-water mussels get stranded. They are an important part of the river system and I don't want to see them dry up or get eaten by those rascal raccoons so I collect them and pitch them back into the river where they are safe. This probably doesn't make the raccoons very happy but they have plenty to eat. Anytime I can help out the wildlife I will do whatever I am can.

One day I was on such a mission when about eight miles up the river from my dock I saw something unusual, not far from the bank. I saw splashing and heard the sound of some critter in distress. As I got closer I could see that it was a very large goose. I couldn't tell what was wrong at first but upon closer inspection I could see that the goose had apparently gotten his big feet tangled in a trotline. A trotline is an anchored line with many hooks and bait, attached to a float. Fishermen set these trotlines, then check them once or twice a day to see if they have caught any fish. Well, this big goose got tangled in one and was thrashing around and flapping his wings, looking rather precarious with that milk jug float hanging from his long neck. This fellow needed help. He was getting very tired and I was afraid he might break a wing with all that flapping and thrashing.

I couldn't get my boat too close for fear of hitting him, so I pulled the boat over to the bank just upriver, put on my life preserver, got out my pocket knife and jumped in. I swam back to the goose to try to cut the lines that held him. He had no trust in me and warned me with some pretty ferocious hisses that I should stay back. I was tempted to abide by his wishes but my determination to set him free was greater than fear of a few pecks on the head. There I was, circling this big goose, looking for a chance to get close and all the while he was circling to face me. It was like two wrestlers in a ring ready to bout. At least his attention toward me caused him to stop struggling with the lines, which was good, but the real struggle was about to begin.

I was afraid to dive down to cut the cord because the line was now wrapped around him and his feet, along with a few hooks that seemed to be attached to him. If I cut him loose he might then be able to get away from me, but still have all that attached to him, which could be very bad. No, I had to get hold of him and hang on while I cut him loose so that I could make sure it was all off, or if he was hurt I would try to take him somewhere for medical help. I saw my chance and lunged for him. Now I've never wrestled a goose before but can say without a doubt that even tangled in fish line he was a formidable opponent, plus he was in his element, as I am basically a land creature. At first I had a bear hug around his torso which kept his wings from flapping but then came those hard pecks on the face that I was expecting, forcing me to hold on with only one arm while protecting myself with the other. With that he had one wing free. I do believe that being slapped with that big wet wing hurt worse than the bites. There was no way I was going to be able to hold him like this and at the same time get my knife from my pocket to try to cut the lines off and pull out the hooks. I had to go to plan B.

It has been my experience with wild animals that if you show your dominance and can constrain them long enough; they will submit and quiet down. I was hoping this applied to geese. With one swift motion I cut the main line that went to the anchor, while keeping my grip on the goose. I then held him tightly while making my way to the riverbank, setting the stage for round two. I was able to reach the muddy bank, then crawl out of the water with the goose held tightly. Then we wrestled some more and I found that he could put up just as good a fight on land. I admit that I have fantasized a time or two about mud wrestling, but not with an angry goose. After rolling around in the mud for a while I was finally able to get a good bear hug on him and at the same time get hold of his hammering beak. Then I just lay there in the mud and held him tightly for what seemed like a very long time. I could feel him begin to relax so I tested the situation by letting loose just a little to see if the fight was gone in him. This test failed a couple of times but finally I could tell that he had submitted. He either knew that he could not beat or get away from this big human beast, or maybe he finally sensed that I was there to help. In any event, he stopped fighting.

I slowly loosened my grip and carefully begin cutting the tangled lines. He watched and gave what I perceived as a couple of approval honks. I then took the risk of pulling one of the hooks out that was snagged on his leg. Fortunately the hooks were not imbedded deep so the barbs of the hooks were not grabbing. He continued to calmly watch. I had to unwrap nylon line from around the webbing on his feet. He watched and made more friendly sounding honks. Then I started checking him from top to bottom to see if he appeared to be hurt, especially his wings. He seemed to be all right and was cooperating with the inspection. When my work was done I sat back and waited for the goose to go back in the river or fly off. There we sat the goose and I, caked in mud from head to foot. Knowing that geese are pretty smart, I figured that he might need to wash off all that mud before trying to fly, and so he finally did. He slipped into the water and began thrashing around, not because he was in trouble like before but because he really needed a bath, and so did I. I slipped back into the river and there we were, bathing together and even carrying on a conversation.

I swam back to my boat, climbed aboard to nurse my wounds, and waited to see the goose fly away. I didn't know geese were so meticulous about bathing because he continued to wash himself for a very long time, but I patiently waited. I wanted to make sure he could fly before leaving him. He finally gave me a few friendly honks, and lifted off. I was very pleased. He circled a couple of times above me, and then headed north. Feeling very good about the whole event I started up my boat and headed

Photo by Author
Lift-off

south toward home. I now needed some care and recovery time after all that. That night I went to sleep thinking about that big beautiful goose and hoped that I would someday see him again, under different circumstances. I have helped many animals in trouble but this one was special. I believe he was thanking me when he circled above me and honked before flying off.

The next morning I set aside time to go to my dock and clean up my boat. I hooked the long length of hoses from the house and dragged them down the sloping bank to the dock. Just as I turned to go back up to turn the water on I heard something very familiar. A honk? I knew that honk! Yes, it was the goose that I had saved the day before, swimming around my dock as if saying "good morning." I was delighted that he came to visit me. He didn't stay long but came visiting again the next day, this time staying longer. Each day I was there the goose would show up and eventually came into the yard. The goose eventually switched his routine and was at my place most of the time and would occasionally leave to visit elsewhere. Years have passed and he is still there. Something very special happened during that rescue. I can't explain it but a strong bond developed between man and goose. We are friends for life. Even though he decided to make my dock his home, I don't claim him as being mine. He is not my pet. He is my friend! He is free to come and go as he pleases and I do not feed him, except for an occasional treat of wheat bread. I do not want him to become dependent on me, as I respect his freedom the same as I do of all wild animals.

Gilligan's Landing....

The big goose had made a home and was becoming well known among the folks who pass or stop by on the river. A couple of visitors were there one day and the lady was fascinated with the beautiful and very friendly goose. She asked me what his name was. I said, "Never gave him a name; he's not mine to name." I went on to explain that even though the landing (my dock) is his home he is a wild animal and so I just refer to him as "the goose." She convinced me that having a name to call him would in no way domesticate him but would, in fact give him an identity, which a unique animal like him deserves. I said, "Ok, so give him a name." She thought for a while and said, "Well, you call the dock "the landing," and for some reason the name Gilligan just comes to mind; maybe it's the dock, like a floating island. Yes that's it. Your dock is Gilligan's Landing." And so from that day forward, the goose is Gilligan and his home is Gilligan's Landing, known by folks all up and down the river. Being the victim that I am, I put a sign on the dock that read *Gilligan's Landing*.

As mentioned earlier, I don't feed him with any regularity. I prefer to allow Gilligan to remain self-sufficient, but do treat him now and then. His favorite is wheat bread. He doesn't care for white bread as it gets doughy and sticks to his beak, causing him to look rather comical as he flips his head around and scrapes his beak on the grass trying to get it off. He seems to know what is good for him and what is not. He will reject anything with sugar or salt on it. No crackers, cookies, or junk food for this goose. His primary food source is from the river and its shore. He comes and goes as he pleases and sometimes goes off by himself for a few days. I understand how a fellow needs some time alone. The first winter he apparently migrated south, but it was a short winter and he returned in about six weeks. Other winters Gilligan has become a snow goose and stayed home at Gilligan's Landing, using the dock as a floating shelter. One winter I built him a floating goose house next to the dock. It had a easy access ramp, straw for warmth, and other comforts, but he apparently preferred his own accommodations and chose not to use it. One day a huge storm was coming in and Gilligan was out exploring along the river somewhere. I looked at the threatening sky and was hoping that he would be all right. Then I could hear the familiar honking in the distance. I saw Gilligan fighting the wind, looking like a B-52 airplane making a circular glide path as he headed for his landing. He made a rather rough landing in the choppy water and immediately took refuge under the dock. What a smart goose, I thought. Under the dock is the best possible shelter during a storm.

Gilligan is usually at his landing as though standing guard. He greets people who pull over in their boats and sounds off to let me know that visitors are arriving. Since the river rises and drops all the time, the landing must be adjusted with cables for the various water levels. Sometimes the river will get above flood stage. When this happens, tending to the landing is very important. One night the river was still rising and I had made what I thought was enough adjustment in the cables to allow for the water to rise more. I had miscalculated the amount and the next morning I looked out the window to find the dock gone. It had broken loose during the night and went down the river. It was winter time and I had no boats in the river to go looking for it so, I drove to every place I could get a good view trying to spot Gilligan's Landing, with no luck. Later that day I noticed no sign of Gilligan. He sometimes would go off to a bluff up the river to wait out the high water, especially when I pulled the dock onto shore, so I figured that's where he was. A week went by with no sign of the dock or Gilligan. For all I knew the dock could be on the Mississippi River headed for the

Gulf of Mexico by then, but I was getting concerned about Gilligan. He could have at least come down from the bluff to visit, even if the landing was gone.

Ten days had passed when a fellow I know came by the house and asked if maybe I had lost my dock. I said yes and he explained that it had gotten hung up near his cabin about ten miles down the river. He had tied it off to a tree so the owner could find it. Well, that was good news! He then went on to talk about this big goose that was hanging around the dock and appeared to be quite protective of it. That was great news! Gilligan apparently felt duty-bound to go with the dock and look after it. The reason this man suspected that the dock belonged to me was that he had heard of Gilligan, so he went on a mission to see who it was who shared some riverfront with this goose and eventually was led to my house. I immediately put a boat in the water and headed out to retrieve the dock. As I approached it, I could see Gilligan still standing guard and he seemed very excited to see me. After having a joyful reunion with Gilligan I hooked a tow line to the dock and proceeded back up the river with it. I had to move very slowly in the swift current and Gilligan swam along-side the dock all the way, happily honking, knowing that his landing had been saved and both he and the dock were heading home. We celebrated with wheat bread upon our arrival.

One of my boats is very unique. It is a paddlewheel houseboat called the *Wabash Queen*. Gilligan has also taken on the responsibility of watching over it in my absence, and occasionally takes a ride in it with me. He prefers to ride on the bow and does an amazing balancing act for a fellow with webbed feet. He likes to ride on the wood railing and look down at the river while cruising. It is as though he is on watch, looking for snags or other hazards. Some friends of mine asked if they could get married aboard the *Wabash Queen*. They are river folks and it seemed the proper way to get married, so I agreed. The plan was for the wedding party to show up at my place and go aboard. Others would arrive by boat, and then we would anchor the *Wabash Queen* in the middle of the river with the other boats tied around it. As the people arrived, Gilligan was on duty, greeting people and scaring some who didn't know that he is an aggressively friendly goose. All went well until the wedding party boarded the boat. When we set off from the dock, Gilligan was obviously upset, as he was swimming along-side making some hostile noises. As other boats arrived Gilligan got in their way, as though trying to keep them from tying off to the *Wabash*

Queen. As the ceremony proceeded, Gilligan circled the boats flapping his wings and making all sorts of noise. There must have been something not quite right with Gilligan, regarding this event. The wedding vows continued despite this distraction. Finally the ceremony was completed, the music was playing, and everyone was laughing about the antics of Gilligan during all this. What was his problem? No one will know but Gilligan. A newspaper reporter was on board writing a story about the houseboat wedding. In the article she listed the bride, groom, wedding party, and one frustrated goose named Gilligan. Maybe it was because he wasn't used to that many people at one time, or possibly he was concerned that we were overloading the *Wabash Queen*. In any event, Gilligan as usual became the star of the show and helped create some humorous memories for the people at the wedding. Following the wedding everyone went to Staff Island for the reception. Gilligan did not attend, but was invited to do so by the bride and groom. Sometimes he goes to gatherings at the island, but he chose the peace and quiet of Gilligan's Landing this time.

Sometimes Gilligan likes to ride in the *Wabash Explorer*. That is the boat I was using when we first met. He will ride on the bow seemingly enjoying the wind as he opens his huge wings and appears to fly while standing still. On one occasion he underestimated the wind while cruising down the river. He opened his wings and had an accidental lift-off. Caught by surprise, he tried to land back in the boat but tumbled backwards on the deck and collided with the center console. This all made him very angry so he made a few Donald Duck-style tantrum remarks, and then decided to go home. He flew off and was waiting for me at the landing when I arrived later. Gilligan doesn't always choose to go with me in the boats, and in fact I don't often encourage him to, but sometimes he can be persistent.

Photo by Author
Cruising

One day I was setting out on a canoe trip. My plan was to put in at Gilligan's Landing, paddle downriver for three days, and then have my son pick me up and bring me and the canoe back home. While loading up the canoe with gear, Gilligan was of course right in the middle of the activity when I pushed off. I am accustomed to Gilligan escorting me for a distance down the river, but he usually turns back at some point. You see, Gilligan can fly but prefers aquatic transportation and so only flies when necessary. There I was paddling down the river with Gilligan swimming along-side. After a couple of miles I reminded Gilligan that I was going to continue for about 100 miles and he might want to turn back, but he apparently had different ideas and continued to stay with me. On and on we went. I made about 30 miles that day and set up camp on a beach. That is, Gilligan and I set up camp. The next morning I expected Gilligan to have gone home, but he did not. I set off and he continued to stay with me, chatting much of the way.

One of the reasons I enjoy canoeing alone is to get some quiet time, but I certainly wasn't getting it on this journey. The second night after setting up camp, I began to wonder how Gilligan was going to go back home when then trip ended. He had never ridden in a truck. What would I do? The next morning Gilligan was still with me and we went on until I reached my destination late that afternoon. I walked to a phone to call my son while Gilligan stood watch with the canoe. We hung out by the river and waited a few hours for my son to arrive, all the while not knowing what I would do with him. When the truck came we loaded the canoe and gear, and then tried to coax Gilligan into the truck to ride back with us. He wanted nothing to do with getting into that thing, and I wasn't about to get into another wrestling match with him. It was a difficult decision to leave him but I had to believe that he would know his way home and take flight. After all, he did leave to go south the first winter and found his way back. As we pulled away, he honked in a way that seemed an approval of his situation. It was not a stressful honk but one as though saying "see you later." On the way home we stopped for dinner and discussed Gilligan, who was on our minds. We pulled into my driveway and the first thing I did was head for the landing to see if there was a chance that Gilligan would be there. That 100 miles of river would only be about 60 miles as the goose flies. No Gilligan! We unpacked and I then went to the landing to drink coffee and watch for that crazy goose. About two hours later I heard a familiar sound in the dark. It was Gilligan, who must have stopped to take some breaks on his flight home. We celebrated his arrival with the usual wheat bread, but I scolded him just a little for making me worry about him like that. As I mentioned my canoe trips are usually solo, but this one was in the company of a very noisy companion, but I must admit that I did enjoy the trip with my friend Gilligan.

Gilligan's social life....

It seemed that Gilligan's popularity had grown considerably. He is, of course, quite a handsome fellow and the life of any party. As mentioned earlier, he does sometimes attend local gatherings of river folks on a nearby island. There he mingles and enjoys an occasional snack of wheat bread. He is often offered much more but kindly refuses anything that may not be good for him. Sometimes he will just show up unannounced and instantly becomes the center of attention. He also doesn't mind posing for photographs and, in fact, will often stop what he is doing when he spots a camera. A local news team contacted me once and said there was a report that an eagle's nest was located along the river within the city limits. They asked me where it was located and I denied knowing anything about it. I told this fib to protect the eagle's location and keep the public from disturbing the nest. The reporter called me again later and said that she was certain there was a nest within the city limits and was also sure that I would know where it was. She had heard that I was a proponent of leaving wildlife alone and figured out why I was denying knowledge of the nest's location. She offered to keep the location a secret if I would take the news crew out in a boat to film the eagle, guaranteeing that they would say only that it was in the city without giving the location. I agreed to that.

Gilligan was there to greet the crew as they arrived at his landing, and of course was a big hit. We went down the river into the city and I showed them the nest. The pair of eagles were there busily shoring it up. They got some great film and I reminded them of their promise. On the way back to the landing the reporter was asking me questions about eagles and the environmental aspects of the river. She said she wished the animals could talk. She was sure they would have some opinions worth airing in an interview. I told her that I know an animal that will give her an interview. I coached her on how to talk to Gilligan. All she had to do was to say whatever she wanted and when she was ready for Gilligan to speak, just say his name very distinctly and he would respond. I also advised her that if a camera was aimed at Gilligan he would sit still for it. He loves being photographed.

Back at the dock I explained to Gilligan what was going on and asked him to come up on the grass. The reporter stood next to Gilligan while I stood on his other side, just out of camera range, and the cameraman began to film. The reporter began talking about the eagles and some environmental issues that affect wildlife. As she talked she said "And it's all for the protection of wildlife like Gilligan here." She lowered the microphone to Gilligan, whom when prompted by hearing his name, gave a very nice triple honk in response. The reporter was thrilled. When the story aired the reporter kept her word and did not divulge the location of the eagle's nest. It was a very nice piece with excellent footage of the eagles, but as usual Gilligan was the star of the show and his interview was a big hit. People called me for days about seeing Gilligan on TV, with many wanting to come and visit him. I kindly explained that Gilligan must have his privacy just as any celebrity needs from time to time.

Calling all geese....

An amazing and wonderful thing happens each fall and spring along the river. It is a migratory path that many flocks of geese

Photo by Author

Gilligan's visitors

travel, on their way south for the winter and north for the summer. As mentioned earlier, Gilligan migrated for one short season but now stays. He does, however, provide a service to his fellow geese and other waterfowl. When flocks are approaching in the sky, Gilligan goes out into the river and begins honking loudly. He appears to be communicating with the transient flock. I can only imagine that he is saying, "This is a safe place to rest" because they circle and land at Gilligan's Landing by the score. Upon landing on the opposite side of the river the geese usually form into small platoons and cross over gradually, escorted and encouraged by Gilligan. He mingles with the geese and seems to enjoy their company. The first few times this happened, I thought perhaps he was going to join the flock and leave but he never did. After a time of rest the flock begins to signal each other in goose language and organize for the next leg of their journey. As they take flight Gilligan stays behind and bids them farewell.

This service Gilligan provides is not limited to geese. He also has called down flocks of trumpeter swans. I can always tell when the swans arrive as they sound like Volkswagen horns. When Gilligan goes out to mingle with those huge swans it is the only time he appears small. Swans are very fussy birds and seem to quarrel amongst themselves a lot, but they never fight with their friend Gilligan. He seems to love and be loved by everyone, except maybe duck hunters! The variety of flying visitors to Gilligan's Landing is incredible. Many types of ducks stop by. Cormorants also land on the large snag across the river to fish, but are not as sociable and will usually fly off when Gilligan approaches to greet them. Less sociable by nature, but not so with Gilligan, are the Great Blue Herons. These birds live in communities but spend their days alone in their designated fishing spots along the river. One heron finally gave in to Gilligan's repeated attempts to be friends and often fishes from his landing. He usually remains there until a humans approach, and then flies away with a sound of disgust for being interrupted.

Many times Gilligan will stand watch at his landing in the setting sun and call out with a mighty honk, over and over again with the echo bouncing up and down the river. It is as though he is letting all know that this is his river but that he welcomes any friendly visitors to join him.

Gilligans many friends....

Most people do not regard geese as being very friendly fellows, but Gilligan is the exception. That isn't to say that he would not and has not defended himself. In fact he has had to teach a few of his living companions some lessons in humility along the way toward a peaceful co-existence. I have other critters living at or around my little cabin on the river, and one of those is Buffy. She is a big fluffy black and white cat with a very sweet attitude. She had no problem making friends with Gilligan and they continue to be buddies. Buffy was a stray that came to the home of a friend, who called to tell me about this really nice pregnant cat and wondered if I knew of someone who could care for her. I agreed to take her in for the winter so she could have her kittens safely, then find homes for them all. After ten weeks and no kittens, I discovered that Buffy was not pregnant at all but simply had a weight challenge. I then put her on a strict diet and exercise program. She slimmed down somewhat and in the meantime became a permanent fixture at my place.

Another arrival that took more adjustment was another stray cat, aptly named Taz (for Tasmanian Devil). Taz is a beautiful long-haired tomcat with a very aggressive attitude. When Taz first came on the scene he relentlessly teased Gilligan. Being so aggressive, he scared Gilligan and so the chase would go on. I tried to intervene and get Taz to stop bothering the goose with no success, so I finally concluded that they would have to work it out between themselves. Apparently that is what happened because one evening I looked out the window and sitting on the deck, side by side, were Gilligan and Taz as though enjoying the sunset together. One day Taz went for a boat ride with my son. As they were cruising up the river another boater passed by and blew his air horn at them while waving. The horn startled Taz so much that he jumped out of the moving boat into the river then swam to shore and ran into the woods. We spent two days looking for him with no luck. After that I guessed we would never see Taz again, being so far from home. About six weeks later I took my daughter with me to rescue some beached mussels one morning and when we landed the boat, Taz came running to us and ready to go home. He is a survivor.

'Bugs' is a rather unlikely name that my son gave to his large dog, and again there was an adjustment period involved for him with the cats and the goose. On his first visit to my cabin Taz attacked the dog. This seven-pound cat showed this 90-pound dog who was boss right away. Gilligan is a very smart goose and has always been wary of and stayed clear of dogs. He always avoided the playful antics of Bugs by flying off or staying out in the river. One day Bugs cornered Gilligan near the cabin. I heard the sound of the confrontation and quickly ran outside to break it up. I was apparently too late. By the time I arrived on the scene, Gilligan was chasing the dog down to the riverbank and it was Bugs who took refuge in the river. They apparently reached an understanding with this event and seem to get along fine now.

One of my favorite of Gilligan's friends is one who is not very sociable and never stops by for a visit, but flies over often. The eagle that lives just down the river hunts the waters in front of the cabin. He then enjoys his freshly caught fish in a dead tree just across the river. There is communication. Gilligan calls out to this majestic creature and he in kind replies with an unforgettable screech. I believe they have a certain respect for one another and salutations are exchanged.

There is a large beaver that living in a den along the riverbank near my cabin and he pays an occasional visit. He is a rascal and when I try to sleep in my houseboat he likes nothing better than to swim around the hull and slap it with his tail. One day the beaver decided to come ashore while Gilligan was on watch, and he apparently didn't like it one bit. I heard the familiar sound of an upset Gilligan, looked out the window, and there was the beaver and Gilligan standing face to face with the goose ranting and raving. The beaver seemed pretty passive and just stood there watching this hysterical goose, not knowing what to do. It was clear to me that Gilligan was about to attack the beaver and swift action had to be taken. I ran out the door, again too late. The beaver slid back into the river wanting nothing more to do with that noisy goose. I was glad he backed off because the beaver could have killed Gilligan had he attacked him.

Other critters are often seen visiting my cabin. I never know what to expect to see or what kind of reaction will happen among the resident critters, but it's always interesting. The one thing that remains unchanged is who is king of the river. It is Gilligan without a doubt and all within his domain know that.

Romance....

Yes, Gilligan has had some romantic encounters. Being such a handsome fellow it is no wonder why that might happen. It isn't really clear just what kind of goose Gilligan is. He seems to be a mixture and looks somewhat like a farm goose, but I've never said that in front of him. Canada geese mate for life but apparently not so in other breeds. He was courting this lovely Canada goose for a while. She would come by almost every day and sometimes he would go off with her. I thought there might be some possibilities for a long-term

Photo by Author
Daddy looking after the eggs

relationship. She seemed so perfect for him and also got along well with all the other critters in the area. She was a bit shy around humans but you can't blame her for that. I was sure that if she decided to stay we would have some little Gilligans before long. I also felt like she might be a good influence on a sometimes-rowdy goose that finds ways to get into trouble. The courting continued for a while and I observed that he was quite a gentleman. Then one day she was gone. I even went up and down the river in my boat to see if she was in trouble, but no lady goose (I hadn't given her a name). Well, I guess things just didn't work out for her and Gilligan and I never saw her again. She may have felt that he was too wild and rowdy for her, but anyone who really gets to know Gilligan is aware of his sweet nature.

The seasons passed and life went on. It was early the next spring when I noticed that Gilligan had not been around for several days. This was not particularly unusual but I was beginning to wonder about him. I knew he liked to go to the bluff in high water, and the river was rising very fast. I decided to take the boat and see if I could spot him. No Gilligan at the bluff. On the way back I was passing under a railroad bridge when I heard the honk of Gilligan coming from a sandbar under the bridge. I pulled back around and there was Gilligan sitting behind some rocks, not moving and calling to me. My first thought was that he was injured, so I pulled up to the sandbar and climbed up to see what was going on. To my surprise, Gilligan stood up to show me something that explained why he had been missing. He was guarding eggs! At first I thought maybe Gilligan must be a she, to be laying eggs but then I saw this pretty young white goose along the riverbank, shy of me and waiting for me to leave. I looked at Gilligan and said, "You sneaky devil, you." But he was being a faithful husband and soon-to-be father, so I was very proud of him. He was apparently proud to show me the eggs, but soon sat back on them for warmth. But there was a problem that I knew was coming. The water was rising fast and I knew that by the next day this little haven they had set up would be washed out by the river and the eggs would be lost.

This called for a plan. I had to move the eggs to higher ground. I don't know why the couple had not chosen the bluff but, that is where I intended to relocate the family. Maybe the lady didn't like the accommodations at the bluff and preferred this beachfront location, but it was a poor choice during the spring rise. Over Gilligan's objections I carefully removed the four eggs and placed them in the boat. I could tell that Gilligan was considering attacking me, but he surely came to realize that I would never harm their eggs and must have a good reason for my actions. Lady Goose continued to stay back and watch the activity. As I slowly pulled away from the sand bar Gilligan followed, making a lot of noise. The bluff was not far away and I hoped that they would both follow me to the new home. If they did not, then I would have to take the eggs home and try to incubate them myself, but preferred to let nature takes its course. After arriving at the bluff I searched for and found the right location; high enough to be clear of flood waters, with soft, sandy terrain. Overhead was a steep bank for protection from the weather and other animals. Yes, this was perfect! I placed the eggs in the sand and piled rocks around the area to simulate the last place as best I could. All the while Gilligan was getting in the way trying to protect the eggs. As soon as I set the eggs in place, Gilligan immediately went to them and covered them with his warm body. Lady Goose followed but stayed in the river. I then left them alone to do whatever redecorating that may be needed to suit them.

By the next morning their former dwelling was under water. For several days after that I went back by the bluff to check on the newlyweds but did not go ashore. I wanted to keep my distance and not disturb them. They had reluctantly accepted the new nesting spot and I was certain that they were happy that I came along and relocated them, considering the floodwaters passing by. It was a very busy spring for me and I had to be away for several weeks. Friends had seen no sign of Gilligan during my time away so I went back to the bluff to check on them. They were gone! No Gilligan, no lady goose, no eggs. There were pieces of eggs, but I could not tell whether they had hatched or been eaten. On the way back I was feeling sad about what I had found until I passed the power plant, which is just three miles up the river from my cabin. There, along the opposite bank was a white goose trying to hide under the brush with four baby geese following her. I wondered if this was Gilligan's lady goose. I suspected it was since white wild geese are fairly rare around these parts. Well, if that was mama and those are the babies, then where was Gilligan?

I found the answer to that as soon as I arrived back at the landing. There was Gilligan, apparently taking a break from his fatherly duties and paying a visit. We celebrated his family with a round of wheat bread and soon he headed back up the river. Time passed and I made regular visits to see the youngsters, without getting too close. They were wild and I did not want them to become too accustomed to humans, as that could be dangerous for them. After the babies lost their fuzz and took on feathers they were an amazing sight, being four Gilligan clones. With the exception of the beak color, they all took after their father in every way. Gilligan has a black beak and Lady Goose has an orange beak. They grew very fast during the summer and in no time all four youngsters were bigger than their petite mother. I camped a few times on a nearby beach to watch them from a distance. Gilligan would be gone a lot during the day, but returned each evening to tend to his family. One night he paid me a visit at my camp and brought the kids with him. I was amazed. I had been so careful not to get close and he brought them to me! It turned out to be a nice visit and they went home shortly afterward.

As fall was approaching I began to wonder what was to become of Gilligan's family during the winter. Would they stay? Would they migrate? The baby geese were flying now. I had watched them practice with Gilligan's guidance. I was doing another camp-over one night and the next morning I woke to the sound of many geese in the water. I looked out to see about 40 geese and among them were Gilligan and family. It was as though a conference was going on. I thought, is this it? Could I be lucky enough to witness an adoption of this family by a migrating flock? It seemed so. After much discussion they began to organize for what I recognized to be preparations for flight. The geese went airborne in groups, re-grouped in the sky into a rough "V" formation, and then they were gone. The flock, Lady Goose, and the baby geese were gone but Gilligan stayed behind. I had expected him to go too, but for whatever reason he chose to stay on his river. It was a tearful event but a happy one at the same time. Gilligan had been a dedicated father. He and Lady Goose had raised four more like Gilligan to grace the earth. Whatever his reason for staying, it was probably the right one, since it was made under completely natural conditions and nature's way is almost always in the best interest of creatures. I realize that I did intervene with nature when I moved those eggs, but have no regrets after this wonderful experience with my friend Gilligan. The next spring I looked for the young geese to come back, not knowing for sure if they would. Gilligan migrated one winter and came back so there was a chance. They apparently chose to go elsewhere. God bless them!

Civic responsibilities....

In the spring of 1999, Gilligan was awarded yet another great honor. Having gained quite a name for himself from all his friends, the television interview and newspaper stories, Gilligan was asked to be the official mascot for the Indiana Waterways Association. IWA is a non-profit organization that is involved with river activities, cleanups, and other environmental concerns. Their primary objective is creating public awareness campaigns and gaining public support for waterway improvements and other projects. They indicated the need for a loveable water-related character to represent the organization, and felt like Gilligan would be perfect along with being well-known locally. Upon acceptance of the honor Gilligan has been featured in several newsletters, posters, and other public relations efforts, along with having his own web page on the Indiana Waterways Association site called "Gilligans Links."

Maiden Voyage....

I have a rather unusual watercraft. It used to be a canoe but is now a dinghy for my houseboat. This alteration came about when I crashed the canoe in rapids, nearly breaking it in half. Seeing my favorite canoe sitting there broken was depressing, but I kept thinking that I might find a use for what was left of it. Gilligan had already been using the upside down vessel as a lookout platform, but I kept thinking that there must be something it could be used for. Then one day while working on my houseboat it came to me. I cut the canoe in half where it was broken, built a transom on the back and painted it. I then had a lightweight dinghy for my houseboat. I powered it with an electric trolling motor since; trying to paddle half a canoe will not bring the intended results. A paddle could be used to steer it like a rudder though. Gilligan didn't seem to mind giving up his perch for the project. I was ready for the maiden voyage. I hooked up the trolling motor, got my life preserver on, put on my special river hat that I reserve for special occasions, and I was ready. While loading up the little craft, Buffy came to the landing to see what was going on. Gilligan of course was there. I carefully lowered myself into the unstable vessel, discovering right away that I would have to sit on the bottom because sitting in the seat caused it to be top-heavy and it tended to roll over. After getting positioned I was ready to go. Buffy decided she wanted to go, too. She is a true river cat and does enjoy boat rides. She jumped in and found the only space available to sit, which was on my lap.

I started the little motor and pulled away with Gilligan swimming along-side as expected. I think Gilligan was a little worried about this contraption that Buffy and I were in as he was conveying some rather stressful-sounding honks. A couple of times Gilligan cut across the bow in what seemed an attempt to get me to turn back. I continued up the river and all seemed well. The boat handled reasonably well as long as I stayed seated in the bottom.

We went about two miles up the river. I felt that it was an adequate test and so turned back. Gilligan continued his vigilant escort and seemed happy about the direction we were now going. While we were gone a friend had stopped by the cabin but couldn't find me, and had walked to the landing to see if I might be there. When she walked out on the dock she could see me coming back down the river. As I approached the dock, she began to laugh. I wondered what was so funny and looked behind me. Hmmm, nothing there! By the time I got to the dock she was almost in hysterics. After getting her composure she explained. "Why, Jerry Hay, you are probably the only man around who one might see going down the river in half a canoe with a cat in your lap and a goose swimming alongside. And that awful hat! Some people just might consider you a bit eccentric." I replied that I saw nothing unusual or anything wrong with being eccentric, if that's what you want to call it. Well, the test was successful and the half canoe became the *Wabash Queen's* dinghy that has served me well. Gilligan has never shown an interest in riding in it but Buffy still enjoys an occasional cruise in it.

No matter what I am doing at the landing or in the yard, Gilligan is always there to give advice and keep me company. He has been there for other maiden voyages, including the arrival of the *Wabash Queen*. He didn't quite know what to make of that floating house coming to his landing and gave it quite an inspection on arrival. After a time he gave a honk of approval and I knew I could keep it. I have to be very careful pulling away from the dock since I must back up first, and when Gilligan is in one of those "you can't go" moods he will get behind the boat and attempt to block it. Those big paddles turning could shred a goose, so I have to call him around to the side of the boat, then back up. Upon going forward he would be gently nudged aside if in the way.

Gilligan has been a real treasure in my life and I value his friendship and trust. When he hangs out with me it is not to beg for food, since that is only for special wheat- bread celebrations. He takes walks with me and is always there, just wanting to be with me. I work on a steamboat and am gone for weeks at a time. During that time Gilligan is seldom seen by those who look after my cabin in my absence. When I return he returns. He has amazing hearing for a fellow with no visible ears. He knows when I come home and apparently hears my voice because soon after arriving I hear him in the distance coming to greet me, and is he happy to see me! Something magic happened between that big goose and myself on the day of the rescue that created a permanent bond. Along with our unusual relationship I have also been blessed with befriending a remarkable animal who is not your normal goose. I have never taken him for granted and enjoy each encounter with him, knowing that one day he will be gone. I continue to respect his freedom and still maintain that he his not my goose. He is here by choice and may leave by his own choice. I could never claim ownership of such a free spirit and part of nature's wonder. He is Gilligan the Goose, the most loveable goose on Planet Earth.

Chapter 7

Rescue From a Dock

I received a call during the winter of 1999 from a lady whose father was retiring. She explained that he had always wanted to take a trip on the Wabash River in a canoe but had never had the opportunity. Then he started planning a trip and looking for a canoe, so she began to take his plan seriously. Knowing that he had no canoeing experience, she was concerned for his safety. The Wabash is a large and sometimes dangerous river, so she was asking for my advice regarding his plan. I told her that it would be a good idea for him to get some experience on smaller rivers, or take the trip with someone with experience. During the next few days she called a few more times with questions. She then called and asked if I would be willing to take him on a canoe trip down the Wabash River for a few days. I agreed to schedule it for the following summer, suggesting that a three-day trip would be plenty for a person who had never canoed or camped before. A three-day trip would be about 100 miles and I would select a good stretch of river for us. A trip from Lafayette, Indiana, to Terre Haute, Indiana, is about that length and is a beautiful section of river.

On June 9, 2000, Ken met me at my riverfront house. My son trucked us to Lafayette for the float back to Terre Haute. It was raining hard when we put in and the river was rising. That first day it continued to rain most of the day, but we had a tailwind and made our planned 33 miles easily. I was pleasantly surprised to find that my paddling partner was in great shape and never tired out. He also adapted to the canoe and paddling very quickly. That evening I found a suitable campsite that had been used often. Luckily I discovered a woodpile with a plastic tarp covering it, since there was no other dry wood for a fire. We were grateful to find the wood and the next morning I left a ten-dollar bill and note in a plastic bag, and attached it to the remaining covered wood. It would not be right to use someone's wood without paying for it.

The next day was sunny with a mild wind, causing things to dry out nicely. We traveled beyond our quota and began looking for a good campsite. I spotted an old dock at a steep riverbank, with wooden steps leading to high ground. Upon inspection it appeared to be a spot frequented by fishermen, with a dirt road coming from a cornfield. I usually stay away from making camp at places that have vehicle access, preferring islands or more remote locations, but we had already hauled the gear up and it was getting late. I made sure there weren't any "No Trespassing" signs and proceeded to set up camp and gather firewood.

While I was busy gathering kindling, Ken yelled out, "There are two cars coming real fast". I went to the opening in the woods and saw a small black car barreling down the dirt road, leaving a huge trail of dust. A Blazer was passing the car and fishtailing on the soft dirt road. My first thought was that we were indeed trespassing and an irritated landowner was in a hurry to chase us off, maybe with a shotgun. As the Blazer approached the turn-off toward the river I told Ken to stay back and cautiously walked toward the vehicle. I found a middle-aged woman whom I'll call Dolly for a couple of obvious reasons, at the wheel smiling at me with a friendly greeting. I asked if we were trespassing and she said' "Hail no, everbody comes here. Wur jest goin fishin'." I noticed a baby with her in a car seat. I told her that she sort of spooked me the way she was driving and she said that she was just having a little fun with her sister in the other car.

When her sister caught up and pulled in I could see a very large man (the name Jethro fits), who unfolded as he extracted himself from the little car. This was the sister's boyfriend. We chatted for a while and they seemed friendly enough. While we were setting up our camp, a pickup truck arrived on the scene. A man got out (I'll call him Buford), and said he was just stopping by to see if anybody was catching any fish. He shared a few of his fish stories, then left. I was beginning to think this was not going to be my idea of a peaceful evening along the river. The trio and baby headed down to the old dock to begin fishing, only to discover that it was listing at quite an angle. It had apparently been tied off at a higher river level and was now partially grounded.

Jethro decided to do something about that so he unhooked the support cables from some trees. He then gave the dock a mighty push, attempting to get it completely floating. As he pushed and lifted at the same time, one of the plastic flotation barrels rolled out from under the dock. Jethro fell over the barrel and face down into the muddy bank. The dock went into the water but was now listing the other way, due to the missing barrel. One corner of the dock was swamped. As Jethro was pondering the situation, Dolly called out to him."Git in the river and lift up the dock, whilst I push the barrel back under it." Jethro reluctantly waded into the river where he was knee deep in mud. He made several attempts to lift the dock with Dolly on it, leaning off the edge and trying to push the barrel under. Getting exhausted Jethro said, "Yer gonna have to git yer big butt off-a-there so'se I can lift it high-nough." She told him to give it another try with more of her weight on the barrel, and her knees on the dock. With another mighty heave, Jethro lifted again while Dolly leaned forward on the floating barrel to pull it toward her and the dock. The barrel went into a forward roll (barrel roll), and Dolly went off the dock, rolled over the barrel and made a not-so-graceful nose-dive into the muddy bank.

Anticipating a possible photo opportunity I had my camera ready and got the shot of Dolly rolling headfirst in mud with her body still lying over the barrel. Jethro tried to help her out of this precarious position but had his own problems. He was stuck in the mud and could not move. Dolly finally rolled off the barrel and partially into the river, and then climbed up the muddy bank.

Photo by Author

Dolly does a barrel roll.

After getting my composure back I said, "I think this project has got you over a barrel." Dolly's sister (I'll call her Pearl), stayed on the high bank with Dolly's grandchild, enjoying the show with Ken and I. Not being ready to give up yet, Dolly got into the river to push the barrel under the dock while Jethro tried to lift it again. This time they were somewhat successful. The barrel slipped under the dock but in a vertical position. The dock was again listing at about the same angle as it had when it was grounded. Dolly said, "To hell with it, we can fish from it like it is." By then Jethro had sunk deeper into the mud. He struggled, while pulling himself upon the dock. He finally freed himself but without one of his shoes.

The three hillbillies and baby finally got onto the dock. The baby was left in the car seat and kept from sliding on the angular dock surface with a bungee cord. They finally began to fish. It was getting dark and chilly but Jethro didn't seem to mind fishing in wet clothes with one shoe. He was proud of his victory over the dock and test of strength, and didn't mind talking about it. It was my observation that they were no better off then when they started, but said nothing. Dolly had a change of clothes in her Blazer. I had a little conference with Ken and asked him if he would mind donating three of his beers. I explained that we really didn't know these people and I figured it might be a good idea to give them an offering in friendship. This would increase our chances of waking up the next morning with all our equipment. He agreed and I took the beers to the misguided fishermen. I went back to our campsite. Each of us had our own tent and Ken had already turned in for the night. Getting to sleep was difficult as the trio had a noisy celebration each time a fish was caught and loud cussing for each that got away. I was getting used to the noise and just beginning to drift off, when I heard a loud cracking of wood, water splashing, and screaming.

I grabbed my flashlight and hurried toward the noise. I didn't know what was wrong, but I did know that someone was in trouble at the dock. The dock had split in half. With the one barrel flipped vertical, the weight on the old dock with those people on it was too much for it. Upon my arrival at the scene, my first thought was the baby. The dock decking had broken and formed a trough in the water, with barrels still holding the outside edges up. The car seat had slid into the trough, but came to a rest between the two halves. Jethro had fallen though and was holding the two halves together to keep the baby from falling between them. Dolly had also tumbled into the broken section and was holding onto the car seat. Pearl had not fallen in but was trapped on the half of the dock that was not attached to anything but Jethro, who was holding on to it. To make matters worse, they had not re-attached the line to the dock, so the only thing holding it all had been the wooden stairs. But the dock had pulled loose from the stairs and the only thing keeping that it in place was Jethro's feet in the riverbed and Pearl grabbing hold of an overhanging tree limb. They were all in big trouble.

I ran to the cable end and quickly wrapped it around a tree. This secured at least half the dock. I raced down the twisted stairs to the end, then down the muddy riverbank within reach of the dock. I pulled hard and was able to get the dock close enough for me to reach the baby in the car seat that Dolly was sliding up the dock toward me. I took the wet baby and climbed back up the bank to the stairway and then to the dry bank above. Carrying a small child is not usually a problem for me but with the car seat, deep mud and twisted stairway, in the dark, this was no easy task. I was surprised that the 22-month-old child remained so calm throughout the event and did not cry out, even though he was wet and cold. I left the child in the car seat, went back to the dock, and grabbed some rope from my canoe and a six-foot wooden plank that lay along the bank. I placed the plank on the mud for a catwalk and attached a rope from a tree to myself for a lifeline in case I slipped into the river. I pitched another length of rope to Jethro so that he could loosely tie the two halves together and climb back out from between them. One at a time, I assisted each of them off the dock and onto the stairway.

We were all finally on high ground. We were wet, cold, and tired, but safe. They were very grateful for my rescue efforts and we reflected on the event. They decided that they had had enough fishing for that evening; besides, all their night crawlers had been dumped into the river. Dolly had dry clothes for the child and after changing him, they all left. I might have wondered why Ken had not come down to help, but was too busy to think about it at the time of the rescue. When I went back to the campsite I discovered that he had slept through it all. Ken got up before me the next morning and as I arose he came to tell me that those hillbillies had really torn up the dock last night, and I should come and see it. While canoeing that day my thoughts went to the hap-hazard group of people and the events leading to the rescue. How was it that I selected this unlikely place to camp? I always prefer remote places, but that night I had been lead there. I remembered that when I reached out to grab the child's car seat, he reached for me with his little hand. The image of that tiny hand reaching for me will be with me forever. I am grateful that I was there that night, not only because I was able to help, but also because I had made some more river friends, which are always valuable to me. We completed our canoe trip with no more life-threatening events. Ken finally got to do the trip that he had always dreamed of. For me the little trip ended with another assurance that there are always new adventures and interesting people to be found on the river.

Photo by Author

The morning after

Chapter 8

The Great Duck Race

Back home when there is a river event or activity, I am often called upon to help with the planning. Since I wrote the Wabash River Guide book, I was the likely person to give advice or become directly involved in a program. One day I received a call from the director of the local YWCA, who told me that they were planning a fund-raising event, which would be called the "Great Duck Race". They were going to rent ten thousand rubber ducks, have people adopt a duck (for a fee), then race the ducks down the river. Prizes would be awarded to the people whose adopted duck placed first through tenth in the race. My first question was, "Where in the heck do you rent ten thousand rubber ducks?" There is a company that does exactly that. They wanted me to plan the race course and coordinate all aspects of the river portion of the event. I knew that the project would take a lot of time, but I agreed to help.

I was told that this type of event had been done in other cities, so I decided to do some research on how it was handled. One of the cities was Chicago, which rented fifty thousand ducks for their event. I called a friend who works at a marina in Chicago to ask if he knew of the event and how it went. He advised me that they had established a starting point on the Chicago River, with the ending point of the race about a mile away. They launched the ducks into the river using dump trucks to start the race. My friend said, "It all went pretty well, except for one little thing. Whoever set up the finish line didn't know which way the river flows and all the ducks went the wrong direction." I said, "Well, I know which way the river flows so that shouldn't be a problem." I had a few weeks to get the plan together and find several volunteers. I would need boats, floats, a duck launching method, and duck retrieval system.

The first thing I did was to put out a few calls for people with boats. That was the easy part, as within a few days I had more than I needed. The boats would be needed to help herd the ducks that went astray by throwing wakes along-side the contestants while they floated down the river. I would also need boats and people with nets to scoop up the ducks at the end of the race. In addition, boats would be needed to chase down any runaway ducks that headed down the river, beyond the finish line. It was important to retrieve the ducks or the YWCA would be charged for them, thus cutting into their potential profit. I had decided that the best launching method to begin the race would be from a highway bridge. This meant having people line up along the length of the bridge with ducks in barrels, washtubs, bags, or whatever, and simply dump the ducks into the river on signal. The YWCA found enough volunteers for the launching. The race's finish line would be about one mile down the river, near the city dock. Needing to test the approximate length of time for the race, I put a rubber duck into the river at the bridge and followed it in a boat to the dock. ETA would be about twenty minutes at the current river speed, as this was a low water time of year. I was concerned that since the current was so slow, a strong south wind might cause the ducks to flow upstream. In that case, the boats would also be needed to use their props to flush the ducks downstream.

The company that rents out the ducks also provided a catch tube. This was a Plexiglas tube of about eight inches diameter, mounted on floats. The purpose of the tube is to have a single source to funnel the leading ducks into, one at a time, and determine a winner. I was happy to see this device since I was having trouble visualizing the challenge of picking the winning ducks if they all came down the river in a large group. The river is several hundred feet wide, so I knew that it would be necessary to create some type of giant floating funnel for race day. The boats could herd the mass of rubber ducks into the funnel, and as it narrowed toward the catch tube the first few would be channeled into the tube and victory. As the planning continued and publicity of the event spread, I realized the scope of the race. By race day it had become a media event and nearly all the ducks had been adopted. Venders would be lined up along the river and thousands of spectators were expected. I began to get a little nervous about my portion of the activities, since the success of the race depended on my plans working. I rechecked all systems and tried to think of anything that could go wrong. On the morning of the race I arrived on the scene at daybreak.

Soon my friends began arriving with their boats. Venders started setting up their tables and tents. It was time to build the giant funnel on the river. I took my twenty-two foot deck boat out 150 feet from the dock and anchored. Another boat came alongside and paid out a line from my boat to the dock at a 45-degree angle. A second line was taken from the other side of my boat at the same angle and distance, where it was attached to an anchored buoy. We then began placing "noodles" on the line. Noodles are Styrofoam tubes used as swimming pool toys. The noodles were hollow, allowing the rope to pass through them, creating flotation and sidewalls for the giant funnel. The first problem encountered was that the noodles would not stay together, and gaps between the four-foot sections would allow ducks to pass through. We also discovered any work on the noodle funnel was difficult from a powerboat, since it was difficult to hover in place and the boats dragged the line if they held on to it. Fortunately, two of our volunteers were an elderly gentleman and his granddaughter. That was fortunate because their vessel was a canoe, the only watercraft maneuverable and light enough to do the job. It was pleasantly ironic that some of the boaters laughed at the thought of those two in a little canoe being of any help, then to have them save the day. They skirted along the lines and attached the ends of the noodles together with duct tape, something most wise boaters carry onboard.

With the funnel now in place and thirteen boats in the river, we were ready. The starting time for the race was approaching. The local Sheriff was onboard my boat. He was to officially designate the winning ducks as they floated into the catch tube, one at a time. I could see the people lining the bridge awaiting my signal to launch the ducks. Spectators lined the shore to cheer on the ducks. Television crews were preparing to film the great event. The weather was perfect with mild wind and slow current, but in the back of my mind I was hoping that none of the ducks would pop over those four-inch diameter noodles as they collided in the funnel. In case a few went past it, we had boats behind the funnel to pick up any strays, so why worry? With everything in place I held up the starting gun and fired.

It was amazing to see the flow of yellow rubber ducks flowing off the bridge a mile away. The crowd cheered and began walking the riverbank alongside. People were apparently cheering on each of their ducks, but I had no clue as to how they would know which duck belonged to whom. The mass of ducks began to spread out across the river, but the herd boats went into action, racing back and forth alongside the group and keeping them in formation. It was a beautiful sight! A few ducks got past the boats and ran aground, but the boaters quickly snatched them up and pitched them into the race lane of the river. Anticipation was mounting as the ducks approached the open end of the 300-foot-wide floating funnel. I thought, "This is perfect, all is well." The leading ducks entered the funnel. They began to fill the wide part of the funnel, and all ducks were on course. As they bumped into the angled sides of the funnel, not one duck popped over the noodles. Instead, the ducks bumped the noodles and hesitated for a second, before the current drew them under the line, where they popped up the other side. Not just a few, but all of them! Every duck was drawn under the barrier the same way and not one duck was diverted toward the boat and catch tube. We stood on the boat in shock as we watched the ducks pass by us and head down the river. Some ducks even went under the boat and popped up the other side. Nothing was stopping the stampeding flock of rubber ducks. Things were out of control! The crowd on shore was gasping. The man calling the race on the loud speaker went silent.

We still needed to determine the winning ducks, but the fellows in the boats behind us raced in to start catching the runaways. I yelled on the loudspeaker to stand down. "Don't touch those ducks," I called. I unhooked the dock and buoy lines from my boat and started down the river to get ahead of the ducks. The hull of the boat pushed most of them aside as we made our way to the lead ducks. By the time we got to them, they had separated enough that we could identify the few ducks that were ahead of the rest. We got ahead of them, turned back toward them, and plucked each of the first ten ducks from the water. After the Sheriff logged them in as winners, we sped back to the dock where people were anxiously awaiting the results. The winning ducks were announced and the happy winning adopters came forward. Then I realized that our work was far from done. There were still 9, 990 rubber ducks going down the river that must be retrieved. The boaters were still waiting for my order to catch the ducks, having heard my last urgent message not to touch them. I got on the loudspeaker and said, "Catch those damn ducks." Then they went into action.

The team went down the river with the faster boats passing the slower boats to begin their work, starting with the lead ducks. Most boaters had fishnets, which were very helpful for scooping up many ducks at a time. There were bass boats, ski boats, cabin cruisers, jonboats, and of course the canoe. All were working together on their mission. They were even flanking the ducks with military-style efficiency. Boats full of yellow ducks could be seen heading back up the river to deliver their payload to the waiting people at the dock. One fellow in a small jonboat was so loaded with rubber ducks that one could only see him and his outboard motor. Our man-and-granddaughter canoe team proved effective for close bank retrieval by skirting along the shallow shore, loading up with ducks, and hitching a tow behind a powerboat upriver to the dock. It was a glorious sight! After about an hour, it appeared that all ducks were present and accounted for. We celebrated our victory, and received applause from onlookers.

A few days after the event, one of the sponsors hosted a banquet to honor the volunteers. The YWCA was very grateful for the assistance of the boaters, particularly their rescue of the runaway rubber ducks. Upon recognizing them for their efforts, each one was presented with a reward...a rubber duck. I don't believe they could have thought of a better way to show their appreciation. Each one of us accepted our duck as though it was a medal of honor. I still have my rubber duck and it travels with me to this day. My duck has been with me on every major river in the United States, traveled with me in many states, and has been onboard with me on flights. It is probably the most traveled rubber duck in the world.

Lesson learned: The little glitch (actually big glitch) was the ducks being drawn under the floating funnel. That should have been tested, and I should have had some idea that it could happen. The following year, they asked me to do it again but I was not going to be available. I transferred the leadership to an able river friend, with recommendations to build a better funnel. He contacted a U.S. Coast Guard Auxiliary and arranged to borrow some spill containment buoys. The large, heavier lengths of flotation worked very well and the next year went much smoother. Another point made in this experience is to never scoff at the attributes of any vessel. Each type of boat has his advantages and disadvantages. Those folks in the fancy boats who questioned the value of the little canoe found this to be true. The elderly man with his granddaughter in that little aluminum canoe proved invaluable. The next year more canoeists were encouraged to be on the team.

Illustration by Author

Chapter 9

Anatomy of a River

The best river to use as an example of waterway anatomy is the mighty Mississippi River. To know the Mississippi is to know all rivers. The Mississippi drainage basin draws from 31 states and two provinces in Canada. It drains 40% of the continental United States. The basin extends from the Appalachian Mountains in the east to the Rocky Mountains in the west. Within the basin are impressive size rivers that have tributaries carrying water from great distances. From each tiny stream to the giant river itself, the waterways have similarities and all are seeking sea level. All converge into the main trunk of the lower Mississippi River.

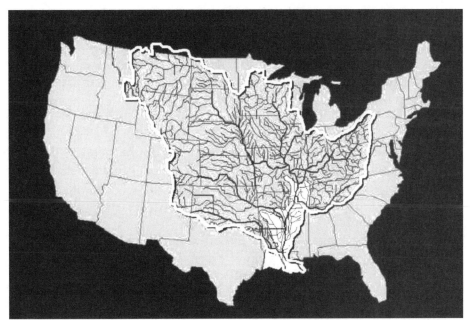

Courtesy of the U.S. Army Corps of Engineers
Mississippi River Drainage Basin

One could put a note in a bottle and place it in a tiny brook in western New York. That bottle could drift down the brook and enter the Allegheny River, then into the Ohio River at Pittsburgh. It could follow the Ohio River to the Mississippi River at it's confluence at Cairo, Illinois. From there it could eventually pass by New Orleans and drift into the Gulf of Mexico. Once in the Gulf it would be possible for someone to find and read the note in Florida, or as far away as Africa.

Early French explorers traveled great distances on the rivers and made amazingly accurate maps. They were astonished by the size of the basin and distant reaches of the tributaries. For many years a Northwest Passage was sought, which would provide a route to the Pacific Ocean. It wasn't until the Lewis and Clark expedition that it was finally discovered that there is none. The Rocky Mountains proved to be the barrier and long portage to waterways running to the Pacific.

Rivers do not follow the compass. Rivers can run any direction as they seek the sea. People have often told me that they live near the only river in the United States that runs north. I then proceed to give names of many rivers that run north. It is true that the general course of most rivers in the United States flows south. That is because the elevation above sea level has a general slope to the south. The facts are simple. Rivers run downhill and in some areas of the country downhill is north. Rivers will also follow a path of least resistance in making diversions in their course, but it is gravity that determines the direction it takes. A case in point is the Niagara River. It flows north from Lake Erie to Lake Ontario. There is a substantial drop in elevation between the lakes, and the river makes a very dramatic drop to reach its destination (Niagara Falls). Along with the general direction of flow, many rivers actually flow all directions. Rivers bend, loop, and double-loop (S bends). When traveling on rivers, people can become confused if they rely totally on the direction that the water is going. A person might wake up one morning and wonder why the sun is rising in the West, if the boat is pointed downriver and the sun is on the right. The lower Mississippi takes a very snakelike path to the ocean. When I am talking about directions on a river, I prefer to use only two: Upriver and downriver, neither of which is on a compass.

Most major rivers have insignificant beginnings. They start as runoff from high ground or overflow from a lake. Some rivers begin with ice melting, such as from glacier country. Rivers can also begin as a confluence of two or more other streams or rivers. As the stream flows, other streams join it. It begins to take on size as it continues to absorb tributaries. At some point it will become a major river. This process is ongoing in thousands of basins throughout the world.

Technically all waterways have a basin. Even the tiniest stream has a small basin of water flowing into it, like veins and arteries. The small basins are part of large basins, which are part of even larger basins. To call the lower Mississippi River a trunk is very descriptive, since its basin resembles a giant leafless tree. Some rivers begin quite large. An example of this is the Ohio River. The Allegheny River flows south and the Monongahela River flows northwest. Where they join is the official beginning of the Ohio River at Pittsburgh. In the truest sense, the Ohio River is the Allegheny; the name was changed at the fork of the Monongahela. Or it could be argued that the Allegheny is actually the headwaters of the Ohio River and should be called the Ohio all the way to its source. There are many rivers that have controversial names. Another one is the Mississippi River. There are those who argue that it should be called the Missouri River from the Missouri's headwaters, past the confluence with the upper Mississippi River and on down to the Gulf of Mexico. This theory actually makes sense because the Missouri River is much longer than the Mississippi at their confluence. In fact, the Missouri River is longer than the entire Mississippi River by about 200 miles. In addition, the Missouri River basin is much larger than the upper Mississippi River basin. If one looks at an aerial view of the confluence, the upper Mississippi appears to be the tributary. The brown color of the lower Mississippi comes primarily from the Missouri River, which has six times as much sand and silt as the upper Mississippi. By world standards, the Mississippi River is measured from the headwaters of the Missouri and not the headwaters of the Mississippi. These are all sound reasons for the name discrepancy but the fact remains that the rivers were named by the Indians and translated or corrupted to European names. Indians named the rivers in a relatively small region. However there were similarities in the pronunciation and meaning of the names given to the Mississippi. The Ottawa Indians called it the Missis-Sepi, the Chippewa called it Meze-Zebe, and the Kickapoo named it Mechas-Sepua. All translate to mean "Large River" or "Great River."

Many of the early explorers traveled down or up the rivers continuing the names given to them by the Indians. With downriver exploration it is easy to understand why they would drift by large tributaries and continue with the name. Going upriver the name continuation would depend on which fork of the river confluence they chose to take. Had upriver explorers taken a left turn at the confluence of the two great rivers, the Missouri would indeed be called the Mississippi to this day. Had they traveled first down the Missouri River to the confluence, it is likely that the river would be called the Missouri all the way to the Gulf of Mexico. Some make a similar argument that the Ohio River carries more water and is much wider than the Mississippi River at their confluence, and should continue to the Gulf of Mexico as the Ohio River. I even had a person ask me why the Mississippi River is named after only one of the states it passes by. While fighting to keep my composure I explained that the river had the name first and that the state of Mississippi is named after the river.

The early upriver exploration of rivers with given names is why we have so many rivers with forks named for the main river. Travelers would be going upriver and come to a split where both

Photo by Author
Mississippi River headwaters

sides appear nearly the same size. Not knowing which one was the main trunk of the river, they would first take one fork and may name it the North Fork. While going up that fork they may encounter another split off to the right and name it the Middle Fork, knowing that there was a South Fork that they had not yet explored. Then, of course, they went back downriver and explored the South Fork. On all rivers with forks, just one of them actually leads to the true headwaters of the river, the true source generally being the longest fork. Many forks are impressive in size and would merit having their own name, rather than being called a fork.

Putting all the name controversy aside, the official source of the Mississippi River is Lake Itasca in northern Minnesota. I visited the lake and waded across the Mississippi as it flowed from the lake over the shallow rocks. Not far from Lake Itasca is Elk Lake, with an overflow leading into Lake Itasca. I wondered why Elk Lake isn't considered the true source, but I am not one to start any trouble so I'll leave it at that. Itasca means "true head", so that's good enough for me.

It is interesting to note the huge difference between the upper Mississippiand the lower Mississippi. These sections are treated as two rivers in most respects, including on river charts. The navigable mileage markers for the lower Mississippi begin at the mouth of the river, below New Orleans, and end at the confluence of the Ohio River at Cairo, Illinois. Mile zero for the upper Mississippi begins at Cairo and continues northward to Minneapolis. Besides the obvious difference in water volume, which is measured in cubic feet per second, there are other distinctions between the upper and lower Mississippi. The upper Mississippi is much older than the lower Mississippi. In fact, the Missouri/Upper Mississippi built the Lower Mississippi. At the end of the last ice age, huge amounts of sand and silt were carried down the river that ended near present-day Cape Girardeau, Missouri. This massive deposit ended there because the Gulf of Mexico went that far north. For thousands of years the Missouri and Upper Mississippi rivers built the delta that filled in the upper reaches of the Gulf. It changed course often, flipping back and forth like a giant hose, depositing more sand and silt and building the alluvial land. As it built more land, with each rise it cut a winding channel through that land. Most people visualize a river as a waterway that has cut a path through existing land. The lower Mississippi built the land that carries the river to the sea. This also creates differences between the upper and lower rivers. The upper is rocky and has a greater drop in elevation per mile. The lower is sandy with less graduation of level per mile. In the lower Mississippi Valley, bedrock can be thousands of feet below the surface.

Making the upper Mississippi River navigable required the building of many locks and dams along the way. Before the dams, the river would simply run out of navigable water. The lower Mississippi, below Saint Louis, has no dams. The swift currents, aided by wing dams, cause a channel to be scoured out, which remains deep most of the time. The land is flat and is not suitable for building dams, as the water needs to back up into a valley behind a dam. Most people expect a river to get wider toward the mouth, but the Mississippi actually narrows as it flows to the sea. One of the reasons is that it has been confined by levees. It is carrying huge amounts of water but is very deep, around 200 feet at New Orleans. The widest part of the river is on the Upper Mississippi, near Red Wing, Minnesota. The sand and silt pouring into the Mississippi from the Chippewa River built a natural dam, closing it off and forming a natural lake over two miles wide. The water backed up for many miles until the river broke through, cutting its present-day channel and creating Lake Pepin.

Rivers have often changed course. The changes are usually small, but sometimes they are big. The most common change occurs in the form of cut-offs. During flooding the waters may cut across the land at a bend in the river. If enough force is in the current crossing the bend it will scour out a new channel, leaving the old channel in what is called an oxbow. The oxbow will usually silt up on the upriver side and form an oxbow lake. Sometimes it will completely dry up, leaving only a scar of the old riverbed. At times the old bend will continue to carry water and the land between the old river bed and the new channel will become an island. Many cut-offs weremanmade to shorten the river and avoid bends that were difficult to navigate. This was accomplished by simply digging a narrow ditch across the bend. Once the ditch is sufficient depth

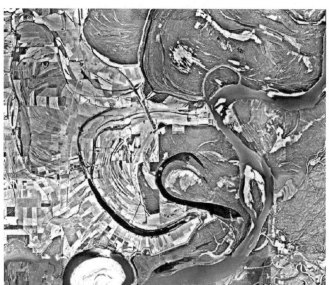

Courtesy of Terre Server Imagery
Satellite view of old bends

the river will take the path of least resistance and scour out the ditch. As this happens the ditch will draw even more water, eventually creating a new channel. The river can also create new bends at relatively straight sections. An obstruction along the riverbank can cause a new bend to form. This could be a tree that has fallen into the river with its roots still attached to the bank, causing sand to build up at this point, and catching other debris coming down the river. This natural wing dam causes the current to be diverted to the other side and begin eroding the opposite bank. As the bank erodes the river will widen at the same time, building up additional sand on the side where the tree started it all. The river literally moves by eating away at one bank while building up the other bank, creating a new bend. Many state lines originally followed the center of rivers. In time the rivers move, but state lines do not. Most maps show the state lines deviating from the river course, indicating where the river once was.

Rivers can also change course in major ways. A river can be self-damming across its entire width. Sandbars and log jams will be so immense that the river will find a different path to the sea. This is the phenomenon that has caused the Lower Mississippi to flip back and forth and build most of Louisiana and Mississippi. The present path of the Lower Mississippi from Angola to New Orleans was formed only about 800 years ago. Over time it has found many paths to the sea from Texas to Alabama. The process continues on all alluvial rivers that build a delta. Even though most people associate the word "Delta" with the lower Mississippi valley, many rivers build deltas, including the Sacramento River Delta. Rivers change course with less frequency than in the past, due to revetments, levees, and other control structures built by man.

Another aspect affecting river anatomy cannot be overlooked. It is the changes brought about by modern man. Native Americans lived along the riverbanks for thousands of years and made no significant impact on them. They learned to live within the limits that nature offered. When Europeans began to travel in America the rivers were the transportation routes. Making their way up and down the wild rivers was difficult, but easier than cross-country. Then settlers began building villages along the rivers. The villages became towns and cities. Watercraft evolved from canoes to keelboats, steamboats, and towboats. Two main issues became apparent that would inspire man to interfere with nature and do battle with it. Those issues are flooding and navigation.

Levees were the first attempts at flood control. A good example of how levee systems got started is to look at New Orleans. New Orleans is an old city, built in a precarious location. The Mississippi River loops around the west and south sides of the city. Further, it is bounded by Lake Borgne to the East and the huge Lake Pontchartrain on the north, not to mention the Gulf of Mexico just a few miles to the southeast. Considering that this area was still in the process of being built by the river, it could be said that the city was built on land that God wasn't finished with yet. To keep New Orleans from flooding a small levee was constructed, only a few feet

Corps of Engineers Photo
Mississippi River levee

high along the riverbank. This kept the water out of the city, but during high water it flowed over the bank on the other side, necessitating a levee to be built on the opposite bank. This constriction of the river caused it to rise higher, so it flowed over the bank in areas above New Orleans, where there were no levees. In response, the upstream communities built levees to protect their homes and plantations. This process repeated itself upstream as the rising river continued to be restricted. As upstream levees were built, the levees at New Orleans were no longer high enough, creating a demand for taller ones to be built. The

entire process of building higher levees went up the river over and over again. The levees on the lower portions of the river now reach upwards of 50 feet high. This scenario has taken place on rivers all over the United States.

The once rich soils are being depleted since the rivers are no longer allowed to provide new soil. As the levees have risen, so have the river levels and the riverbeds. New Orleans is now located in a ring of levees, much like a bowl. Not only must the surrounding waters be kept from pouring into the city, but rainwater must be pumped out. As the rivers, lakes, and sea level rises, New Orleans continues to sink each year, with parts of the city now below sea level. The Crescent City is in trouble with no easy solution. The very levees that were built to protect the city have become the instrument of dangerously high water. Levees have shut off natural flood plains, so now flooding occurs in places where the river never used to overflow.

An example is my own home on the Wabash River. The site had only flooded once during the great flood of 1913. Since downriver levees were built to protect farmland, the river rises higher and my home site has flooded often. One year, the only thing that kept my home from flooding was when that levee broke, releasing the river to its natural floodplain. Building a levee on one section of a river simply sends the problem to another area. Farmers complain about flooding but do not realize that their land needs an occasional over-flow to add nutrients to the soil. During the devastating floods of 1993 on the upper Mississippi, there was a story of a local farmer who blew up his levee to save the town. It was an honorable thing to do but in reality, the farmer created the problem for the town to begin with by building his levee on a natural flood plain. The "lev-ees only" system of flood control continued until the awful flood of 1927, when it proved to be a failure. That failure didn't mean that levees would be removed but that, at times, the river must be allowed to go where it will do the least damage. Those projects are discussed in chapter 15. The levee system on the lower Mississippi River is the longest continuing levee on earth. It does prevent flood-ing most of the time, but if a levee fails the results are more disas-trous. Before levees the rivers would flow over their banks gradu-ally. When a large levee breaks there is usually a wall of water that will destroy anything in its path.

Making the rivers suitable for year-round navigation has also had a major impact on the rivers. The lock and dam system does not contribute to dangerous flooding as the levees do. The dams are built to hold water back in a pool, causing the water to be deeper. As the ele-vation of the riverbed drops, another dam is built to maintain the depth. Locks are built to allow vessels to pass through the changes in water level. The biggest impact of locks and dams has been increased

Corps of Engineers Photo
Locks & Dam

river commerce. After World War I the government recognized a need for better transportation of bulk items during wartime, there-fore an aggressive program was begun to build and improve exist-ing lock and dams. One must pass through 26 locks when traveling from Saint Louis to Saint Paul.

Environmental issues have risen regarding locks and dams, including the flooding of land for the pools, various marine life that have problems living in deeper, colder water, and obvious problems for migrating fish. Anything man does in his attempt to control nature will cause other problems. Man also has a history of exploitation. From decimating the great river forests to over-harvesting the fresh-water mussels in search of pearls, we have taken our plunder and not given back. We have regarded the river as a convenient sewage disposal. Factories have pumped their refuge into what seemed to be an endless, bottomless wasteland. Everything that went into a river just went away, or so it was thought.

The good news is that most rivers in the United States are getting healthier. With the continued efforts of environmental groups and the Clean Water Act of 1972, there have been great improvements in the past 30 years. Agricultural runoff and urban pollution remain the greatest challenges to overcome. There is still more to do, but we are going in the right direction. Unlike polluted land, rivers are self-cleaning to an extent. If the source of pollution is stopped, the river will eventually heal with enough clean water from its sources. Too often we try to repair damage or correct a problem at its location, without looking at its source. This type of action will only result in temporary maintenance. Long-range improvements will only happen if the source of the problem is identified and corrected. Dredging is a good example of that. Millions of dollars are spent each year in dredging sandbars deposited by the rivers. This is a temporary solution for a river that has been choked with silt because the unchecked agricultural runoff and bank erosion will just bring it back again.

Calling this chapter the anatomy of a river may seem ludicrous to some. After all, how can water have an anatomy? Those of us who know the rivers have no problem understanding the concept that the river is a living thing. It creates its own energy, it provides life-giving food and water, and it even carries us on its back. It is a restless body, seeking new territory. It can be temperamental and angry. It has great power that man has a delusion of controlling. It is a builder and destroyer of land. Yes, the river is a living thing!

Chapter 10

Language of the Rivers

There are many words and phrases we use today whose origins are unknown. Phrases are often used with little thought of why we say them or where they come from. Some of those words and phrases originated from the rivers and the riverboats. I have compiled a list of them, including their meaning and source.

High Falutin'

Steamboats had tall smokestacks. The boats originally had boilers fired by wood. Along with the smoke there would often be flaming embers coming up from the furnace and out of the top of the smokestack. Those embers could and did start fires when they landed on the top deck or cargo. Tall stacks would give the embers a better chance to burn out before reaching the deck. In addition, the top of the stacks were "fluted". Fluting consisted of wire or steel mesh and acted like a small fence that would break the embers into small pieces. Smaller embers were more likely to burn out faster than larger pieces. As fancier boats were built, the fluting became very ornamental and eventually came to be considered an essential decorative element of the smokestack. Those vessels with the fancy smokestacks and decorative flutes became known as high-falutin' boats.

Well Stacked

Men will often use this term to describe the admirable attributes of a female, but that isn't its original use. As steamboats evolved from modest packet boats to multi-decked vessels of grander design, some had the appearance of giant wedding cakes going down the river. Some were stacked with five to six levels of cabin and lounge decks. These boats were considered well stacked. Another use for the term was in reference to the tall, ornate smokestacks of the fancy boats.

Blow Your Stack

Steamboat smokestacks would often have a buildup of soot inside. This buildup could catch fire in time, and needed to be removed. Steam lines were installed to the smokestacks with a valve. To prevent the soot from building up to dangerous levels a valve would be opened, sending a blast of steam into the stacks. This would break the soot loose and send it out the top. Meanwhile the smoke and embers would still be coming up the stack from the furnace. Added to that was the violent hissing and vibration of the steam injection, resulting in a rain of soot falling from the sky. Passengers would often think the boat was blowing up. They would also be unhappy to find the soot landing on their clothes and chairs. Many captains would warn passengers of the event so they could go inside, then deckhands would clean up the mess on the deck. During special events on the outer decks the captain would often be asked not to "blow his stack."

Rock Bottom

This is a very common phrase that is normally used to describe a person who is down and out. It came from a fear of flatboatmen, keelboatmen, and steamboat pilots. If the riverbed was sandy or muddy, there was little fear of splitting the hull, in the event of grounding. A rock-bottomed river was much more dangerous; hitting bottom on rocks was the worst possible conditions to run aground in (to run a-rock might be more descriptive). Gradually, anyone at the lowest possible point in life was referred to as having hit rock bottom.

Oh, Hogwash

Early river transportation included livestock as cargo. One of the more undesirable animals to transport was hogs. They were stubborn to move, noisy, and would emit a foul odor. The animals were normally placed on the forward main deck for easier loading and off-loading. This meant that crew and passengers were often situated downwind of them. The captain would often order a deck hand to wash the hogs. Afterward, the mess left on the deck had to be washed off. This mess was called hogwash. The job of washing the hogs and deck was not one of the more desirable assignments of the deckhands. In time, any undesirable task given to someone was called hogwash. This term eventually evolved into meaning something that is ridiculous, useless, or a lie.

Hillbilly

Many boys and men in the early 1800s were named William, Wilbur, or Willie, which may have occurred due to the large influx of German or English settlers in the Ohio River valley. Steamboats landed in towns on the Ohio River, along southern Indiana and Kentucky, and often young men from the hills would be hired as roustabouts to load and unload cargo and passenger bags. Since many of them bore such a common name and came from the hills, the roustabouts became known as hillbillies. The word eventually evolved into representing anyone with a backwoods style.

Outlandish Behavior

The origins of this phrase have some similarity to the word "hillbilly." In the 1800s all lands west of the Mississippi River was called the outland. As with boats on the Ohio River, steamboats hired local residents to serve as roustabouts. The men coming from the states of Arkansas and Missouri had a reputation for being hard to manage. These rough and tough fellows from the outland were rowdy and fights would often ensue. Over a period of time, anyone misbehaving was considered to be having outlandish behavior.

Letting off Steam

This term is pretty easy to understand, since its present-day meaning is similar to the original use. Steamboats built up a head of steam when power was necessary, which was then let off when it wasn't needed, to prevent dangerous build-up of pressure and subsequent explosions. Letting off steam relieved the pressure. Letting off steam today usually means to speak out to relieve the pressure of holding it in.

Fiddlin' Around

Musicians would often come to the steamboat landings to play. These were usually fiddle players, who would sit by the landing and play their tunes, hoping for coins to be tossed into their cup or hat. Sometimes they would be allowed to play on the bow of the boat as a welcoming for passengers. Other times the captain might give the fiddle player free passage on the boat in exchange for entertainment for his passengers. If the player was really good, he might even get paid for his services. The deckhands and other members of the crew did not have high regard for this fellow who was not really working; he was just fiddlin' around. In time the term came to identify anyone doing useless activity.

Bitter End

The "bitter end" is commonly used in reference to a bad ending of a story or movie. In nautical terms it means something more literal. When paying out an anchor line, one sends out the rode, which is the length of the rope in relation to the water depth. Sometimes people will forget to tie off the end of the line to the kevel on the boat. This results in seeing the end of the line slipping through one's hands and into the water, losing the line and anchor. The end of that line disappearing into the water is called the bitter end. The frayed end of a rope is also called the "bitter end."

Dead Head

Truckers often use the term "dead head" when they are making a run with an empty trailer. After unloading cargo they may have to dead head to another location to pick up a load. Dead head was first used in the days of steamboats to account for non-paying passengers. A manifest may list cargo, passengers, crew, and dead heads. Dead heads were non-paying passengers who might be anyone not included in passage revenues. It may be a special guest, or even the captain's wife. While working on the steamboats, I would hesitate to call the captain's wife a dead head. Somehow it just doesn't have a charming sound to it. Dead head also refers to a vertically floating log.

Stateroom

Most passenger ships call their cabins "staterooms", as do some hotels which use the term to refer to their nicer accommodations. The word has an interesting history that evolved from Texas becoming a state. In 1845 a new steamboat was being built. In honor of Texas becoming a state in the same year, the builder named the largest deck the Texas deck. At the time, Texas was the largest state. The builders carried the naming of the deck a step further. They named the cabins on the Texas deck after each state, and called those cabins on the staterooms. The tradition continued to modern times, and the steamboats operating today have a Texas deck and staterooms.

Hayburner

This is a word that is commonly used in describing horses or a horse-drawn wagon or carriage. Another use of the word was to describe a type of watercraft on the river. Some of the early ferryboats had no engines, but were propelled by sidewheeler paddles and powered by horses. The vessel was steered by a cable attached from each shore and through pulleys on the ferry. A large turntable or conveyer was installed on the deck and attached by gears to the paddlewheels. Horses were made to walk the devices while harnessed to a stationary horizontal pole. This would cause the platform and paddlewheel to turn. The vessels were called hayburners, since that was the only fuel needed for the horses.

Bushwacking

If a person would tell someone that they had been "bushwacking", it might mean that they were waiting in hiding to ambush an unsuspecting victim. Farmers often use the word to indicate clearing a field before tilling. Bushwacking originated in the keelboat days when the boatmen would pole the boats upriver. They would often skirt along the shoreline if currents were strong or the poles would not reach the river bottom. They would pull on the bushes, trees, and shrubs along the way to help move the boat. They called this bushwacking. A related term still used by boats running very close to the bank is "Runnin' the willers", meaning getting very close to the willow trees along the shore.

Stick in the Mud

This phrase also developed from the keelboating days. The boatmen handled long poles that would be used to push against the river bottom. They would walk the length of the boat backward on each side, then lift their poles and quickly go to the bow to push another stroke. This provided continuous power until one of the boatmen would get his pole stuck in the mud. When this happened, it would hold up progress and he was called a "stick-in-the-mud."

I Cotton To You

Anyone who has spent any time in the South, or watched movies about the antebellum South, probably heard this phrase. It is a romantic term used to indicate an attraction for another. The roots of the phrase are from along the riverbank landings of the lower Mississippi River. When cotton was king, huge amounts of cotton bales were loaded onto the steamboats for delivery to distant places. The workers loading and unloading the bales would become covered with the cotton that stuck to their clothes and hair. Since it tended to stick so well, the phrase came to mean that someone would like to stick with another.

Decked Out

When we get "decked out" it usually means that we are dressing up. The phrase was actually more literal in its original use. Steamboat captains would often need to make changes to the deck to accommodate unique cargo or special events. This may be as minor as moving some deck chairs around, to building a structure on the deck. The reason for the changes could range from accommodating a cargo of hogs to setting up for a musician. Any time the deck space was altered, it was being decked out.

Sold Down the River

If we hear someone say they have been "sold down the river", we expect that they have been cheated or deceived. It may also mean that a person has unfairly lost something, or possibly has been told on for something they did. The original use for the phrase developed along the Missouri border of the Mississippi River. Missouri was a slave state and known for better treatment of their slaves than the southern states. If a Missouri slave became lazy or unruly, the owner would hold a threat over his or her head. "If you don't do better you will be sold down the river." This would mean that the owner would sell the slave to a landowner in the deep South. The slaves knew about the harsh conditions they would face down the river and may be inspired to improve. The phrase, "Being sent up the river" is related, but applied to someone being sent to prison, since many prisons are built along the rivers. This phrase developed on the Hudson River, about those being sent up the river to Sing Sing prison.

Come Hell or High Water

When people use this phrase they are usually not referring to navigation, but intend to complete a mission or goal regardless of the challenges. This is a phrase that began in the early days of steamboating and still applies today. Low water periods made navigation very difficult. Running aground and striking shoals were much more likely during low water. High water was almost always preferred for running steamboats, at least until low bridges were built. For a captain to state that he intended to make a run "Come hell or high water" was to intend to go, regardless of the river stage. Hell, of course is low water.

Hot Toddy

We usually think of this as an alcoholic drink concoction that may relieve the symptoms of a cold. It was originally a drink favored by the keelboatmen to warm the insides and provide nutrition. A baked apple was place in a mug of heated rum. It is said that the keelboats used no fuel since they had no engines, but in reality there were huge amounts of rum and apples that fueled the keelboatmen.

Towhead

This word is normally used to describe a blond child. It is a river name for a small island or spit of land extending above or below the main or large island. It may or may not be recently formed. The generally accepted difference between a towhead and an island is that an island is a natural formation and a towhead is formed as a result of an unnatural occurrence. Towheads can be formed from dredge spoils, sunken vessels, and other things that will cause a pile up of sand and silt in the riverbed.

Hit a snag

We all have hit snags in a projects, meaning something has caused a delay. Women also get snags in their hosiery but the real meaning has to do with a hazard on the rivers. A snag is a sunken tree with one end protruding above the waterline. Hitting one with a small boat, or even a large wooden hull boat can lead to serious consequences.

Running off at the mouth

Most rivers have a source at the beginning and a mouth at the end. This is where the river flows into another river, lake or sea. There is a constant flow running off, that goes on an on. Some people tend to do the same thing in their conversations. There never-ending rhetoric can be called "running off at the mouth".

Get off on the right foot

One of many superstitions on the rivers was that a person should always step on or off a boat with their right foot, for good luck. Consequently stepping off or on with the left foot was bad luck.

Chapter 11

Nine Days on a Towboat

During my extended time off from working on the steamboats, I do a great deal of research and travel to augment my job as Riverlorian. One of the things I had always wanted to do is ride on a towboat, and specifically to learn all I can about life on one to share with our passengers. The passing tows are often an interesting sight and the subject of many questions. I wrote to American Commercial Barge Lines (ACBL), and asked if there was any way for me to ride along on a tow for this purpose. I was delighted to receive a call from Bill Kinzeler, vice-president of River Operations, who said he would be happy to accommodate me. Everyone loves the *Steamboats* and having that going for me helped open the door. He said if I wanted to go right away he could put me on a boat in Jeffersonville, Indiana and take a trip up to Pittsburgh, get on another tow going downstream to Paducah, then jump on another tow heading back up to Louisville. I said, "When do you need me to be in Jeffersonville"? He said, "Day after tomorrow". I said, "I'll be there".

ACBL is based out of Jeffersonville but I was to go to the Kentucky side and find the Louisiana Dock Company, a division of ACBL. There a towboat would pick me up and take me to the *Ron Shankin* when she passed by. Following is a log of my experience from the time I arrived at the dock:

Day 1

11:30 A.M....I arrive from my four-hour drive at the Louisiana Dock Company. After signing in I sit on a line (rope) coil to wait for someone to find me. Soon Bill Kinzeler arrives to see me off. Bill says that the *Ron Shankin* has been delayed and will be arriving this evening. The towboat *O'Neal* is docked at the repair facility and I am invited to wait aboard her. I select that option over sitting at a hot dock on a pile of ropes. The repair crew is very hospitable as they show me around the boat. There is an air-conditioned lounge, with satellite TV, and plenty of goodies in the galley. OK, I can live with this! This is to be the first of the many waiting games inherent to life on the towboats, but it is comfortable. After meeting several towboatmen, including deckhands, executives, mechanics, and an engineer, I soon discover that telling river stories is as much a part of towboat life as other forms of river travel.

2:15 P.M....While chatting with some crew members in the galley I notice that there is of tow of eight coal barges drifting on the river, but no boat. I ask if that was not unusual and all hands immediately go out to see what is going on. Now I assume that this is indeed unusual. One man immediately goes to the pilothouse to radio the news of the loose tow. About that time a towboat with a single coal barge is heading for the drifting tow. It quickly adds the single barge, and then circles around to hook up to the stern of the entire tow. They are apparently saving some time or money by releasing their tow long enough to add another barge without assistance. There is very little current at this low river stage and the tow doesn't drift far, but it does look rather precarious as it drifts at an angle to the river. This procedure could never be done on the lower Mississippi, with its swift currents. After that little excitement I continue my wait.

6:00 P.M....I meet the chief engineer for the *O'Neal*, who stays with the boat during repairs. Everyone calls him Rosebud, but I never find out why. Rosebud is from Greenville, Mississippi and asks if I could get him on board the *Steamboats* for a look when we are in Greenville (assuming he isn't on the river). He begins to tell me some good river stories. He has had many adventures in his 35 years on the rivers. Interestingly he says, "I've wasted my life on these rivers and wish I would have taken a different direction, maybe lived a normal life." I point out to him that I'm certain that there are many people out there who have spent their lives on a nine-to-five job with no real adventures, and would envy his life. My point was well taken and not challenged.

8:15 P.M....The *Ron Shankin* has finally passed through McAlpine Lock and is headed our way. The towboat *Georgia*, (used for local transfers) comes to the dock to pick me up and deliver me to the *Ron Shankin*. The first thing that I notice is the cargo, which includes chemical barges filled with benzene, liquid propane, and caustic acid. There are twelve barges with a combined cocktail that would make an impressive mushroom cloud in a mishap. The *Ron*

Shankin is a handsome 148-foot triple-deck towboat. I climb aboard the vessel and after a quick tour I am taken to the pilothouse to meet Captain Dennis Mize. Captain Mize is a friendly, laid-back fellow from Missouri. He welcomes me aboard and we swap a few river stories, which is a pilothouse tradition. He informs me that he has played a joke on the cook by telling her that I will have very special dietary needs, due to my religion and allergies. She is in a tizzy and doesn't know how she is going to feed me. Practical jokes are a way of life on the river. From my conversations with the crew I soon discover whom it is that one needs to get along with on the boat. It is the cook. She has the power, and I found she is a great source of information. She is the queen and held in high regard by all. I begin thinking about that joke the captain is playing and realize that I might be off to a bad start with her before even meeting her.

Photo by Author
Ron Shanklin Towboat

I go to my cabin, which is normally used as an officer's lounge. It has a hide-a-bed couch and is all made up for me. It is a nice cabin on the third deck. I open the door to the bathroom to find only a closet. I think, "Well we must have a community bath here somewhere." I walk the halls on all three levels, reading the signs on each door. No bathroom to be found. After much searching I finally get desperate enough to ask a deck-hand "Where in the heck is the bathroom?" He says, "Why, they are all over the boat. Every couple of rooms shares one, but the officer's lounge doesn't have one. You can use the Captain's. It's shared with the pilot's cabin." I begin to figure out the system. The Captain and pilot alternate six-hour shifts so they are never in their cabins at the same time. It makes sense to have a bathroom between the rooms. I will go through the cabin of whichever one is piloting, while the other one is sleeping to use the bathroom and shower. I am being careful to stop and think about which man is piloting before using the facility, as I don't want to disturb the one sleeping. I spend the evening meeting most of the ten crew members and enjoying the river from the pilothouse deck.

Day 2

7:00 A.M....I rise to a hazy morning on the river near Vevay, Indiana. I head down to the galley for coffee where I expect to meet the cook. I feel like someone who might be going for an important interview and hope to make a good impression. The crew has already finished breakfast and is busy at their jobs. I introduce myself to Gay McGrew. She is from Paris, Tennessee. It doesn't' take Gay long to fill me in on the current crew, her background, and other useful tips. Gay has beautiful hazel eyes that are filled with the spirit of the river. I have come to recognize that kindred spirit during my 30-plus years on the rivers. The crew of the *Ron Shankin* is a family and she is mom. She tells me that many young men who have been without families and sometimes without a home have found their way to work on the towboats. These "boys" have discovered not only employment, but also a home and family here. It is no wonder why so many stay with this life for so long. My first meeting with Gay is a success. I was in! There is the ultimate compliment one can receive on the river. It is a very short sentence that lets one feel accepted. It is "Yer awe right". I'm about to leave the galley with my second coffee. Gay notices that I ate no breakfast, and is probably apprehensive about my dietary needs but says, "Just what is it that you can eat for breakfast?" I explain that I am not a breakfast eater, and then get a short lecture on the importance of a wholesome breakfast.

10:30 A.M....We are transferring a couple of barges to another vessel and are picking up two more. This is a slow and careful process. All things are in slow motion on the towboats. Waiting is a way of life. Waiting to board, waiting at the locks, waiting for barge transfers, and waiting at narrow channels. The vessels move slowly and all work is done carefully to insure safety. This would not be a profession for an impatient person. It is, however, easy to adapt to the pace, and one can imagine that anyone living this life for any length of time would have difficulty going back to the fast lane. That isn't to say that there would not be some fast and furious action taken in an emergency. An emergency could be loose barges, fire, sinking, crew injury, or any number of things that can happen.

12:10 P.M....We are about to enter Markland Locks and Dam. On approach to the lock I see the towboat *Red Eagle* with twelve barges run aground on a sand bar. She apparently got straddled on the bar just after leaving the lock, heading downriver. I can see the sandy-colored water about midway on the tow where it is resting on the bar. The boat is running hard reverse trying to back off. Mud is being kicked up from the prop wash. The low water is causing some problems and Markland is allowing no water to pass in order to maintain the upper pool stage. With no water flowing below the dam it becomes shallow in that area. Captain Mize would have tried to help with a tow line but no help was requested from the *Red Eagle*. I have been on the river long enough to know that a pilot will try everything possible to get off a bar before resorting to being pulled off. It's a pride thing. As we leave the Markland lock heading upriver toward Cincinnati, I check the schedule for the *Mississippi Queen*. She is in Maysville, Kentucky today and we will meet her at some point. I am hoping to spot her and maybe call the pilothouse to say howdy.

6:30 P.M....I just enjoyed a delicious dinner and am chatting with the deck hands. More good river stories! We are about 35 miles below Cincinnati. The pilot, Ronnie Prater, advises me that we are running slowly because a barge is supposed to be picked up along the way and it isn't available yet. Rather than sit there for five or six hours, he would rather run slow and conserve fuel. We expect to pass Cincinnati around midnight, but the unexpected is common out here and changed schedules happen often. The *Mississippi Queen* is now en route from Maysville to Cincinnati.

7.45 P.M....The test. I am hanging out with the crew on the bow and they are interested in knowing more about the *Steamboats*, which being my favorite subject, I am happy to oblige. John is one of the crew and apparently a river history buff. He is curious about my job as Riverlorian. Then John begins testing my river knowledge. "What is the deepest river in the country? How did Meriwether Lewis die? What Kentucky town used to be called Limestone?" The questions continue and I am impressed with his knowledge, since I'm sure he is asking questions that he knows the answer to. I answer to his satisfaction, but can sense his frustration. He really wants to stump the Riverlorian. In apparent desperation he grins and asks a really dumb question. "How many glasses of water are there in the Ohio River?" I reply with a question. "Would that be 12-ounce or 16-ounce glasses?" The session ends with a good laugh by everyone and John says the magic words, "Yer awe right." I am discovering several differences between life on a towboat and a steamboat. Since the cargo on steamboats is passengers, we make frequent stops along the journey at historic towns. This often gives the crew a chance to take a walk or get some needed items. On the towboats there are no such stops. When crew members do their four- or six-week rotation they are on the boat the entire time. Towboats are constantly at work and there are no landings at towns.

11:30 P.M....I am walking the decks with nearly a full moon above me. It is a beautiful night. I go aft on the second deck, then down the stairs to the main deck where the prop wash from twin 16-cylinder engines is. The feel of great power is present. The incredible turbulence created by the nine-foot diameter propellers is amazing, and I can sense the danger beneath me. This violent action of water is an awesome display of man's and nature's power. Cincinnati is nowhere in sight, so I turn in.

Day 3

7:15 A.M....I am told that some people have trouble sleeping when first getting used to the constant vibrations of a towboat, but not me. It makes me sleep better and I find myself sleeping later than usual. This morning I wake up to find us tied off to another barge just below Cincinnati. We arrived at this destination during the night and are still waiting for the barge to add to our tow. The captain is now expecting to get underway around noon. The deckhands have already repositioned some of our barges to make room for the addition. The *Mississippi Queen* should be docked at Cincinnati all day and provide a good sighting as we pass. Knowing that it is a turnover day (taking on new passengers), I don't expect to see much activity on the *MQ* at noon. Captain Mize tells me that his longest delay during his 33 years on the river was waiting for 26 days at Lock 26 on the upper Mississippi River. The lock was being repaired and the tows could only push one barge through at a time. I will soon discover that a similar thing is happening on the Ohio River and will affect our plans. The *Ron Shankin* is registered out of New Orleans and spends most of her time on the Mississippi River. Some of the crew have never been on the Ohio River before, so this gives me an opportunity to serve as a tour guide for them. They are impressed with the size, amount of traffic, and the beauty of the Ohio and its communities.

9:30 A.M....I receive a call on my cell phone from a friend who is checking to see if I am going to a meeting tonight. I am on the board of directors of the World Hovercraft Championship. I explain that I would not make the meeting and advise him that I am on a towboat, on the Ohio River. He says, "You're the only person I know who could tell me a story like that and I would believe it." He knows me.

11:45 A.M....The additional barge has been delivered and we are getting underway. There are barges fleeted (tied off) directly behind us and more barges a short distance in front of our tow. Just ahead is a bridge. I am interested in watching this maneuver as we pull away. A deckhand releases our lead barge along the port side from the stationary barge we are tied to. The Captain is reversing, while using the flanking rudders to cause the stern to swing out. He continues to reverse while straightening the rudders so the tow begins to back up. At a point that only experience could know, he leaves the starboard engine in reverse but pushes the port engine into forward. The stern of the vessel then swings back toward the bank with just enough clearance to miss the fleeted barges behind. He now has the tow positioned so that it is pointed toward the bridge span and clear of the fleeted barges. Both engines are put in forward with steering rudders now being used. We glide under the bridge. Very impressive!

12:15 P.M....We are approaching downtown Cincinnati. I got on the radio to say hi to Virginia Bennett, whom I had met on the steamboats. Virginia is called the "Mother of the Ohio River". She comes from several generations of river people, and lives in an apartment overlooking the river. She also has navigation lights on her balcony and spends a lot of time talking to passing river pilots on her radio. The U.S. Army Corp of Engineers think so much of her that they named a nearby daymark after her. I now see

Photo by Author
Mississippi Queen at Cincinnati

the *RiverBarge* passenger boat, and then the *Mississippi Queen* landed just ahead of it. I get on the radio and hail her but there is apparently no one in the pilothouse. I then go onto our pilothouse deck and have the pilot blast the horn, while I wave both arms to anyone who might notice me. She is a pretty sight to see after many months of being out of service, in lay up in New Orleans. We proceed on upriver in a mild rain. In the galley, Gay is glued to the window, looking at all those big fancy homes on the bluff just above Cincinnati. I don't think fancy beats what she has here.

5:00 P.M....Approaching Meldahl Locks and Dam. There are several tows ahead of us so we expect a long wait, particularly since the main lock is in repair and only the auxiliary lock is open. The auxiliary lock is only 600-feet long, which means longer tows must double-lock. That is, to break up the barges into two sets and pass them through separately. Estimated wait time is around ten hours. I watched the pilot skillfully keep the vessel in a holding pattern. It is more difficult to keep a tow stable in this slack water. If there is a current the engines and rudders can work against it and help hold the tow in place. Without current, the boat tends to drift with a slow pivoting motion and requires more throttle and rudder action to keep it in check. He decides to nudge the tow into the bank. The pilot keeps busy running the two engines in forward, then reverse, individually. He is also operating the rudder sticks, watching the vessel's movement in relation to the shoreline, and keeping an eye on the depth gauge. At the same time he is talking on the short-wave radio to the mate located on the lead barge looking for a tree to tie off to. There is no good tree within reach, so he gently nudges into the shallows to stabilize the head of the tow, and then keeps an engine in forward to hold it there. We now hear that wait time may be 18 hours.

9:00 P.M....Update. We are still on hold at Meldahl. There are still eleven tows ahead of us and most need to double lock. Estimated wait time is now 24 hours.

Day 4

8:10 A.M....After having my morning coffee "meditation", I decide that today will be an excellent time to really explore the boat, since we will likely be here all day waiting to lock through. The engine room is very impressive. Those huge engines are noisy and put out a lot of heat. They are mounted in the lower deck, which is below the water line. On the main deck above them is a large area housing the engineer's office, work shop and rudder controls. The controls are hydraulic-powered rods. There are two sets of rudders and the rod and connections appear to be complex, but are easy to understand when the pilot activates them. Chief Engineer Steve Wells is a friendly fellow with a permanent smile beneath his white handlebar mustache. He keeps a surprisingly clean engine room. The floors shine and tools are neatly in place. I can see none of the dirt, rust, grease, or anything else that resembled my concept of a towboat engine room. In fact, the entire vessel is like that. I have seen kitchens of nice restaurants that are not as clean and well organized as the galley on the *Ron Shankin*. The waiting time at the lock is used efficiently. Since only one engine is needed to hold the tow, Steve is doing oil changes and other maintenance as the engines are shut down alternately. The deck crew is busy washing the exterior. This is not just hosing it down, like I do my boat. They wash everything with soap, brushes, rags, and high-pressure water. Gay is busy in the galley and concerned about the long delay because she needs items for the boys from the boat store that delivers supplies to towboats. It is located above the lock. Gay knows what they all like and tries to accommodate them. She even knows what each one doesn't like. I listen to her express concern about how one of the crew isn't eating enough. I no longer perceive her as Queen. She is Mom. The crew can order personal items also by listing them on a sheet in the galley.

4:00 P.M....The weather has changed today. It has cooled off, to our delight. The humidity is down and we have a light breeze. I brought the book *Trail of Tears* with me, which tells of the Indian removals in the 1830s. I decide to read, which leads to a rather comical quest for just the right spot to do so. I started in my air-conditioned cabin, and then felt guilty. It's so nice out today, why waste it in here? I find a folding lounge chair in the closet, gather the book and other things I may need, stop by the galley to get iced tea to go, then proceed to a shaded spot to settle in. I find a place on the main deck, port side near the bow. It doesn't take long to discover that the breeze has turned into wind and wakes hitting the stern barge are providing me with an unwanted shower. I pack up my chair, book, iced tea, and cell phone and move to mid-ship along the same shaded side, only to find that the engine noise is not conducive to peaceful reading. I look toward the stern and check it out. There is shade, relatively quiet, breeze, and the pleasant sound of water thrashing from the propeller. Yes, this will work! After settling in I notice some activity on the deck above me. Suddenly huge amounts of soapy water come pouring over the side of the deck about 20 feet from me and closing in. The deck crew is still washing the boat. It is time to move again. I gather my stuff and, remembering that the pilothouse has a nice deck around it with an overhang roof, I continue my search for sanctuary. Once again I am settled in. The pilothouse is quite high and a good place to enjoy the wind. In fact, the pilothouse deck is higher than the smokestacks. It just happens that this wind is a tail wind, and the deck I am on is in the direct path of the smoke from those stacks. I try to tough it out and ignore those fumes, but can endure it no more. I then remember a place where I can read in comfort. There is no smoke, noise, water, or other distractions. I go back to my air-conditioned cabin and settle in to read.

7:00 P.M....A decision must be made. Captain Mize advises me that the towboat *Warren Hines* is delayed below the Montgomery lock, near Pittsburgh, for several days. It must still turn around and go back through the lock to meet us. That lock is also under repair and their auxiliary chamber is only 300 feet. This means only one barge at a time can be locked through. Why is this important? The *Warren Hines* is the turnboat that I am to get aboard for the trip up to Pittsburgh, then back downriver to Paducah. A turnboat is when two towboats are headed toward each other and when they meet they exchange their tows and turn around. This keeps the boats from having to get too far away, particularly when a crew change is coming up. Being concerned that I might get stuck above the Montgomery lock for weeks, I tell the Captain that I will just stay on the *Ron Shankin* for the return trip.

9:00 P.M....Good news for Gay and crew! The boat store has put their order in a van and brought it around below Meldahl lock where we are still holding up. They will be at a nearby boat ramp. The lead man (2nd mate), and a deckhand lower the yawl into the river and speed off to pick up the order. They must hurry because we are finally next up to lock through. A few minutes later the small craft is cutting across the setting sun on their return. The long 30-hour wait at the lock is nearly over.

10:00 P.M....As we enter the lock the deckhands are preparing to untie the first four barges that we will send through. These are called cuts. When double-locking these are the first cut, then the rest of the barges, including the boat, is the second cut. I watch from the pilothouse as Captain Mize eases the tow into the chamber, while the lead man, Steve Birney, is calling approaching distances to him. I

Photo by Author

Towboat entering lock along guidewall

remark on how smooth we slip into the chamber with so little clearance. Upon disengaging the engines and seeing the huge tow drift into its predetermined position, Captain Mize says that liquid tows are a bit trickier. Too sudden of a stop will cause the liquid to shift forward and create an unwanted forward surge in the vessel. Once in position the hands secure the four barges, and then release them from our tow. The Captain then backs out of the chamber with the remaining barges. The gate closes and the first cut is locked through by being pulled out by another tow that has secured its barges and unhooked from them. It will then lock through, going downriver. There are a couple of other methods used for sending a cut through. I had seen a system in the Illinois River locks where they use what is called a mule. This is a mechanical device that runs along the guide wall, pulling the barges through, much like real mules pulled flatboats in the canal days. The third method is interesting, and can only be used going downriver. Upon opening the lower gate to allow the cut to exit, the lock operator will open fill valves that are located in the bed of the chamber. When done skillfully with just the right surge of water, the barges will drift to a stop at their destination along the guide wall where a deckhand will tie it to a pin and await the rest of the tow. Steve tells me that riding that loose barge when too much water pushes it can be a real adrenaline rush, particularly since he must catch a pin and stop it before leaving the lock area. I would call it barge surfing. We lock through and hook back up to our first cut and by midnight are on our way again.

Day 5

6:00 A.M....I wake up to find us still moving, which is encouraging. We are around mile 400 and running a little faster than previous days. The *Warren Hines* has finally locked through Montgomery Lock, picked up our tow in Pittsburgh, and is now back at Montgomery, waiting again to lock through to meet us. We are still 370 miles apart.

7:00 A.M....Fog moves in. It is much cooler this morning and with the warm water, I expect to see some fog. It isn't thick enough to stop us and begins to burn off in an hour. As the sun rises and the fog lifts this morning it reveals the beauty of the upper Ohio's waters, hills, forests, islands, and riverside communities. The crew often has safety drills. Captain Mize tells me a story about the day he decided to have a man-overboard drill. If a person is overboard the first step is to stop engines, then man the throw rings. Pitching the throw rings takes some practice, so he decided to give them a target. He found a full trash bag, tied the top, pitched it into the river, and sounded a man-overboard alarm. At exactly the time he pitched the trash bag into the river, he noticed a Coast Guard boat was approaching from behind. By the time he got to the pilot-house to explain to the Coast Guard what he is doing, the efficient deckhands were already manning the life rings. One can only imagine the surprise of the Coast Guard officials to see a trash bag thrown in their path and then to see the crew effect a rescue mission of the bag. They just had to believe the Captains story, especially when the crew lowered the yawl to complete the rescue of the disabled trash bag.

9:00 A.M....I am sitting in what has become one of my favorite spots. I continue to be drawn to the stern, near the propeller wash. The waterfall sound is violent but relaxing and there is usually shade to be found. I spend a lot of time in the sun, as is obvious by my dry tan skin, but when I relax I am a shade worshiper with no desire to broil in the sun. While here I notice another interesting thing that happens when the rudders are turned. The pivoting of those huge rudders causes the stern of the boat to lurch sideways. Though not enough to see, I can feel it. Considering that we have nearly 6,000 horsepower, spinning two nine-foot propellers and pushing thousands of tons against a dense substance like water, there is an incredible amount of pressure on the rudders when turned. Steering a towboat is much like pushing a wheelbarrow. The back must swing out to point the front in the right direction. When going downriver with a strong current, towboats must "flank" around the bends. The engines will be run in reverse, letting the current push the head of the tow into the turn, then shift into forward when the tow is positioned to steer out of the bend. The second set of rudders is called flanking rudders and are located in front of the propellers so that a reverse thrust is directed into them. Boats have more control while running against the current due to increased resistance against the hull and rudders, creating more responsive steering. That is why downriver traffic has the right of way. They have less maneuverability. All vessels must mover faster or slower than the water to steer. Tows use flanking buoys that are attached to the stern barge by a line. These show whether the vessel is moving faster, the same as, or slower than the current. They indicate this by floating with the line stretched, drifting aimlessly, or drawn up against the barge.

1:15 P.M....We are passing Portsmouth, Ohio. I notice deck hands walking around the edge of the barges. They are opening hatches and looking inside. The barges are double-hulled and the hatches are above the space between the hulls. A visual check is made every six hours to insure there is no water leaking through the outer hull and no chemicals leaking from the inner hull. If a leak would start, it would be confined to a section of the hull. Bulkheads divide it so that the entire barge cannot easily be flooded. There is another change in plans. The *Warren Hines* is still stuck above Montgomery lock so the *Northern* will now be our turnboat. She is closer and the *Ron Shankin* will exchange tows with them before turning back. Captain Mize wants to know if I still want to go to Pittsburgh; and I say I don't want on any boat that will end up above Montgomery Lock. I'm staying on the *Ron Shankin* back to Louisville.

3:00 P.M....I'm chatting with some crew members taking a break, and mention how impressed I am with the smooth lockings, some without as much as a bump. The mate says, "Yep, it sure ain't like that with old Harvey." It turns out that there is an infamous pilot on the river who just can't keep from banging those lock walls hard. "You better hang on or sit down going through a lock with Captain Harvey at the helm." I wasn't told, nor did I ask what his last name is, but he is known only as Captain Harvey Wallbanger.

4:30 P.M....We are entering Greenup Locks and Dam at mile 336, with Captain Prater at the helm. Our tow nudges up along the guide wall while waiting for another tow that is locking through going the same direction. Suddenly the head of the tow begins careening to the right for unknown reasons. I had noticed that we were kicking up mud on the lock approach, indicating shallow water, but that shouldn't make this happen. The 1,000-foot tow is moving into a very precarious angle, pointing off to the right of the lock wall. The lead barge is getting very close to the riverbank. The pilot immediately goes into hard reverse and the tow begins to slip backward, but the stern is now heading for the guide wall. He uses flanking rudders to shift the stern to starboard, while still backing away. He calls a deckhand to take a line to the port side of the stern barge, and directs him to throw a line over one of the pins at the end of the guide wall when he gets within range. After several attempts the deckhand loops the line over the pin and secures it to a kevel on the barge. The pilot then starts running the port engine in reverse and the starboard engine forward, sending intense vibrations throughout the boat. The action is an attempt to twist the boat into alignment with the wall.

In fact, the maneuver of running the engines in reverse of each other is called twisting. The line attached to the wall is used as a pivot point. The stress on that line is incredible. It is squeaking, popping, and beginning to smoke. This is called a hot line. The deckhand wisely removes himself from the area. Slowly the tow begins to move back to the guide wall. Another deckhand is sent to the lead barge on the port side to hook another line on the wall to keep the tow in place this time. After passing through the lock I ask Captain Prater about that maneuver, which he explains to me like it is routine, before admitting that in over 30 years of piloting it is the first time he has done it. The lockmaster indicates that others have had a problem with that lower sill but that they haven't figured out what is causing it.

8:30 P.M....We hold up at Ashland, Kentucky to have a barge removed. It is the empty we picked up a couple of days ago below Cincinnati.

10:30 P.M....Passing Huntington, West Virginia, at river mile 311. Huntington is an impressive-looking city from the river at night. I remember to ask someone about a posting I saw today on the bulletin board. It lists the dress codes for the crew. Most of the criteria are as I expected until I got down to the item that says "ball caps in darkness". What's up with that? I wear a ball cap in the sun to shade my eyes and keep the sweat off my face.

Why do they require ball caps at night? With that question still on my mind, I go below to the forward deck and ask. The deckhands must go out on the barges during dark hours for various tasks. To help them see, the pilot will turn on those powerful Xenon searchlights. In order to see what they are doing they must avoid being blinded by the light and the ball cap shades their eyes. Makes sense now!

Still interested in their equipment I ask John Scroggis, the mate, to pose for me with his safety gear on. I choose John because he has that riverman look that most of us envision. He's big with huge tattooed arms, full beard, pirate-style headwear, and a few scars with stories behind them. John agrees and

Photo by Author
Mate John Scroggis

tells me that this is his modeling debut. I have known many river folks over the years and often find that people aren't always as they appear. John is a sensitive guy who cherishes his 10-year-old daughter, of whom he has custody. I also know how this river gets in one's blood. John first took a job on the river for a little getaway, with no plans to continue it for any length of time. That was nine years ago. When fitted up to go out on the barges crew members must have steel-toed boots, back-support belt, reflector straps, flashlight, gloves, shortwave radio for onboard communication, flotation device, and, of course, at night a ball cap. The gear is no fashion statement, but the work is dangerous and safety has first priority.

Day 6

7:00 A.M....We are at mile 268 which is between Gallipolis, Ohio and the mouth of the Kanawha River. The *Ron Shankin* is tied off to a landing barge (permanently moored), and the deckhands are busy preparing to remove two of our barges. The small towboat *Iron Duke* pulls behind us with six coal barges, then ties off. She unhooks them and comes around to extract the two barges from our tow. Our turnboat, the *Northern,* is waiting upriver for us to exchange tows when we are finished here. I watch Captain Mize maneuver the *Ron Shankin* sideways to change positions on the tow. There are no bow thrusters on this boat so the sideways maneuver is done with skillful use of throttle and rudders. I notice that each time a barge is removed from our tow that a deckhand takes a long pole and pushes out any debris that collects between the barges. This is to insure a snug fit of replacement barges.

10:00 A.M....*The Northern* brings down the exchange tow which has 11 barges. All are empties except for one liquid propane tanker. The *Northern* eases in carefully and ties off to the port side of our lead barge. We then cut loose our tow, leaving two deckhands on it, and go to the lead barge of the *Northern* to transfer depth-gauge units, lines, and other equipment. We then go behind the *Northern* and wait for her to unhook. When she is clear, we go to the lead barge of the tow we are leaving and pick up our deckhands, then finish the equipment transfer. We then swing over to hook up to our new tow while the *Northern* is hooking up hers. I notice that every contact with the barges being moved around are made with lines secured to the towboat, however brief. During the transfer, no barges are left unsecured or unmanned. These fellows work a lot more carefully than those on the coal tow that was left drifting on my first day at Louisville.

11:45 A.M....We are now underway with a different tow. The tows are actually still going the same direction as they were, but the two towboats have turned around. We are now traveling down-river toward my destination of Louisville.

1:00 P.M....I notice that we are going much faster than I've seen on this entire trip. Going this fast I had to go see that prop wash that I am so fond of. It is really boiling now. I am almost mesmerized by the power and fury of the heaving water. I can't help myself and stand there doing that famous Tim Allen grunt. Soon the engines throttling back interrupt my power thrill. We are approaching the Robert Byrd Locks and Dam at river mile 279. I go to the pilothouse to find that we were had been running at 11 mph. That's lightnin' fast for a towboat. While approaching the chamber a deck-hand comes on the radio to warn that there is a notch on one of the starboard barges. The pilot indicates that he guesses he won't walk the wall with this one. Of course, my questions followed. A notch is any protrusion along the side of a barge that sticks out enough to catch those vertical cutouts in the lock wall that house the floating pins. Floating pins are tie-offs for the barges that float up or down with the chamber water level. Walking the wall is to gently "tetch" the wall and slide along it. I have already observed that pilots take pride in sliding along the wall as close as possible without "teching" it. One can see by the condition of the walls that they get "tetched" plenty. Our tow slides into the chamber, running along the wall within inches without ever touching it. The pilot says nothing but I could see a faint grin as he looks my way. I reply with a subtle thumbs up sign. Enough said.

8:00 P.M....We have a nice afternoon of cruising. I spend most of my time parked in the lounge chair watching the river. I remember a quote, "A successful man is one who can sit and watch the river all day without feeling guilty about it." I can relate to that. My peace is broken by a swift and furious thunderstorm. The sudden cool winds ahead of the storm gets my attention, so I look downriver to see it coming. By the time I gather up all my standard lounging equipment I return to the cabin soggy. The storm has little affect on the boat, even with nearly horizontal rain, pushed by a strong head wind. It clears up in about 15 minutes and all is well. One of the crew remarks that there will be no need to wash down the decks this evening.

9:00 P.M....Approaching Greenup Locks and Dam. The captain decides to hold up well above the lock to wait for our turn. I notice a small cruiser sitting in the channel with no navigation lights on.

As we get closer Captain Mize slows down, and then reverses to a stop. We are planning to stop anyway, but the folks in that cruiser could not have known that. I can't imagine why anyone would want to flirt with disaster by sitting in the dark, with no lights, with a 1,000-foot vessel coming their way. They finally turn on their lights and saunter off, long after we have stopped. It is not uncommon to see people doing foolish things around towboats. Unfortunately, it is also not uncommon to hear of tragedies resulting from these stunts. These huge vessels do not maneuver quickly, cannot be stopped quickly, and the pilot can't see for several hundred feet in front of the tow. If one of those wave runners would dump over while cutting across the bow, there would be practically no chance of the rider's survival. Boats getting too close to the stern can be pulled into the churning waters by the prop wash. Captain Mize is not one to over-react or lose his temper. If he sees someone in his path he will do everything he can to stop or maneuver around them. I would probably be one of those who I have seen blasting the horn and shaking my fist. In the case of this cruiser, the captain was concerned that they may be in trouble, since it was drifting with no lights. If that was true he would have sent crew in the yawl to help.

Day 7

8:00 A.M....My journal begins later this morning. Last night I hung out with the crew in their work station on the main deck, swapping stories and drinking coffee until the wee hours. By then, I was wired with caffeine and read in my cabin. It must have been around 4:00 am before I fell asleep, waking up a few hours later with my book still in hand and reading glasses on. We are a few miles from the dreaded Meldahl Locks and Dam. This is the one we waited at for 30 hours when going upriver. We had been informed that the repair would be done by Friday, which was yesterday, but no one believed that would happen. They were right! We must double-lock again and are not yet certain of the waiting time. This morning there is a heavy overcast with a thick haze on the river. Cool, but very humid. It feels, looks, and smells like rain will be upon us soon. I go to the galley for coffee and Gay informs me that today is steaks n' burgers day. I can choose which meal to have; steak or cheeseburgers, and I chose steak. She knows by now that I have no special dietary needs. I must say that being a person who usually views food as simply fuel for the body, with no great passion for eating,

I have come to look forward to meals on the *Ron Shankin*. It is excellent and Gay adds a touch of TLC with each serving.

9:15 A.M....We come to a stop on a bend just above Meldahl. Unless the main 1,200-foot chamber happens to open today, we are expecting an 18-hour wait. It will not open today. It's raining now and the crew is busy cleaning the inside of the boat. I learn a new word today. While looking over the bulletin board again I notice a "sooging schedule." That is what they call washing and cleaning any part of the vessel. Nobody seems to know where the word sooging come from, but they all know what it means. I have always had an interest in the origin of words and phrases, so I intend to research this one when I get back home.

4:00 P.M....OK, today I am bored for the first time on the trip. We are still waiting above the lock. I have drunk too much coffee, have finished reading my book, have taken a nap, and am now scrounging through a crew magazine pile. I'm not a fan of *Hot Rod* or *Hustler* but did find an issue of *Workboat* that looks fairly interesting. I look out and discover that while I was napping the boat has moved across the river and closer to the lock. We are now tied off to two other tows, all waiting. It looks like a city of barges out there. Occasionally we pull away to let a tow out. All the while additional tows are joining our fleet. On a day like this I envy the crew as they always have things to do. As I stroll aimlessly around the vessel I see crew working on machinery and painting the smokestacks. This scene reminds me of Tom Sawyer getting another boy to paint the fence. I would gladly paint the stacks if offered a brush. On second thought, it's pretty darn hot out here. I think I'll get a glass of iced tea and read an old issue of *Mechanics Illustrated*.

9:00 P.M....Still waiting our turn to lock through. The evening has rewarded us with another beautiful sunset. I'm watching it from the pilothouse while chatting with Captain Mize. We discuss passing the "gauntlet" tomorrow. That will be Cincinnati on a Sunday afternoon. I've been there. Pushing a tow amongst all the recreational boats can be nerve- wracking. They have as much right to be there as we, but hope they will use common sense and keep clear of us. I tell him of the time my anchor broke loose on my houseboat and drifted into the channel while sleeping. I woke to blasting horns and blinding lights as a towboat was trying to signal me, while attempting to stop and steer clear of me. I was able to get out of the way and learned a valuable lesson about the importance of proper anchorage.

Day 8

7:00 A.M....We are finally locking through after 22 hours. As we approach the lock I can see cranes in use and repair work being done in the main chamber. It doesn't appear to be anywhere near ready. Emergency gates are dropped into slots located along the walls. These are in place to keep the water out of the lock when the movable gates are open, while work is being done. Our first cut of the barges is in the lock and we are waiting for it to be pulled through.

9:00 A.M....After that 22-hour wait we can use a little excitement, and it comes to us. While in the pilothouse, Captain Mize sees something strange on one of his barges. He looks through his binoculars and confirms what he suspects. We have a stowaway running along the starboard stern barge toward the boat. Captain Mize gets on the radio to alert the crew of the intruder, a large rat that has set a course for the food and refuge of the *Ron Shankin*. The rat patrol goes into immediate action, as the critter leaps from an empty barge down to a full barge, which sits lower in the water then the crew intercepts the rat before it reaches the boat and gives chase. The patrol breaks formation and flanks the intruder on both sides, with impressive military-style strategy. The rat attempts to retreat by changing its course 180 degrees. A quick and nimble deckhand is closing in fast and at just about the time his steel-toed boot gets within striking range, the rat leaps into a dark crevasse to hide. Unfortunately for the rat, that crevasse is a small gap between two barges, which leads to the turbulent water below. The crew members are pleased with themselves for fulfilling their mission of keeping an unwanted guest from the boat. I go down to the bow to congratulate them on their success. My only regret is that I have no video camera to record the heroic event.

11:00 A.M....We approach Cincinnati and pass under a bridge being repainted purple. Purple? There does not appear to be much traffic on the river this morning. The high winds and threatening clouds may have something to do with that. As we pass the busy docks I notice another difference between riding on a towboat and a steamboat. While aboard the beautiful steamboats, I am accustomed to the boats receiving a lot of attention as we travel the waterways or make port. Some small communities keep track of our schedules and announce our passing or landing. Some even make an event of our arrival. Many people come time and again to watch the boats and hear the calliope play. All along the rivers people wave and gather at locks we pass through. At night we see porch lights blinking to signal a greeting to us. We also receive waves from passing boaters but for the most part, towboats get little attention. Unusual cargo may attract onlookers. A few years ago a tow carrying a Boeing 727 up the Ohio River got my attention. It had been used to make a movie plane crash scene in *U.S. Marshals*, and was being transported back to Pittsburgh.

12:00 P.M....Having passed Cincinnati, we are now holding just below the city, waiting for two more barges to be added to our tow. An empty grain barge and a full machinery barge arrive. The machinery barge is added to the front, which makes our length 1,176 feet. The grain barge is placed into a three-sided slot just in front of the boat. The slot is created by a barge at the front, a barge along the side, and the front of the towboat, that extends about eight feet from what will be the center barge. A towboat is shoving the grain barge into the slot, but it doesn't quite fit. It pushes harder with no luck, and then pivots to the side corner and pushes. Still no luck! Our able-bodied mate, John, walks to the winch holding the rest of our tow to the boat and releases some slack in the wire. Now the barge slides into the slot and John re-tightens the wires. The crew commences to secure all the wires of the additional barges and we are underway in a short time.

3:30 P.M....The winds have increased, but since they are pretty much direct head winds, they are having less affect on the tow than if they were crosswinds. I go to the pilothouse and have one of my frequent conversations with Captain Mize. This soft-spoken gentleman is not what some may visualize as a riverboat pilot. He could pass as a school principal if he had a suit on. But his laid-back style and mannerism do not diminish his authority. His crew respects him and follows his orders to the letter. He is an excellent leader and an inspiration to deckhands, since he spent his first 13 years on the river as one. Captain Mize is also a humanitarian. He and his wife of 26 years are foster care parents for several children. He also has an assortment of cats and other wayward critters. He takes no chances, particularly when pushing chemical barges. I am constantly impressed with his skill at the helm. On the approach to one of the locks, and expecting a delay, he decides to hold up along the left bank of a very wide section of the river. He is going to turn upriver and gently nudge the tow against the bank, since it is easier to control the boat while facing the current. He begins to make the left swing, and then pulls the engines out of gear, knowing exactly where the vessel is going to end up. At about the time, the boat and tow are straddling crossways in the river with no propulsion, the chief engineer comes up the stairs and into the pilothouse with a "what the hell" look on his face. He apparently has just noticed that the boat is crossways in the river with no props turning and thinks something is seriously wrong. We have a good laugh as the vessel gently drifts into the holding position that the captain is aiming for.

6:00 P.M....The *Ron Shankin* is steaming along in good time and should pass Louisville tomorrow morning, but we still have another lock to go through so that could change. At least the Markland Lock chamber is not being repaired. The number of recreational boats has increased this afternoon. The deck crew and I are watching them and commenting on the boats we like best. Our taste in boats is similar. The older cruisers with clean, traditional lines get the highest praises, like Chris Craft, Marinette, older Starcrafts, Lone Star. Those are real boats. A deckhand says, "A real riverman wouldn't be caught in one of those boats shaped like a half-used bar of soap." Another said "What about those candy-ass bass boats? Does anyone really need to go 80 mph to get to a fishin' hole? Then you got to worry bout puttin' a scratch on that purdy paint job." The discussion becomes lively, but ends abruptly. It is time to inspect the barge hatches. We all disperse.

11:00 P.M....We're entering Markland Locks and Dam after three hours of wait time, which doesn't seem as long to me as it used to. On day two, I mentioned the towboat that was stuck on a sandbar just below Markland. In its place is now a dredge boat, removing the sandbar. That is pretty fast action by the Corp of Engineers, considering the complex vessels, piping, and machinery that must be transported and assembled. Of course, the *Red Eagle* may not have been the first vessel stuck there.

Back in the engine room I am talking to the chief engineer about the drive system of the boat. The two nine-foot Propellers are housed in circular bands, looking much like a jet engine. This is called a kort nozzle system. It protects the propellers and funnels the water more directly into the rudders. There can, however, be some disadvantages. In two different incidents a loose buoy has become drawn into the kort nozzle. Those buoys are made of steel and weigh around 600 pounds. One time a buoy lodged between the propeller and the housing, causing the engine to bog down and stop. It was jammed so tight that nothing they did would free it. They managed to run on the other engine to a place where a diver was hired to cut the buoy up with a cutting torch and remove it, one piece at a time. The next time it happened, it caused a more serious challenge. A buoy was kicked up by the powerful propellers into the hull, piercing it. Water began gushing in but quick action saved the vessel from sinking. Watertight hatches were closed to contain the water in a limited area. The chief knew there was a lot of pressure on the hatches so he spot-welded them closed, just for good measure. Not all trips go as smoothly as this one has.

Day 9

5:00 A.M....I am up early to pack and be ready to disembark as the *Ron Shankin* passes Louisville, en route to Baton Rouge. I make a final round to visit the crew, and of course look at that prop wash one more time.

7:15 A.M....We are approaching the Louisiana Dock Company dock, where I left my vehicle. It is directly across the river from JeffBoat. Both JeffBoat and LDC are divisions of ACBL. JeffBoat built the *Mississippi Queen* in 1976 and is still turning out boats and barges, a sign that the business is still thriving. I go to the pilothouse to find that Captain Mize has already arranged for what I'll call a shuttle towboat to pick me up. I then take my bag to the forward main deck. The mate and deck hands are there, looking for my ride. They know it has been dispatched, but see no sign of it. Surprise! It's already waiting for me at the stern of the boat. The mystery of the missing towboat is solved and I take my bag to the stern. I board the towboat and bid farewell to the crew of the *Ron Shankin*, who come back to see me off (well, they also had some boxes to unload). The tow takes me to the dock where I jump off and head for my truck in the parking lot.

8:00 A.M....I am driving on I-71 during rush hour in Louisville. There are some delays but something has changed in me. So what's a few, or several minutes slowed down or stopped on a freeway anyway? It is nothing compared to 30 hours at a lock. I believe that I am completing my journey a more patient man. The highway I'm on now runs along the river and I pass the canal leading to McAlpine Locks and Dam. I see the long line of towboats waiting their turn. I know that I will be home in about four hours, while my friends on the *Ron Shankin* will still be here waiting to lock through.

I would like to thank all the fine people who made this experience possible. Bill Kinzeler arranged the trip. It is a complex operation considering all the tows, transfers, locks, and many changes that occur. Bill called the boat one day, not knowing that I had changed my plans. He was worried that they may have lost me, but I was in good hands. I appreciate his efforts and concern. I came to know Captain Dennis Mize the best, and am a better person for it. Integrity, skill, compassion, and leadership are words that come to mind when I think of Captain Mize. We had two pilots who transferred mid-trip. Captain Ronnie Prater was generous with his knowledge and a very nice guy. Captain Harry Simpkins piloted the return trip, and also had a few good stories to tell. Thanks to Chief Engineer Steve Wells for his stories and allowing me free access to his engine room domain. Chief Wells reminds me of Scottie on Star Trek. Assistance engineer Randall Husky, known as Mo, helped keep the trip interesting. Mo is the prankster and jokester on the boat. Mo included me in on one of his creative pranks on Chief Wells. As I mentioned, Gay McGrew is mom to everyone. She even puts up with Mo's pranks (to a point). I think Mo knows the limits he must stay within with regard to Gay. She was a delight and I felt adopted. Mate John Croggis is a solid guy who I would pick to be responsible for my life, if needed. He has the skills, attitude, and look of a veteran riverman, and I'm certain serves as a mentor for others. Lead Man (pronounced "leed") Steve Birney impressed me with his decision-making skills. He also likes to talk and we shared many good stories. Deckhands Larry Cantrell, John Embry, and Jerry Ryan were just great. They accommodated me in every way, always happy to explain what they were doing and willing to share their space, coffee, magazines, or whatever. A fine bunch of guys.

American Commercial Barge Lines is a first-class company and my impression from the crew is that they treat their employees well. If my experience with the *Ron Shankin* is indicative of life on the towboats, I am impressed. The work on the boats is hard and responsibilities are great. There are times of waiting and times of fast action and danger. My perception of life on the tows has changed somewhat. As I pass these huge vessels while aboard the *Steamboats*, I will visualize a professional crew, clean living conditions, and a family atmosphere. I was accepted as part of the

Photo by Author
View from the Pilothouse

family from day one, and made to feel at home, as the crew of the *Ron Shankin* quickly discovered that I was "awe right".

Chapter 12

Navigable River Know-How

In the chapter *Reading the River*, much is discussed about traveling remote rivers with little or no navigational aids. Those would be described as non-navigable rivers, even though they can be navigated in the right watercraft. The other side of river travel is trips on navigable rivers, which are maintained by navigation of commercial vessels. They are different from non-navigable rivers. This chapter is not an effort to teach a full course in river navigation. If one is serious about traveling rivers in a powerboat, he or she should take a course with a qualified organization, such as those the U.S. Power Squadron or the U.S. Coast Guard Auxiliary has available. What this chapter will do is provide a brief description, history and provide some specific navigation information. It will also explain the hazards and advantages of cruising on a navigable waterway. If the reader finds this information interesting and wants to learn more, then I recommend seeking qualified training.

In the early days of the development of navigational aids on the inland waterways, the methods were simple and by no means totally reliable. Steamboats that ran on the rivers in the early 1800s provided their own methods. The first, most important and still most reliable navigational tool is a good pilot. River pilots had to learn the river like the backs of their hands. Modern-day pilots still do. It was the pilot who was king of the river and was held in high regard by everyone. He indeed demanded and got paid handsomely for his services. Good pilots were the ones with the mansions along the rivers. Pilots knew difficult sections of the river and knew where they needed to steer around obstacles like snags and shoals. When approaching a known shallow area they made use of a leadline, which was a length of rope with a weight on the end that could be tossed into the river by a leadsman to find the water's depth. It also served a dual purpose by having a hollow end that was coated with beeswax or other sticky substance. When the weight dropped into the riverbed, it might bring up a plug from the bottom. This plug would let them know if it was sandy, muddy or gravelly. If nothing stuck in the weight the pilot proceeded with even greater care, since that would indicate a rock bottom.

The line was divided into fathoms and quarter fathoms, with one fathom equaling six feet. The leadsman would toss the line out, and then grab the line near the boat deck when it was in a vertical position. Allowing for the distance from the deck to the water, (freeboard), he would sing out the sounding as the vessel proceeded slowly ahead. The first mark on the line was one strip of leather, which is one fathom, or Mark One. Between marks was color-coded cloth woven into the line to indicate Quarter Marks. Six feet is very shallow water for any steamboat and the pilot would be hoping for deeper water as the leadsman sang out Mark One. If things were going well, the water depth would gradually deepen and the leadsman would sing out the greater depths as follows:

Mark One . . . . .6 feet, one strip of leather (one fathom)
Quarter One . . . . .7-1/2 feet, white cloth
Half One . . . . .9 feet, red cloth
Quarter Less Twain . . . . .10-1/2 feet, black cloth
Mark Twain . . . . .12 feet, two strips of leather (two fathoms)
Quarter Twain . . . . .13-1/2 feet, white cloth
Half Twain . . . . .15 feet, red cloth
Quarter Less Ta-Ree . . . . .16-1/2 feet, black cloth
Mark Ta-Ree . . . . . .18 feet, three strips of leather (three fathoms)
Quarter Ta-Ree . . . . .19-1/2 feet, white cloth
Half Ta-Ree . . . . .21 feet, red cloth
Quarter Less Four .22-1/2 feet, black cloth
Mark Four . . . . .24 feet, four strips of leather (four fathoms)
No Bottom . . . . .Any depth over twenty-four feet

Many of the very early steamboats did not travel by night, unless there was a full Moon, but competition forced the captains to start taking chances. The leadline was very valuable to them for night navigation. If the dark waters were known to have snags, along with being shallow, the captain would send men ahead of the boat in a skiff to heave the leadline and call back to a deckhand on the bow, who would in turn call up to the pilothouse. Another system for getting through a snag row at night was to have the men on the leading skiff show the way through by lantern light, and in some cases, using a system called "eating up the lights." This method utilized candles in floating cups, which were placed in the river ahead of the steamboat. The pilot would run over the candles thatwere in the same general path that the skiff was taking.

Courtesy of Gary Lucy Gallery
Eating Up The Lights

By 1852 the U.S. Government stepped in to help make the inland waterways safer. By then many of the snags had been removed by specially designed snag boats. Folks called the boats "government tooth pullers." Lanterns were also installed along the river on poles that could be used as a visual target for steering. Lantern keepers were hired for tending the lanterns, keeping them fueled and wicked. One of the problems with this system was that people stole the lanterns or the fuel. The lantern keepers were diligent in keeping their assigned lanterns lit in all kinds of weather. They were also armed to deal with any thieves they may catch.

There were many collisions on the river between steamboats, particularly at night. Two things were developed to deal with the problem. First, fire pots were hung on the boats and kept lit at night so that others could see them coming. Second, whistle signals were developed so pilots could communicate their intentions in advance, preventing last- minute failed attempts to avoid a collision. For passing, a pilot may give one short blast if he intended to meet the oncoming vessel on the port side, or two short blasts for the starboard side. The signal would be agreed upon by the oncoming vessel, which repeated the same blast. Sometimes pilots would disagree on the side to pass on and blast opposite signals, creating many close calls and collisions by virtue of stubbornness. This was overcome by a law that gave downriver traffic the right to decide on which side to pass another vessel.

Today there are many navigational aids, with the most common being buoys. The U.S. Coast Guard maintains channel buoys, which are floating steel cans that indicate where the channel is located. In most cases the U.S. Army Corp of Engineers is in charge of keeping an open channel of sufficient depth and width to accommodate commercial vessels. This depth can vary, but one can be certain that a buoyed channel has plenty of depth for any pleasure craft. The channel buoys are normally about nine feet tall and weigh around 600 pounds. They are anchored to the riverbed by a 1000-pound block of concrete, attached by cable or chain to the floating buoy. The buoys are color-coded to indicate the edges of the channel. The inland waterways system has green buoys along the right bank of the channel and red buoys along the left bank.

What are the right and left banks? All rivers have a designated left and right bank, and these are always the descending bank. In other words the left and right banks are as we face downriver. Right and left bank designation does not change in the upriver direction. We must simply be aware of that and think the opposite. What is along the left bank going downriver will still be along the left bank going upriver, but will be on our right side. Sound confusing? How about this! When mariners are returning from the sea, they go up the rivers to their home port. All red buoys are on the right while they are returning, hence the saying; "Red, Right, Return".

If we stay between the red and green buoys we are assured of a deep channel. If there is only one color of buoys, we know that there is a channel between those buoys and the opposite shore. An example of that would be if we were traveling downriver and we see a line of green buoys, we would keep the buoys on our starboard (right) side, and be assured of deep water to the bank on our left (left bank). Green buoys are called cans and red buoys are called nuns. There are buoys for several other purposes, such as mooring and danger, but our main focus in this writing is channel buoys. Remember, however, that all buoys that are red and white are a warning of some kind and should be paid close attention to.

There are also signs along the river called daymarks. The daymarks are color- coded the same as buoys with the red-right-return rule. The passing daymarks have different shaped signs on them to indicate which side the channel is on, or if the channel crosses the river. This is more important for commercial vessels than with the more maneuverable pleasure craft. What is of interest to all is the

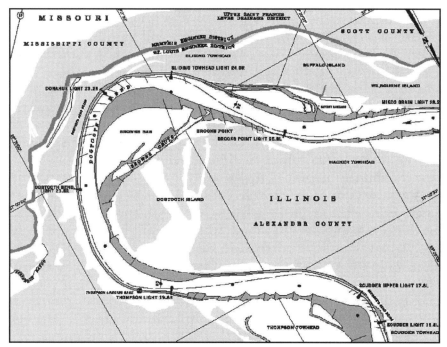

Courtesy Army Corps of Engineers
River chart

secondary sign with numbers on it. This is the river mile marker. Anyone traveling a navigable river should have a chart of the river with him or her. The chart will show where the mile markers are located and provide a means of knowing where we are and how far it is to anywhere else on the river. The markers show the mile to the tenth, so one may show "123.5" as the mile. As an example of this, let's say we are traveling down the lower Mississippi River and are passing Memphis. We want to know how long it will take to get to Helena, Arkansas. Memphis is mile 736 and Helena is mile 663, which is 73 miles. Our boat will cruise at 12 mph, making our cruising time about six hours. On most rivers this is the mileage from the mouth of the river, which means that the numbers get smaller as one goes downriver. There are some exceptions, like the Ohio River. Mile zero is at the beginning of the Ohio at Pittsburgh where the Monongahela and Allegheny rivers meet. The chart will also show the channel, tributaries, power lines, bridges, and all other details relative to the river.

Some daymarks are called lights because they have a flashing light on top. The color and flash sequence can tell the mariner something about the river ahead while cruising at night. The color green, as with buoys, tells us that the light is located along the right bank; red is along the left bank. The green light will be seen as a single intermittent flash, and the red will be seen as two intermittent flashes. Some have white lights flashing with the same pattern. What does all this tell us? While traveling on the river at night it is often difficult to distinguish the right bank from the left bank at a distance ahead of the vessel. Seeing the color and/or rate of flash with tell us in advance where the right and left banks are. These lights are usually found on the approach to or on river bends, with the white lights telling us that the channel is crossing toward or away from the outside of the bend. Knowing this will help to prepare for a bend in the river that cannot be seen. If we are traveling downriver at night and see a white double-flashing light, we know that there is a channel crossing toward the left, leading into a right bend. As we round the bend there will likely be green single-flashing lights to target as we round the bend. Most channels go toward the outside of bends. If we are traveling upriver into the same bend, the only difference is that we would know that we are coming into a left bend. If the lights were single-blinking and green in the bend it would be a left bend going downriver, or a right bend going upriver. Large towboats often target the lights in order to steer or flank around the bends. It is important for all mariners to know as much about an approaching bend at night in order to prepare for unseen oncoming traffic and also to prevent running aground.

Sometimes pleasure boaters pay no attention to the navigational aids indicating where the channel is, thinking that only deep-draft vessels have to worry about that. This is often true but when traffic is clear, it is wise to stay in the channel to avoid unseen dangers. Many rivers have rock wing dams. These are piles of rocks that run perpendicular to the shore to direct the flow of water toward the channel. During periods of low water, the dams can usually be seen. During normal and high water the rocks are submerged, sometimes just below the waterline. Hitting one can wreck a boat. Wing dams are shown on the charts and sometimes have a buoy at the end of them. Going on the wrong side of the buoy can be disastrous. The wing dams are another very good reason to have a chart and know where we are on the river. Many wing dams are also located on the riverbank side of an island, extending from the island to the shore. They are there to prevent the main channel from shifting to that side. When taking the off-channel side of an island, proceed with caution. During the day the turbulence created by the wing dams can be seen by an alert mariner, but at night they are much harder to spot. While traveling at night, one must also watch the navigational lights on other vessels to determine their course, and any special light signal that may be showing. This chapter will not get into details of onboard navigation lights, as anyone who owns a boat should already be familiar with them or learn them in the training recommended earlier.

We will discuss rights-of-way because there are some differences on rivers that are not present in lakes and open waters. Most of us know that when approaching an oncoming vessel, the general rule is to pass port to port. For pleasure craft this is true, but with another dimension. For commercial traffic on rivers the downriver traffic has the right-of-way. This is because large boats going downriver have less maneuverability than upbound vessels. With the current pushing the boat there is less resistance against the rudders, and they must outrun the current to steer. Large vessels also take much longer to stop when traveling with the current. With all motorized vessels, there is better steering control while pointed against the current. That is why vessels will often turn into the current to hold in place. It is also the reason we all turn upriver to dock or land a boat. What it all boils down to is that the least maneuverable vessel has the right-of-way. A collision between a ski boat and a boat under sail will almost certainly be considered the fault of the operator of the ski boat. We all know that a towboat with fifteen barges is not a very maneuverable vessel. It starts slow, turns slow, and stops slow. We all should know the danger of 25,000 tons of boat and material gliding in water. Pleasure craft are expected to stay out of their way from any direction. I have seen people in pleasure craft cut across the bow of towboats. The pilot of the towboat cannot see for several hundred feet in front of the lead barges, so if the pleasure craft should stall or flip over, there would be little chance of survival. Even if the towboat captain could see them, there would be no time to stop or turn away. There are other specific right-of-way aspects to be learned in a boating course. We should always relinquish our right-of-way to avoid a collision. This makes sense, because isn't it better to give up our right-of-way than our lives?

When traveling many navigable waterways we encounter locks and dams. Dams were built to hold water back to keep a pool stage of water deep enough to maintain a navigable channel. Some dams also provide hydroelectric power and flood control. When water is dammed, it will naturally have a higher level above the dam and a lower level below. In order to allow for vessels to pass through, locks

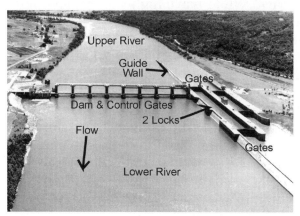

Courtesy Corps of Engineers
Lock & Dam

are constructed to lower or raise boats from one level to the other. The locks and dams could best be described as watery staircases. Before the days of locks and dams, many rivers became too shallow to navigate during low-water periods. These structures allow for year-round navigation. When descending a river lock and dam and upon approaching a lock, the chamber will have been filled to the upper river level. This is done by the lockmaster opening valves in the bottom of the chamber that lead to the upper river. The water will flow into the chamber by gravity and stop filling when the level in the chamber is the same as the upriver side of the closed gate. The gate will then open and allow vessels to pass into the lock chamber. The gate behind the vessels will close, and then valves open to drain the chamber to the level on the lower side of the dam. The lower gate will open to allow vessels to proceed down the river. The procedure is simply reversed when locking through upriver.

It is a good idea to know locking procedures before taking any cruise that will require passing through a lock and dam. There are vessel priorities at locks. Some vessels will be allowed to pass others waiting to lock through. The highest priority is given to government vessels, such as U.S. Coast Guard and Corp of Engineers. The next in line are passenger boats on a schedule. Following are commercial boats, such as towboats, workboats, and commercial fishing boats. The last on the priority list is pleasure craft. Anyone in a pleasure craft, whether it is a canoe or a yacht, should be prepared for a wait. Boats with no marine radio must approach the lock guide wall and pull a cord to await instructions from a loudspeaker. It is advisable to have a VHS radio on any vessel for communications with locks, other vessels, marinas, weather, and emergencies. By hailing the lockmaster by radio, one can call in advance of arrival to get an idea of lock conditions and traffic, along with advice on possible delays. Very often the lockmaster may advise the boater that the lock is opening soon on their side and to come on in. Without calling in advance one stands a greater chance of just missing the closing of the gate and must wait until the next opportunity. That is, unless a towboat comes along, then the wait may be even longer. Often more than one boat is invited into the chamber; pleasure craft are usually grouped together. Pleasure craft may also lock through with a commercial vessel if there is room and the pilot of the commercial boat gives his consent. An important thing to remember about locking is that the lockmaster is truly the master of his domain. It is this person who calls the shots and can help make the locking a pleasurable experience with minimal wait, or make you jump through hoops with maximum wait. The lockmaster must be treated with respect, so it is wise to be humble and not demanding.

Now that the basics of locks have been covered, following are actual procedures:

1.) Call ahead by stating the lock name and/or number. State your type of vessel, boat name, direction being traveled, location, and that you are requesting to lock through. An example might be, "Markland Lock, this is the pleasure craft *Key West*, southbound at mile 363 requesting to lock through." The lockmaster may be busy and not respond immediately, so be patient. If there is still no response after a reasonable time, repeat the request.

2.) If you have no marine radio, go to the end of the lock guide wall and pull the identified cord. This will signal the lockhouse that someone is requesting to lock through. Wait for instructions to be given on a loudspeaker.

3.) If your vessel is close to the lock gate, the lockmaster may advise you to hold up off to the side of the guide wall, as there may be a vessel coming toward you in the chamber and you would be in the way. You may also have to wait due to the priorities discussed earlier.

4.) Just like roads there will be a red light and a green light. Always wait for the lock gates to open completely and for a green light before entering, unless instructed otherwise by the lockmaster.

5.) Proceed into the lock slowly, as all locks are no-wake zones. Someone will wave you over, or tell you which side of the lock chamber to secure the boat to. Make certain that anyone outside the cabin of the boat or in an open boat has a life preserver on. This is required. Also, no smoking is allowed in the locks.

6.) Have boat fenders ready to drop in place on the side of the boat that will be secured to the lock wall. The walls are rough concrete and can damage a boat. Also, have a pole or paddle to push against the wall during locking to keep the boat away from the wall as much as possible.

7.) There are different ways to secure boats in locks, depending on how they are constructed and the preference of the lockmaster. Some will pay out one or two lines to you for holding, to keep the boat stable and close to the wall while the water is filling or draining. Do not tie the lines to any part of the boat. You must be able to control the slack and tension of the line by hand. If you are locking down, you will pay out line as the water drops. If you are locking up, you will take slack out of the line as the water rises. Some locks have floating pins to tie off to. The pins are located in vertical slots in the lock wall. As the water rises or falls the pins and your boat will rise or fall with the water while remaining secured. Do not draw the line tight from the floating pin to your boat. Leave some slack so that you can keep the boat from scraping along the lock wall as the water level changes. Sometimes the pins will temporarily hang up in the slot. Larger boats will pull it loose as the water rises or falls. Smaller boats may tip if this happens, so be ready to unhook the line if necessary. The third method of securing will be to not secure the boat at all. The lockmaster may instruct you to stay in the middle of the lock chamber while under power and keep the boat stable with the propellers, while the water level changes.

8.) Do not unhook the boat, let go of the line, or start the engine until instructed to do so, or the gate has opened completely and you hear a blast signal. Proceed out of the lock slowly and continue slow ahead until you have reached the end of the guide wall or signs indicting "No Wake" have ended.

Locking through is not as scary as it may sound. After a few times, one becomes accustomed to it but the first time is always exciting. I am reminded of the day I was locking through on the Illinois River. The lockmaster had put several pleasure craft in the chamber at the same time. We were going downriver and were provided lines to pay out as the water and our boats lowered. A man in a motorsailer was directly in front of my cruiser. He tied the line off to a kevel on the stern of his boat, and then busied himself with something in the cabin. The first thing I noticed was that the water and my boat were going down, but the aft section of the sailboat was not going down. He finally noticed the list to the bow end and came running out to untie the line. By then the rope had so much pressure on it that he could not get it to release from the kevel. I was amazed that the kevel had not torn loose from the decking. I yelled to the rattled sailor to cut the line. I could hardly believe it when he said he had no knife. A sailor with no knife? I reached in my pocket and removed my knife, gave it a toss that I was proud of as it landed in his hands, all while his boat stern was still rising. His nervous fingers finally got the knife blade open and slashed the line. The boat came down with a tremendous splash, creating a wake that knocked the other boats in the chamber around. He thanked me and we discussed how he had learned some lessons that day. Don't tie the line to your boat while locking and always have a knife handy. We were all impressed with the construction of the decking and strength of the kevel mount to lift that much weight.

Some navigable waterways, such as the lower Mississippi, have few marinas to purchase fuel or to dock for the night. It is advisable to purchase a cruising guide for the rivers that will be traveled. A few are available that will provide that information, along with other tips about a section of river. I prefer to spend my nights in remote locations than to tie off to a dock at a busy marina. It is important to select the right place to do so. This is pretty easy if the vessel is a canoe, as it can easily be pulled from the water. For motorcraft, one needs to be careful not to anchor or ground the boat at a location that is likely to have a lot of wake from passing vessels. The wake action can drive the boat farther onto shore and cause the boat to be stuck by morning. Large wakes can also break a boat loose from the mooring.

When I am seeking a place to spend the night, I will look primarily for two things. A non-navigable tributary provides safe anchorage with no commercial vessels passing by. Care must be taken when entering the tributary, not to run aground or hit a sub-merged object. Proceed slowly. The other option is the back side of an island, away from the channel. The same caution should be observed while entering this type of area. One can set an anchor or carefully ground the boat and tie off to a tree. Often the riverbank and water depth will determine the choice. An accessible tree-lined steep bank will provide the most stable anchorage. The boat can be tied to a tree from the bow, and from the stern. This will keep the boat against the bank and keep the stern from swinging out. If the river is falling, or one doesn't know if it is rising, stationary, or falling, check the river's edge on a regular basis to make sure that the water is not going out from under the boat. We have all heard of boats running aground. This would be a case where the ground runs aboat. A stick or rock placed at the water's edge is the best method for gauging this.

I was on the Ohio River one day and came upon three men who had landed for the night on a beach on the channel side of the river. During the night they not only had a lot of wakes pushing against the boat, but a falling river. By morning the bow of the boat was sitting high and dry and listing. The outdrive was still in the water but could never pull the boat back into the water. Upon talking to them, I was surprised that they had slept through it all but then not so surprised when I saw the litter from their evening's ardent spirits. My friend and I stopped to help and we all worked for hours digging a canal under the boat to the water's edge. That, along with a great deal of grunt labor, finally got the old Starcraft cruiser back into the river. They were grateful for the help and preparing to leave when I told them that our work was not done yet. I could not leave this place with the damaged beach and litter. I explained to them that everyone should leave no trace that they were there. They were shamed into pitching in and restoring the beach. Then they collected their litter before heading down the river, with a couple of lessons learned.

Sometimes we can find neither an island nor a tributary, but must sleep. Look for a steep bank, which is an indication that the water is deep along the shore, then tie off the boat parallel to the bank with two lines. This will prevent possible damage to the bow and keep the boat from driving into the bank. The night may be spent with a little rockin' and rollin'. Abandoned piers are good for mooring, as long as there are no signs to indicate that it is not permitted. Public landings, docks, and piers can be used for overnight stays as long as there are no signs indicating that it is not allowed.

Never tie-off a watercraft to another vessel without permission. Never land at an active commercial pier, as you may get woken up in the most annoying way an aggravated towboat pilot can think of. Never land at a private dock without permission. All this changes in emergencies. In an emergency, make a landing at the nearest available safe place.

Cruising on navigable waterways can be an enjoyable and safe journey. One must be well equipped, respectful to other traffic, follow the rules, and most important-be alert. I have spoken of priorities in locks and rights-of-way on the river that must be observed, but everyone and every type of vessel has a right to be there. Sometimes one must be very patient. If you are a horn-honking, tailgating, aggressive driver in your car, you had better change your attitude or stay off navigable rivers.

Photo by Author
Canoeing through a lock

Chapter 13

Bizarre River Experiences

Airplane on the river

I have often been asked about what strange or unusual things I have seen during my river travels. I must say that nearly every trip on a river provides something that would fit that category. One of the most unusual sights I encountered happened while on a river trip from Chicago, Illinois, to Evansville, Indiana. A friend asked me to accompany him to Chicago where he had made a deal to purchase a used 32-foot Marinette cruiser. Rather than to transport the boat by land he wanted to pilot it to Evansville. The boat was located on the North Chicago River.

One of my friend's employees drove us to the harbor on the North Chicago River where the boat was docked. Upon signing the deal, we looked the vessel over and decided to stay there for the night to get a fresh start in the morning. The boat was a twin-engine vessel with a fly bridge. That evening we planned our cruise. To get the boat to Evansville, we would take the Chicago River to the Illinois River, then down the Illinois to the Mississippi River above St. Louis. From there we would cruise down the Mississippi to the Ohio River at Cairo, Illinois, then up the Ohio to the marina at Evansville. The canal that the boat was moored in was very narrow and boats were double-docked, meaning that one was tied to the dock and another was tied to that boat. Fortunately Dennis' boat was on the outside lane so we would not have to move another boat to get out. Dennis and I looked at the narrow canal and could see that there was no room to turn the boat around. A short distance ahead it appeared to be just wide enough. Dennis had never operated a twin-engine boat before, so he was rehearsing how he might operate the throttles in reverse of each other to spin the boat around. As I looked ahead I could see some overhanging trees along the port side and predicted that we could very well find ourselves among the bird nests if he didn't maneuver just right.

The next morning we pulled away. Dennis was impressively skillful at handling the boat and steering with the throttles, however, we did end up among the bird nests for a time. After finally getting turned around we went into the main river and stopped at Windy City Marina to fuel up. The boat was in great condition and performed flawlessly. We cruised on down the Illinois River in perfect weather. Each night we found a nice cove or island chute for anchorage. We then entered the Mississippi River at Grafton, Illinois, and continued past St. Louis. On the fourth day of the journey we turned into the huge Ohio River, with a stop-over at Paducah, Kentucky, before proceeding up to Evansville. We were within a few miles of Golconda, Illinois, where I was scanning the river with binoculars, with Dennis at the helm. I saw something that just didn't seem right. This must be an illusion! I looked again and told Dennis that I thought I could see an airplane in the river, a big one.

Dennis didn't believe me or thought I was mistaken, so he asked for the binoculars while I took the helm. He gazed for a while and said, "Jerry, there is an airplane in the water, a big one. I think it's a Boeing 727". The closer we got the more convinced we were that this was a plane crash. There were many boats around a barge. The barge had a large crane on it that was lifting the plane out of the water. The plane was upside down and the wings were broken off. The window openings bore black streaks, which had been caused by

Photo by Author
Cranes lifting airliner onto a barge

flames. The tail section was heavily damaged and had been on fire. We couldn't believe what we were seeing. We had heard nothing of a plane crash, although we had a radio. We might not have been listening at the right times. This was terrible! I got out my camera and begin taking photos as we got closer. Now we could see that the plane had actually slid into the river there was a path of broken trees and brush leading to the river adjacent to the crash site. It must have attempted an emergency landing on shore and then gone off into the river upside down. We got even closer, then a U.S. Coast Guard boat came our way and ordered us to stay clear of the area. We headed on up the river, numbed by what we had just witnessed.

We needed to fuel up, so we pulled into the Golconda Marina a few more miles up the river. We went into the marina store and of course asked about the plane crash. There was one man behind the counter and two sitting at a table. The man at the counter said, "Plane crash?" I couldn't believe that they would know nothing of it and as I looked at the men at the table I could see a little grin growing on one of their faces. When the others saw that their friend had blown their cover of ignorance they all began to laugh. At first I thought, "What the hell is so funny about a plane crash?" But then I realized that there must be something fishy going on. Upon regaining their composure the men explained what we had just seen. It was a movie set. They had just completed making a movie that included a plane crashing into the river and were beginning to clean up the site. The movie was *U. S. Marshals*, starring Tommy Lee Jones and Wesley Snipes. We didn't find out much more about the plot of the movie, but were very happy to discover that it was not a real plane crash. I must say that they did an excellent job of special effects, since I was right there and could not tell that it was a movie set. I didn't even mind the teasing and fun they all had with us at the marina. At least I got some good photos and I definitely had to see that movie.

When *U.S. Marshals* came to the theaters I went to see it, and later purchased a videotape of it. It is fun to push the stop action and compare the scenes to my photographs. In the movie, the plane was carrying a cargo of prisoners being transferred around the country. After an explosion the plane attempted to make an emergency landing on a road that runs along the river. Upon coming to a bend in the road the plane went off the road, down an embankment and landed upside down in the river. At least the assessment that I had made at the site was correct about how the plane got there, even if it wasn't real. They say you can't believe everything you hear. Well, I learned that you can't always believe what you see.

The Arrowhead

The experience with the airplane in the river was strange but totally explainable. Even though we imagined the worst, the sight was a deception. Sometimes an experience cannot be explained. I am very objective about encounters considered to be spiritual and try to look at them from all points of view, while at the same time seek practical reasons for the occurrence. There can be single or multiple reasons for my taking a canoe trip. It may be for the scenic beauty, or the adventure, or just to get away from it all. I also enjoy collecting fossils and other artifacts along the river. I had heard that one had a good chance of finding Indian arrowheads in or along the West Fork of the White River in Indiana. This river was traveled heavily by the Shawnee and other Indian tribes. There are even stories of Chief Tecumseh traveling the waterway in 1811 seeking the support of other tribes including the Delaware, Miami, and Potawatomi to fight the white man. I decided to canoe a section of that river in search of arrowheads. I am not an avid collector of arrowheads, and indeed never developed an eye for spotting them, but it gave me a mission.

I set off just below Muncie, Indiana, and intended to travel for three days. The water was low and clear. This meant portaging in some shallow areas, but it made it ideal for fossil and arrowhead hunting in the sand and gravel bars. On the first day out I searched all the shallows, bars, and along the shoreline. I traveled very slowly, making only a few miles, but was in no hurry. I did manage to find a few interesting rocks and fossils, but no sign of an arrowhead. While floating down the mild river I often found myself deep in thought of the Indians traveling through this very area. There were hunting parties looking for deer that came to the river's edge to drink or beaver from which to make pelts. There may have been war parties looking for settlers, with rascally intentions on their minds. They may have been traveling to other villages for trade or communication. Whatever their reasons for being there, I felt myself as one of them, even with my plastic canoe and modern equipment.

After an all-day search I never found an arrowhead. At around 5 pm I spotted something very interesting in the middle of the river. It was a large rock about the size of a truck. I looked up and could see that at some time in the past the rock had dislodged from the high bluff along the right bank. I thought, "What a crash and splash that must have made." Two Canada geese occupied the top of the rock, which appeared to have a fairly flat area on it. The water split

Photo by Author
The rock

around the rock and entered into a section of mild rapids just below. It was a beautiful spot in the river and would make a great camp for the night. It was a little early to set up camp, but I quickly decided that I wanted to sleep on that rock with the sound of the moving water and the sight of the tall trees beneath a full moon. It was perfect. I pulled the canoe up to the rock and found a smaller rock on the downstream side to tie off to. Now I would have no problem keeping company with the geese; however, they chose to move on with a few honks of disapproval. The boulder was a bit difficult to ascend but after pitching the needed gear onto the top, I finally managed to get myself up there too. It was even flatter than I had thought, making a nice level surface. It appeared that the geese had spent a great deal of time on that rock, based on the amount of coating they had left there. I am not squeamish, but would prefer to not sleep on goose excrement if I can help it. I went back to my canoe and fetched my bailing bucket, a rope, and some sand from the river bank. After hoisting the equipment up on the rock I proceeded to clean myself a large spot on the rock with sand, water, and the soles of my shoes. After completing my task, I sat on the rock listening to the sound of the water as it cascaded through the rapids below and around the huge boulder. This was a remote location and fortunately not accessible by any way but water. I could be certain that at least this little section of river looked much the same as it did when Tecumseh traveled it. It happened that I had brought a book with me that told the story of Tecumseh and his brother, the Prophet. I sat on the rock and read until dark, stopping occasionally to watch a beaver emerge and enter his tunnel in the bank of the river. He was doing his thing and I was doing mine. The geese made a couple of flyovers but must have chosen a different site for the evening. I had no problem with that, but would gladly have shared the rock with them.

After dark I sat on the rock watching the glimmer of the moonlit waters, listening to the sounds, and feeling myself drawn back in time to when the Native Americans were here. I conjured up images of small villages along this stream with warm lights glowing on the river. I imagined being at their ceremonies, and pictured myself passing by them on the dark river and watching as I glided silently by. It was time to get some sleep. I didn't set up a tent but chose instead to simply roll out my sleeping bag and sleep under the stars. I thought again of the Indians as I drifted off to sleep to the sounds of the water and night critters. With this setting, my thoughts, and reading the book that I had, it is very logical that my dream would be inspired as it was.

In my dream I heard distant voices that I could not understand. I heard the sounds of thrashing water and feet along the shore. I dreamed that I had woken up on that rock. I dreamed I sat up and listened for the sounds, straining to see where the sounds of humans had come from. I could see nothing but the moonlit waters cascading in the rapids below me. I was compelled to climb out of my sleeping gear and crawl to the pointed top of the rock. When I looked down toward the water it was unusually still just below me, providing a mirror image in the moonlight. The image that I saw was the shadow of the rock with my reflection looking down over it. It was me but with a very different appearance. I was older with long gray hair. I was wearing skins and some sort of ceremonial headwear, but not feathers. I was shocked to look at my reflection and see an old Indian. Confused, I looked around me to see who else was on the rock, but I was alone. I was confused but not afraid. In fact I felt very calm and comfortable with what I saw. I carefully went back to a tattered blanket where my sleeping bag had been. I lay down and drifted back to sleep.

When I woke up the next morning I did what I normally do first, which was to reach for my thermos of coffee that I had heated up the night before. It wasn't until I had begun my coffee meditation that I began to think about that dream, which became clearer and more real as I recalled it. It was an amazing dream that consumed me for a long time. I even looked at my clothing and sleeping bag to make sure that it was a dream and that I had not been magically sent back in time. I did not want to leave that rock, but it was now late morning and I had to move on, as I still wanted to find at least one arrowhead. Everything I did that morning was done with the thoughts of that dream. A dream like that is unusual for me, particularly since it was a dream of me waking up and going back to sleep. I don't usually remember details of dreams as I did with this one. I can recall it and rewind it as though it was a video. I rolled up my sleeping bag and made a few careful trips packing the gear down to the canoe. When breaking camp I always go back to scan the area to make certain that I have left no trace that I was there. The only difference I had made was to clean the area on the rock, but I was certain that the resident geese would waste no time restoring it to its natural condition. As I scanned, something caught my attention where my sleeping bag had been. Upon closer examination I found something that stunned me. I kneeled down and looked at it closer before touching it.

Right where I had slept was an arrowhead in perfect condition. I picked it up and at first thought, "Wow, I am not very observant to have missed that yesterday." But wait a minute! I had scrubbed that entire area with sand and water. I used my shoes to scrub it by sliding my feet around the spot. How could this be? How could I have done that without disturbing or not seeing that arrowhead? How did it get there during the night? Then I wondered, was it a dream? Was it a spiritual experience? Was it magic? Does it relate in some way to a past life? Or was it coincidence and imagination inspired by the river and my thoughts?

I admit that sometimes I am not all that observant, but then I thought about my mission. I was looking for arrowheads and had tuned in to spot them. I also wonder about the dream, if it was a dream. Why did my reflection show me as an Indian, and why was I old? There were many questions and no answers, but I cherish the experience and the gift I received on the rock that night. Since then I have had a strong desire to read and do research about our Native Americans, and gained much respect for their heritage. Perhaps there was a reason for the experience (or dream). If so, it has not been made apparent to me yet. The mystery of the experience and the arrowhead has never been solved. I spent the rest of that canoe trip trying to come up with a rational answer. I still think of that night and wonder about it each time I look at my prize arrowhead.

Up the Creek

One spring evening I was sitting on my dock on the Wabash River with my friend Tom. We were discussing the high water and watching large trees go by, as the river was above flood stage. We heard the distant drone of an outboard motor from around the bend. As the noise grew louder we saw another friend coming up the river in his old 24-foot Lone Star cruiser. Steve was never one to be all that careful, and we could see him plowing up the river zigzagging to avoid hitting the debris. His not-so-careful ways are indicated by the large number of dents in his aluminum boat. Steve saw us on the dock and pulled over. He had a couple of buddies with him and were setting out to have dinner somewhere on the river. He had a gas grill attached to the railing of the boat and plenty of food, along with a supply of ardent spirits. It was getting late in the afternoon so both Tom and I turned down Steve's offer to join them. I had things to do and Tom had to go to work a midnight. Steve assured us that we would be back early and frankly, it didn't take that much convincing to get us to change our minds when we saw the steaks and other good food. We got onboard and headed up the river.

The boat labored against the strong current with the heavy load, while we looked for just the right place to have dinner. All the good landings and islands were under water and there was too much floating debris to anchor in the main stream. As we approached the mouth of a stream coming into the river from the west, Steve decided to go up it a short distance to find a nice spot. The stream is usually too shallow for a big cruiser to travel on, but near the mouth it seemed plenty deep enough. We continued up the creek much farther than we expected to be able to go. Steve said he planned to keep going until he hit bottom. At one point there was a minor log jam, which Steve conquered by pushing through it and adding another scrape or two to the hull, which he calls "character marks". Further up a tree was lying across the creek with no apparent way to get through. That is until Steve made another bold decision. The creek was well over the bank so he turned toward the woods and simply piloted around the creek, deftly steering between the trees. We were all busy holding up or breaking off limbs that got in the way. We couldn't believe we were getting this far up this normally tiny stream in such a large boat. I was trying to keep track of our position and number of miles up the creek we were going. On we went, forgetting all about time and circumstances that could cause us problems. We were now on an exploration mission and determined to take this creek as far as it would allow us. We passed under a bridge with only inches of clearance. If the river was still rising we would not have gone any farther for fear of getting trapped above the bridges, but the river was falling. Two more bridges were just as close and at one of them a group of people were watching. I am certain that they had never seen a 24-foot cabin cruiser going up that creek before.

As we proceeded, both sides of the creek were flooded over farm fields and the only way we knew where the creek channel was located was to stay within or along the tree line that indicated the creek bank. We did take a couple of side trips to go cornfield cruising, but kept our bearings on the tree line. There were several places where there were no trees along the bank on either side, but we could see them farther ahead, so we continued in a direction that re-entered the known stream. We were all getting very hungry and decided it was time to stop and prepare dinner. In addition, we needed to allow enough time to get back so Tom to go to work. It was getting dark and I suggested that we ought to get back downstream past the open areas before stopping, but Steve said he had a fix on our position and getting back would be no problem. Steve fired up the grill and we enjoyed some of the best steaks I ever had, along with baked potatoes and other great side dishes. We ate and chatted well into darkness. By the time we had finished dinner it was 10 pm. We were in backwaters with no current to indicate the direction of the main river, so it would be important to follow the tree line back down the stream. We had no GPS, but did have a compass, so if there was any problem we knew that we were west of the Wabash. All seemed to be going well, but it felt very strange cruising between the narrow rows of trees on that black night. We kept sweeping the searchlight back and forth to keep our bearings and felt comfortable that we were heading back down the stream.

Our comfort diminished when we came upon a bluff where the stream was supposed to be. It was like a dead-end stream, so we knew that we were not on the stream at all. Somewhere, we had gotten off the stream and into some woods. Steve started backing the boat out, and then found a large enough place to turn around. There were five of us on the boat with five different ideas of were the stream would be. After coming onto more dead-ends, we started paying more attention to the compass and decided to find the main river by traveling east, regardless of where the streambed was. Each opening in the woods led us across fields and to more places that we could not get through. Knowing that the water we were in was backwater, we could only hope that there would be some opening to the river that would accommodate our boat. One place had possibilities until we came up to an elevated road. We couldn't help but laugh at the sight of a truck stopping along the road, with the driver surely wondering why there was a boat going alongside him in a cornfield. At another location we passed between a farmer's house and his barn, but it didn't look like anyone was home to give us directions to the river. Besides, we would never have asked. As we entered what appeared to be an open area I was watching for a crosscurrent, or any current at all to indicate that we were close to the river. It was now past midnight and Tom was already late for work.

Steve came up with the idea of dropping anchor and staying for the night, then finding our way back to the river in daylight. I reminded him that the river was falling and that we could find ourselves sitting in a muddy cornfield by morning. He then agreed that we had to find our way to the river. It was hard to tell, but I had a sense that we were making progress on our easterly direction. Fortunately Steve had plenty of fuel. The bottom of the boat was taking a beating and the prop was getting chewed up on all the objects that it hit, including a fence. Who would have thought that five experienced river men would get lost going up a little creek? To make matters worse, fog was moving in, which made our searchlight practically useless. There were times when we didn't know something was in our way until we bumped into it. Our plan was to go east until we hit something, then turn north in search of another opening to the east. Then we finally got to an opening that appeared to have some current. We joked about the old saying, "When in doubt, always follow the bubbles", and that is just what we did.

We followed the bubbles until we saw what I had been looking for all night. There was the strong current of the Wabash crossing our bow from left to right. We finally made it back into the river at some unknown opening in a cornfield. After a brief celebration we headed down the river and passed the mouth of the stream we had entered. It was about six miles downriver from where we found our way back into the river, which confirmed that we had traveled cross-county by boat. We finally got back to my cabin just after 3 am. Tom hurried off to work. I went to bed, glad to be back home. Steve and his friends slept in his boat at my dock. The next morning we discussed our adventure and all the things we did wrong. Our situation was humorous and did not seem life-threatening at the time, but when I think about the consequences of getting stuck in a flooded field or woods many miles from assistance, it could have been very dangerous. There would have been no way to walk in that soft mud, so the only option would be to put life jackets on and swim, but to where? Even that would be dangerous with the fences, trees, and snakes. We were out of cell phone and marine radio range and when we were missed, rescuers would have had no idea to look for us in the woods far from the river. In addition, how would Steve recover his boat, left in the woods

Photo by Author

The next morning

Lessons learned: Don't get so carried away with a mission that you forget about the consequences. Waterways look much different at night so don't rely on landmarks viewed in daylight if returning at night. A tracking GPS would have been very helpful but the most sensible thing to do would have been to turn around with plenty of time to get back to the river before dark

Chapter 14

The Evolution of Riverboats

The rivers of America were the original transportation routes, dating back to the Native Americans. Dugout, bark, and animal skin canoes were the vessels used. As time passed, explorers, fur traders, settlers, and boatmen devised other types of watercraft. This chapter will discuss the evolution of various watercraft and their use on the rivers.

Traders, merchants, and farmers had a need to transport their goods to expanded markets. With roads non-existent, overland transportation was difficult and dangerous. Flatboats were built to fulfill the demand. The first flatboats were simply watertight boxes built of wood, with tar sealant. The box was enclosed to protect the goods and provide cabin space for passengers. The boats varied in size and most had an oar at the stern to help steer, called a sweep. Flatboats might begin their journey far up the headwaters of great rivers or on tributaries. Many flatboats were pulled by mules or horses on

Library of Congress
Typical flatboat

the canal systems. The boatmen would usually tie off in groups at night for safety from Indians and pirates. The Ohio River was particularly plagued with pirates, who would swoop down upon the sleeping boatmen, kill them, and take their cargo. Sometimes the pirates would appear to be stranded on an island or along the shore. When the good-samaritan boatmen stopped to help, they became victims. Flatboats were also subjected to the whims of nature. Many were destroyed during high water, as they were swept down the river into log jams and shoals. Fire was also a big threat, as open fires were used for heating and cooking, and the flatboat could quickly become a tinder box engulfed in flames. A flatboat may have started out from Louisville, from where it drifted down the Ohio River to the Mississippi. Their destination could have been Memphis, Natchez, or New Orleans. When they reached a place like Natchez, they would sell their goods or receive payment for delivery. The boatmen would then disassemble the vessel and sell the wood. The boats were literally disposable. Most of the ports had many diversions to offer the boatmen, which included numerous ways to relieve them of their hard-earned money. Saloons, gamblers, floozies, and con artists often relieved them of their cash, and they headed for home empty-handed. The way home for most was to walk. From Natchez, they would walk the Natchez Trace up through Mississippi, Alabama, and Tennessee. The Natchez Trace was simply a trail, and those going home with money or goods would often lose it to robbers along the way. Even worse, many lost their lives to the bandits or Indians. It was a very difficult way to make a living.

Later, keelboats developed. These boats had rudders to steer; the bow and stern were pointed. Many were very large and carried as much as 80 tons of cargo and passengers down the rivers. Most people regard pre-fabricated housing a fairly modern concept; however, keelboats often carried a cargo of walls, already built and ready for assembly. The big difference between keelboats and flatboats was that keelboats could also be taken back up the rivers, which made possible the first two-way commerce. The keelboatmen were a rough and tough breed of men. Using long poles, they pushed the boats back up the river. The crew worked on both sides of the boat, walking along the edge, pushing against the poles in rotation. It was extremely hard work that required a lot of muscle and endurance. The keelboatmen worked hard and played hard. Each night they would drink, sing, and dance. Their favorite drink was called a Hot Toddy, which was heated rum with a baked apple in the mug. Some claim that the keelboats used no fuel, but actually it was huge amounts of rum that fueled the keelboatmen. A legendary character emerged from the keelboat days. His name was Mike Fink. Mike claimed to be able to out-shoot, out-fight, out-drink, and out-anything else any man on the river. He was typical of the keelboatman's image and many stories are written about Mike, including various reports of his violent death. For a man who only lived once, he seems to have died many times and in many places. Even these hardy fellows would fall victim to the same losses as the flatboatmen, particularly at the saloons and brothels. The most famous keelboatmen were those who

Library of Congress
Keelboat

made up the Corp of Discovery. This was the Lewis and Clark expedition that pushed and pulled a large keelboat up the powerful Missouri River. In addition to poling, keelboats could be taken up the river using sails, paddling with oars, and pulling them with ropes strung from the river to trees along the bank. River conditions and weather would determine the best method to use.

Many other specialized vessels could be found on the rivers. Shantyboats usually congregated in floating villages. These boats did not usually travel great distances, but a neighborhood squabble could be settled by simply drifting or being towed to another spot. Great rafts of logs could be seen floating down the rivers, particularly the Upper Mississippi. The logs were lashed together and a small cabin was built on the raft. Two or three tillers were installed to help steer the vessel. Floating sawmills could also be found, making temporary docking to cut logs into boards. Merchants built mobile stores and sold their goods to other boatmen and villagers along the river. From gristmills to blacksmiths, just about anything that was available on land could be found on the rivers. This was very beneficial to the early settlers in remote locations, who otherwise would not have access to many items and services.

In the early 1800s, another vessel appeared on the river. It was a revolutionary boat that would change the rivers forever. In 1811 Robert Fulton, who had built the steamer *Clermont* on the Hudson

River, wanted to bring the steamboat business to the Ohio and Mississippi rivers. He built a boat, much like the *Clermont* and became partners with Nicholas Roosevelt. They were very confident in their boat having named it the *New Orleans* after building it in Pittsburgh. Roosevelt planned to take it to its namesake city on her maiden voyage. Much has been written about that first steamboat journey, so I will not go into great detail in this writing. The trip was very risky, even with ideal weather and river conditions. But it was anything but that, for 1811 was a very strange year. If there had been prophets walking the streets displaying a message that the world was coming to an end, many would have believed it. The year began with an unknown comet dominating the night sky for months. It was simply named the Comet of 1811. Plagues of small pox, cholera and yellow fever was spreading along the river towns, resulting in mass graves. Chief Tecumseh was traveling to other Indian tribes, seeking support against the white men. Pressure was building again with the British which erupted the following year as the War of 1812. The rivers were running at record lows and record highs in the same year.

The under-powered, deep draft, wooden-hulled *New Orleans* set off on her historic journey with the odds stacked against her. Mr. Roosevelt had yet another challenge along the way. The New Madrid earthquake, centered at New Madrid, Missouri, shook the entire Ohio and lower Mississippi valley for weeks. This caused banks to cave in, a huge amount of trees to fall into the river, and great upheaval in the land and the river. Today, the estimate of the initial quake would have registered 8.6 on the Richter scale. Even with all the events of 1811 against them, the crew of the *New Orleans* succeeded in their journey to New Orleans, beginning the era of the mighty and magnificent steamboats.

The early steamboats could carry huge amounts of freight and many passengers. They could go downstream and upstream, to the amazement of all. A boat that could go up the river at an incredible four miles per hour was a miracle. The steamboats were giant belching monsters that the Indians called "fire canoes". The boats burned wood or coal, depending on what was available. The first steamboats were deep draft side-wheelers that ran on the Hudson River. The western rivers required some design modifications. All rivers west of the Allegheny Mountains were western rivers, so even though we think of the Ohio and Mississippi rivers as in the eastern half of the country, they are still called the western rivers and the boats are western steamboats. The western rivers had many more hazards than did the Hudson. Fluctuating river stages caused many shallow areas during low water. The primary difference between the Hudson River boats built by Robert Fulton and the western riverboats first built by Henry Shreve was that the western boats needed a flat bottom and shallow draft. To achieve this, the engine was brought up from the hull and placed on the first deck. Also needed were more powerful engines to buck the swift currents.

A favorite brag among captains was that their boat could run on heavy dew. Some of the huge vessels would draft as little as two feet. The boats were built as fast, cheap, and light as possible. The fragile construction of the boats, along with the natural hazards of the rivers, and

Harper's Weekly

Exaggerated snag cartoon

primitive machines resulted in great lose of lives and property. On the average an early steamboat may last only three to five years.

Snags were the number one boat killers. Snags are trees that have been dislodged from the bank and have floated down the river. Eventually the root end of the tree becomes so saturated with water that it sinks and imbeds itself into the riverbed. The rest of the tree sticks up like a giant spear. Some snags were exposed above the surface of the water. Other snags would lurk just below the surface. It was those   unseen snags that would often pierce the wooden hull of a steamboat, sending it to the bottom of the river. It is estimated that 40 percent of all steamboat losses were the result of hitting snags and sinking. Steamboats running at night were in the most danger of hitting an unseen snag. One of those boats was the *Arabia*, which hit a snag on the Missouri River and sank in deep water. Many years later the *Arabia* was discovered in a field, after the river had changed its course and left the boat behind. The *Arabia* site was excavated and tons of artifacts have been restored. The Steamboat *Arabia* museum is in Kansas City, Missouri. While visiting the museum I viewed the piece of the boat hull that was punctured by the snag; alongside it is the actual snag that punctured it. When a steamboat hit a snag, a hazard was not always the fact that the boat may sink. The vessels were often heated with oil and lit with oil lamps. Upon hitting a snag, the boat would list or come to a sudden halt, causing the burning oil to spill out. The wooden structure would quickly become an inferno.

Rocks, shoals, and sandbars also made navigation difficult for the steamboats. One might easily imagine what a hard hit against rocks or rocky shoals might do to a wooden hull. Sandbars were less hazardous but more frequent and often difficult to get free of. Sand and gravel bars could form quickly during high water, particularly at the mouths of tributaries. Steamboat pilots running aground had several methods of attempting to get off of them. The first step was to try backing off the bar by running in reverse, while pivoting the rudders back and forth. This swinging of the stern would often break the suction and allow the boat to pull loose. This method worked better if the boat was heading upstream, since the current would help back it off. If backing off failed the crew would determine how far along the hull the boat was aground by throwing a lead-line along the side until the water depth was greater than the hull. This would help decide whether to continue to pull back or go forward through the bar. Crewmen were also sent wading or in yawls to determine the width or length of the sandbar. If the river was falling, work must be done as quickly as possible for fear of getting stuck even worse.

The next step would be to transfer weight to the stern of the boat. If that failed, freight and passengers would be taken to shore to lighten the boat. Next, a line would be strung from a tree to the capstan, a steam- or hand-powered winch that was capable of pulling the boat across the bar while the paddlewheel pushed. Some boats were equipped for a method called grasshoppering or sparring. Long poles (spars) were attached to the sides in an angled vertical position on a pivot point. The poles were set with the lower end in the riverbed. The tops of the poles were attached by a line to the capstan. With the capstan drawing the line, the top of the pole would be drawn forward, causing the lower end to move backwards. This would cause the boat to "walk" off the sandbar a few feet at a time.

There are stories of captains having the passengers of grounded boats get into the shallow river and walk laps around the boat
for hours to make the sand shift in their favor. Rivers form natural
dams of sandbars that are unavoidable. The boatmen would push,
dig, and even dynamite sandbars and shoals to open a channel. This
may work for the time being, but the natural dam had been main-
taining deeper waters above it. When the dam was breached the
water would drain from the upstream pool and create longer
stretches of low water. Sometimes boats would have to wait for high
water to continue. This meant unloading cargo and passengers to
another boat or wagons. One such steamboat was the *Virginia*.

The *Virginia* was one of two boats owned by a Pittsburgh man.
He had been struggling to keep his boats full, as competition and
railroads was eating away at the steamboat business. He had finally gotten a full load of freight and passengers for a cruise down the
Ohio River. While the final arrangements were being made for the
journey, far-away rains were causing the Monongahela and
Allegheny rivers to rise. Those rivers converge to form the Ohio,
which was also rising rapidly. With the Ohio River above flood stage
and huge amounts of debris on the river, a prudent boatman would
have chosen to wait it out but the owner's desperate need for funds
prompted him to take the risk, and he ordered the captain to gather his crew and set out. They didn't get far.

Upon rounding a bend on a dark night, the powerful current
swept the *Virginia* into the inside of a bend and out of the main
channel. The pilot knew that he could not get the boat across the
current, with its battering ram of drifting logs. He fought to keep
the steamboat straight and attempted to cross the shallow inside
bend. The *Virginia* came to a halt on a sand bar. Attempts to back
off against the current were futile. The only option was to push forward and wiggle the boat with the rudders. This would either push
them to deeper water or cause the boat to run further aground.
Unfortunately, it became even more stranded. They worked all
night attempting to free the boat but discovered that the river had
crested, and was then beginning to recede. A day later the *Virginia*
was sitting high and dry in a cornfield. In a few days the Ohio River
was no longer over its banks and the *Virginia* was several hundred
feet from the water. The freight was unloaded and transported
overland. The steamboat in the cornfield became an attraction,
with people coming from miles around to see the unusual sight. The
owner did not share in the excitement. He needed to get the
Virginia back on the river as soon as possible to provide needed

income. He and several consultants spent a great deal of time at the site trying to figure out how to get the boat back into the river. It could be a very long time before the water would be high enough to float the boat again, with no assurance that it would even be released when that happened. The owner of the cornfield demanded to be paid for the space the boat was taking. The owner was advised to scrap the boat, particularly since the hull was draped over a mound with the hog chains broken. (Hog chains are heavy chains hooked from towers near the center of the boat to the bow and stern to keep the ends from sagging and creating a hog's back shape to the boat.)

The owner had heard of a man who had an excellent reputation for moving houses. The man agreed to look at the boat and determine whether he could put the 250-foot steamboat back into the Ohio River. A contract was signed that indicated payment would be

John Hartford collection
Steamboat in a cornfield

made upon his putting the *Virginia* back into the river. If he was not successful, no payment would be made. Even though it was a risk, the house mover was challenged by the project and accepted the job. He and his crew arrived at the scene and

began the very slow process of moving the boat. Before starting, the crew re-fastened the hog chains and little by little drew them tighter to keep the hull from sagging and possibly breaking open. A method to move her much like the ancient Egyptians moved huge blocks of stone was devised. With powerful winches anchored into the riverbank and logs positioned to roll under the hull, the boat was moved inches at a time. Repairs were also made to the hull and the wood was kept wet to prevent shrinkage of the planks. Caulking was added to any gaps that formed between the planks. After all, it would do no good to get the boat to the river, only to have her sink.   Several weeks passed while the crew continued to move the boat toward the river's edge. This too, became a spectator event. Slowly and carefully the crew finally succeeded in moving the vessel to the riverbank. But then another problem arose. The river had dropped well below the bank and there was a considerable drop from the bank to the water. Now the crew had to figure out a way to lower the boat to the water. A holiday weekend was coming up so the house mover and his crew took a few days off while he made plans to launch the boat. He had decided that the riverbank would have to be excavated into a sloping ramp and wooden planks would be built to slide the boat sideways into the river.

During the long weekend it began to rain. The Monongahela and Allegheny rivers begin to rise, as did the Ohio River. This was good news to the house mover, as there would be less distance to lower the *Virginia*. The crew arrived at the site to begin digging the slope out of the steep riverbank. To their shock and pleasant surprise they found the *Virginia* floating. A line had been left tied to the winch and had held her in place. They no longer had to lower the boat to the river. The river came up to the boat. They celebrated and called the owner to have a boat crew take the *Virginia* to her home port in Pittsburgh. In a few days the pilots, engineers, and deckhands arrived, got up a head of steam, and took the *Virginia* home. Upon arrival the house mover went to the office of the owner to get paid. The owner laid out the contract they had signed and pointed out that the house mover had not complied with the terms of the agreement. The terms stated that his crew would put the *Virginia* into the river, and the owner pointed out that they had failed to do that. He claimed that it was an act of God that put the *Virginia* back into the Ohio River; therefore he had no obligation to pay him for his work. Naturally this upset the house mover, who had made a huge investment in time and money on the project. He filed a lawsuit in an attempt to obtain at least partial payment for his efforts. After much deliberation the judge pronounced his decision. The judge agreed that the defendant was correct in his assessment that the river had come to the *Virginia,* and that it was an act of God that provided for the flotation of the boat. He went on to say, "However, this man and his crew put the boat within God's reach and they will, by God, be paid."

Boiler explosions were another hazard that took many lives during the steamboat era. The early boilers were poorly constructed and often had defective release valves and no pressure gauges.

Engineers used guesswork to judge how much pressure the boilers could take. They were often wrong. When the boilers blew on a steamboat it was literally hell on water. The initial blast would send iron fragments, boiling water, and splintered wood throughout the forward section of the vessel. Missiles of burning wood or coal from the furnace would set fire to what was left of the boat. Passengers and crew who survived the initial explosion could choose between burning to death and jumping into the turbulent river. Many of the steamboat explosions occurred while the boats were near or at port. Steam would not be used to operate the paddlewheel and would build up pressure, causing explosions. The boats used river water in the boilers to generate steam. The sand and silt in the water could build up inside the boiler, and if not cleaned out frequently, the material built up inside the boiler tubes. This would create a hot spot in the boiler and cause it to become weak.

The steamboat business became very competitive. The competition to be first to a port or make a speedy run often resulted in the machinery being pushed beyond its limits. Races between steamboats became frequent. Sometimes the races were simply in the spirit of competition, with one steamboat pilot not wanting to let another overtake it. Passengers would often get into the spirit of racing and prod the captain to race an overtaking steamboat. To get up steam quickly, the fireman would be ordered to burn pine knots. Pine knots produce natural turpentine, burning very hot and fast. Barrels of lard or oil would also be on hand to dip wood into before putting it into the furnace. There are stories of chairs and shutters being broken up and thrown into the fire during the heat of a race. Unfortunately, these quests for speed would sometimes result in a horrific boiler explosion.

The worst boiler explosion was on the steamboat *Sultana*, which arrived at Vicksburg, Mississippi at the end of the Civil War. Captain Mason brought the boat there to transport Union prisoners of war back to their homes in the north. The boat had a troublesome boiler, so it was patched in order to take advantage of the lucrative business. The government was paying five dollars a head for the run up the Mississippi. The soldiers had been prisoners at Andersonville and Cahaba Camps. Conditions there were horrible so most of the surviving soldiers were weak and frail, but were happy to finally be going home to their loved ones. As trains delivered the soldiers to Vicksburg, their numbers grew into the thousands. Several steamboats had arrived to transport the men, but only one was being loaded. The *Sultana* was designed to carry 276 passengers, but the number of soldiers being herded onto the boat greatly exceeded that. There was also a large amount of freight and livestock put onboard, along with civilian passengers. The exodus from Vicksburg to the *Sultana* continued; while other boats were sent away nearly empty. There has been an investigation of bribery as the reason the *Sultana* was overloaded and other boats were ignored, but it has never been proven.

Soldiers were converging on the landing in such numbers that it became impossible to get an accurate count of their numbers; therefore it was decided to count them as they disembarked at their final destination of Cairo, Illinois. Reasonable estimates of the number of soldiers and civilians packed on the *Sultana* are around 2,200. One can only imagine the hot, crowded conditions and lack of sanitation. As bad as it was, it wasn't as bad as the prisoner of war camps. The river was flooding, so strong currents made for slow headway. The *Sultana* struggled up the mighty river with coal fires burning hot to keep up a powerful head of steam. They landed at Memphis, Tennessee, to exchange some civilian passengers and cargo. Some of the soldiers got off the boat to enjoy the night-life of Memphis, and few of them did not make it back to the boat in time for depar-ture. They were disappointed to have missed the boat, but had no idea of how lucky they were. Captain Mason pulled the *Sul-tana* a-way and across the river to take on more

Harper's Weekly
The Sultana explosion

coal. The overloaded vessel then proceeded upriver toward Cairo, a destina-tion she would never reach.

The *Sultana* was pushing hard around a bend about seven

miles above Memphis. At about 2 am, April 27, 1863, the boilers gave up. The Sultana had seven boilers, and when the weakened boiler that had been patched gave way, the others soon followed. The explosion could be heard for many miles and the flash of light could be seen from Memphis. All who saw the sky light up to the north knew it had to be the *Sultana*. The explosion destroyed the front section of the boat and fire quickly consumed the rest of it. Many of those who survived the blast and fire had to face the cold dark water of the Mississippi. They grabbed for anything that floated and hung on for their lives. A downriver steamboat was first to spot the debris and survivors. Small boats from the Mississippi and Arkansas banks of the river were put in to pick up anyone that could be found. Confederate soldiers, who themselves had just been released from Union prisoner of war camps, were in the river trying to save their former enemies. Some survivors drifted all the way to Memphis before being rescued, but mostly bodies floated past the riverfront. The hospital in Memphis treated hundreds for injuries, scalding, and exposure. Of the seven hundred rescued, three hundred more died within days. Reports vary about the number on the boat and how many died. What is clear is that it was the worst maritime disaster in American history. The highly publicized sinking of the *Titanic* had an official loss of 1,502 lives. Reasonable estimates of the *Sultana* disaster are from 1,600 to 1,800 lives lost.

As mentioned earlier, fires were and still are one of most deadly hazards on all boats. In addition to boiler explosions and wrecking, fires were often started from the smokestacks of steamboats. Burning embers from the wood-fired furnace often flew up and out of the stack, sometimes landing on the top deck and catching fire. Boats carrying cotton stacked high on the decks were particularly susceptible to fire. As a preventative measure, decks were often coated with sand and fire buckets were in place. Stacks were built as tall as possible to give the burning embers a chance to burn out before landing on the deck; this also allowed the smoke to be emitted high above the boat. Many of the steamboat landings at larger ports were crowded with steamboats. They were nosed in, side by side, to get as many packed into the landing as possible. More than once a boat would catch fire, sending the flame and burning embers to the next boat, then the next. In St. Louis a single boat caught fire, but resulted in dozens of other boats burning, along with several downtown city blocks.

Of the estimated 6,000 steamboats that plied the rivers in the 1800s, none are left. All sank, burned, blew up, or were scrapped for salvage. The Steamboat Safety Act of 1852 spelled out safety procedures that became law. Those included better boilers with safety valves, an engineer license program, passing signals, navigational aids, and fire safety methods. The Act had good intentions but was for the most part non-enforceable. Safety valves would be held down in the heat of a race and no enforcement agency was present on the rivers. This is evident in the *Sultana* tragedy, which happened eleven years after the passage of the Act. At about the time regulations were enforced and steamboats became safer, the era of the steamboats was passing. Increased competition from railroads caused them to gradually disappear from the rivers.

There were other boats that made their mark on the rivers. Those were the showboats. Unlike the Hollywood version of the vessels, most were humble and did not move under their own power. The majority were simple barges with a building on it. Some showboat owners would use the same method as the flatboats by building a boat in Pittsburgh, and then drift from town to

Photo by Author

Showboat in Cincinnati

town until they reached New Orleans, where the showboat would be scrapped for wood. Others would hire a towboat, or owned their own towboat to push the boat up and down the rivers. There were a few grand paddlewheel showboats that were considered floating palaces. The showboats brought entertainment and culture to river communities that could not offer such things, as the bigger cities could. The owner would send someone ahead of the boat to post their upcoming arrival. The entertainers would often get onto the gangway (stage) and do a teaser performance to entice folks to purchase tickets for the big show. The variety of entertainment often included singers, musicians, actors performing Shakespeare, or circus acts. The showboats were a welcome sight to the entertainment-starved residents of villages along the rivers. The performers were quite motivated to provide a good performance. In some of the rough frontier villages, the people were known to burn a showboat if they felt cheated.

Steamboats surviving into the 20th Century were towboats designed to push barges loaded with huge quantities of material. If it were not for the development of the towboats, it is likely that the government would have eventually ignored the entire river navigation system. Paddlewheel towboats proved that the river was still a viable transporter of bulk goods. Huge quantities of grain, rock, coal, salt, and eventually chemicals could be shipped economically in barges pushed by towboats. The passenger trade of the 1800s was replaced to a great extent by the shipping industry. Paddlewheel towboats became larger and more powerful, pushing more and more barges up and down the rivers. The largest paddlewheel towboat was the *Sprague*, affectionately known as Big Mama. She held the record for many years by pushing sixty barges at one time. The *Sprague* was eventually retired and became a showboat in Vicksburg, Mississippi in 1948. In 1974 she caught fire, but plans were being made to restore her and convert the big boat into a museum. Unfortunately the river dropped suddenly while the boat was moored and the pressure broke her in half. Dynamite was used to blow up the remaining hull, in order to keep the channel open. It is a very sad ending to a magnificent boat.

Modern towboats emerged with the conversion to screw (propeller) drive and diesel engines. The much more efficient towboats

Photo by Author

Modern Towboat

now dominate the waterways. Some towboats have three 16-cylinder engines generating 10,500 horsepower. Three nine-foot propellers can push an amazing amount of tonnage. The record tow to date is 72 barges, pushed upriver past Memphis, Tennessee. The efficiency of the towboats is easy to measure. Each barge carries an equivalent of 58 semi-truck loads of materials or 15 jumbo hopper railroad cars. That means that a typical towboat of 20 barges can haul as much as nearly

1,200 trucks. That would be at least that many truck drivers being paid to haul what a crew of ten does on a towboat. The cost of fuel per ton is much less, along with fewer emissions. The towboats are the giants of the river, with some as long as 1,500 feet. They are an important part of American commerce and national defense. It was discovered during World War I that United States railroads and trucking were inadequate for transporting equipment and supplies during wartime. Thus, serious projects to improve river navigation were begun. By World War II, the rivers and towboats were serving the nation well for moving new vessels, large items, and materials to the lower Mississippi ports and on to overseas destinations. Commercial vessels have changed greatly from the crude flatboats to the mighty towboats. All have been important in their time. Although the evolution of vessels will continue, it is interesting to note that one form of transportation is seldom completely replaced by another. Paths across the country became wagon trails, and those became roads, then superhighways. Rail transportation has probably undergone the least physical change of any form of travel. Rivers are still rivers with navigational improvements. The big change in river transportation is the vessels. As I visited the huge Jeff Boat Company in Jeffersonville, Indiana, I witnessed new vessels being built. I watched new barges on an assembly line style production, headed for their eventual launching into the Ohio River. I visited the Avondale Shipyard in New Orleans and saw a variety of ships and river vessels under construction. This tells me that the river business is still healthy, and I cannot imagine how it could ever be replaced by a better method of bulk transportation. I believe that for as long as our nation and other nations need chemicals, petroleum, grain, coal, rocks, salt, steel, and raw materials, there will be some type of boats moving it up and down the nation's rivers.

The Restless River

Chapter 15

Restless River

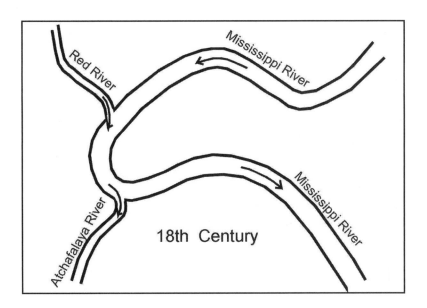

Once upon a time there was a bend in a river about fifty miles northwest of Baton Rouge, Louisiana. The bend was named Turnbull's Bend and the river is the lower Mississippi. On this bend, shaped like an extended thumb, another river flowed into it. This was the Red River, a tributary that flowed all the way from Texas. On the lower part of the bend was a distributary, which means that the water flowed from the Mississippi into it. This distributary was an ancient course of the Mississippi River and was known as the Atchafalaya River. This location on the lower Mississippi sets the stage for a dramatic story that began hundreds of years ago, and is still going on today. The story may end with some major changes that will affect many cities, industry, and a way of life for millions.

The lower Mississippi has been developing for thousands of years. It has migrated back and forth across Louisiana many times, like a giant hose flipping in slow motion. With each change in course it formed a new delta by depositing tremendous quantities of sand, silt, and clay. When the first European settlers arrived, the lower river was pretty much on the same course it is following today. The natural order of things had not been interfered with. The great river would have continued to build fertile land, absorb tributaries, and create outlets to the sea, but that all changed with man's manipulations. As steamboats plied the rivers during their heyday in the mid-1800s, rivermen found ways to make navigation safer and faster. In 1831, Captain Henry M. Shreve dug a cut across the narrow neck of Turnbull's Bend. The river accepted the shortcut and abandoned its old channel, the upper part of which silted up, leaving the lower section. This lower section of the old channel became known as Old River. The Red River had no place to flow but directly into the Atchafalaya, and no longer into the Mississippi River. The Old River channel connected the Red and Atchafalaya rivers to the Mississippi River. The current normally flowed from the Mississippi through Old River and into the Atchafalaya; however, during high water on the Red River, the flow sometimes reversed.

Since the Old River connected the Mississippi to the Red and Atchafalaya rivers, interest grew in navigating them. The problem

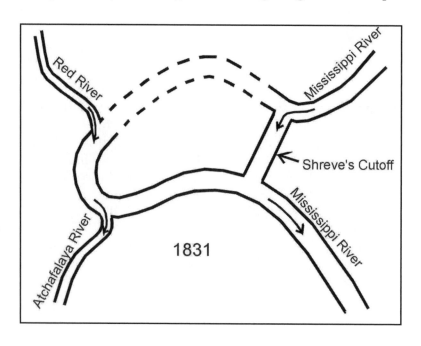

on the Red River was a huge log jam that piled up from its mouth to about 160 miles upstream. The "raft" of logs was said to be so dense that wagons could cross over it. Henry Shreve, who designed and built the first snag boats, arrived on the scene. Under government contract, he and his crew took on the difficult three-year project of removing the log jam. After successfully opening the Red River for navigation, Shreve founded the town of Shreveport, Louisiana. The Atchafalaya River also had a massive 30-mile long log jam from its source at the Old River that defied efforts of the settlers to remove it. In 1839, the state of Louisiana began to dislodge the raft and open up the river as a free-flowing and navigable stream. In time the former Turnbull's Bend had transformed into an "H" shaped configuration. The right side of the "H" was the Mississippi River; the left side was the Red and Atchafalaya rivers; the middle cross was Old River. All navigational challenges were solved, but other problems would surface many years later.

The increased volume of the log jam-free Red River now flowed completely into the Atchafalaya River. The removal of the log jams provided an opportunity for the Atchafalaya to enlarge, becoming deeper and wider. As the Atchafalaya grew deeper it demanded more water, and drew even more from the Mississippi River. During the 1930s the Corp of Engineers dredged much of the Atchafalaya River to improve navigation, which also increased the flow and demand for more water. Since more water was being diverted from the Mississippi River into the Atchafalaya, the Mississippi began to silt up below Old River. This caused even more water to back up and flow into the Old River channel. Another factor that caused changes was that the Atchafalaya offered the Mississippi waters a shorter route and a greater drop in elevation to the Gulf of Mexico. Predictions of a catastrophic course change were made as early as the 1920s, but went unheeded.

By 1950, it became apparent to the Mississippi River Commission (MCR) that the Atchafalaya River would eventually capture the entire Mississippi River in a massive course change. It was also apparent that something must be done to stop this process. If the Mississippi changed course it would turn the present channel into a saltwater estuary, since the waters of the Gulf of Mexico would meet no resistance in flowing up the old channel, since its riverbed is below sea level. The effects would be catastrophic. Corporations have constructed billions of dollars worth of petrochemical plants, refineries, grain elevators, and electric power plants, most of which rely upon fresh water from the

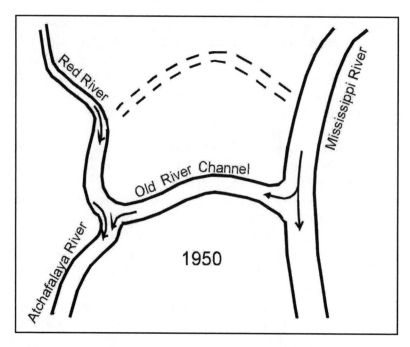

river. Also, cities below Baton Rouge, including New Orleans, would be hard-pressed to find drinking water. The change of course would come relatively sudden, during heavy flooding. The Atchafalaya Basin could not handle this much flow without massive flooding there and extensive relocations. The new route would render billions of dollars worth of flood-control projects useless along the lower Mississippi River, and expensive control projects would be required in the newly created Mississippi's course. A tremendous volume of shipping between the nation's heartland on the upper Mississippi and the ports of Baton Rouge and New Orleans would be disrupted.

Something had to be done. In 1953, a report by the MCR recommended that the diversion of flow from the Mississippi into the Atchafalaya should be controlled by a complex of structures, to be built at the Old River crossover. Engineers proposed a plan to dam Old River and build three control structures, one to operate at all times and stages, and the other to operate only during floods. A lock would also be needed to pass traffic between the different levels of the Mississippi and Atchafalaya-Red rivers. The plan was not to divert water back to the Mississippi, nor to reverse what had already taken place. It was to hold the flow at its present distribution. It was determined that approximately 30 percent of the total volume of the Mississippi River was flowing into the Atchafalaya

River in 1950. This is the amount that would be allowed to continue to flow, so that natural conditions in the Atchafalaya would not be affected. The Atchafalaya Basin is one of the last great primitive areas, and one of the largest wetlands in the nation. The extensive plant and animal life in the basin's swamps need fresh water. Construction began on the three structures in 1955. The Low Sill structure (a dam with control gates) was built between the Mississippi and Red rivers, and then an outflow channel was dug to allow the controlled amount of water to pass through. Next to the Low Sill structure, the Overbank structure was constructed. This would serve as a levee, but would also have gates that would allow additional water to flow into the outflow channel in an emergency. The third structure was the lock, which was built parallel to the Old River. A canal was dug to allow vessels to pass from the Mississippi, through the lock, and into Old River and Atchafalaya River. When the lock was completed the Old River's mouth was dammed so that water could pass only through the control structures and the lock. The entire complex was completed in 1963 at a cost of $67 million.

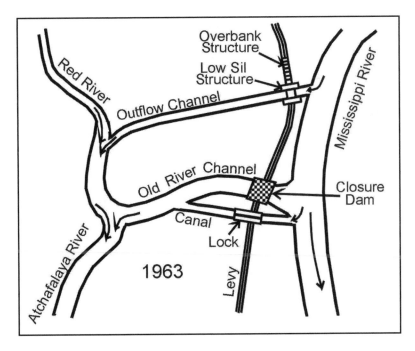

The force of the water being channeled into the Low Sill structure to the outflow was often very strong. It was so strong that on two different occasions, loose barges were drawn into the structure from the Mississippi River. The barges were very difficult to remove from the gates. One was cut up and removed in pieces and the other was finally drawn through the open gates. The Corp of Engineers knew this was a dangerous situation, but didn't know the extent of the damage that had been done to the structure. For a time a towboat was stationed at the inflow to catch any loose barges before they could enter the canal. Later it became illegal to moor barges within 20 miles upstream of the facilities. All appeared well with the control systems and confidence was high that the problem of the Mississippi River trying to change course was solved. The last major flood on the Mississippi River had been in 1950, so the control structures had not been put to the test-at least not until 1973.

Persistent, heavy rains during the fall of 1972 and the winter and spring of 1973 in the central plains and the Mississippi and Ohio River valleys caused many of the Mississippi's tributaries to rise above flood stage. The Mississippi crested several times that spring, and a prolonged flood fight raged up and down the big river. The sheer volume of water passing through the Old River structures was awesome, and the Low Sill structure bore the brunt. Due to increased constraints over the years, the Lower Mississippi could not hold as much water as it could before 1950. At the same time, the Atchafalaya could hold, and demanded, more water, increasing the pressure on the structures. During the times that barges had become stuck into the Low Sill structure, the foundation was damaged and the force of the water was scouring out the footing beneath it. One of the two 67-foot-high concrete guide walls came crashing down, further preventing the effective use of the gates. Large scour holes developed in the outflow channel above and below the structure, exposing the steel pilings that support the entire structure. The Low Sill structure vibrated under the enormous pressure. Emergency spillways, including the overbank structure, were opened to relieve pressure. Emergency procedures went into effect during the flooding in an attempt to prevent the structure from collapsing. It was a frightening situation. The river finally crested to the relief of everyone involved. It was a very close call. If the control structures had been breached, the Mississippi River would have made its dreaded course change and the Atchafalaya Basin would have experienced devastating flooding. Morgan City would have been directly in the path of the rampaging water, and may not have survived.

After the flood, the fallen guide wall was replaced by a rock dike. The large scour holes were filled in with thousands of tons of rocks, brought by barges. Large holes were drilled down through the structure and into the foundation, and closed-circuit television cameras were lowered into the holes to check the damage. Engineers expected to get a look at any fractures or other deterioration of the foundation, but saw only water. It was shocking to see how far the raging water had undercut the structure, nearly breaking through. If the water had broken through, the structure would have been swept away in a mass of muddy water, crumbling concrete, and steel. A specially developed cement grout was pumped into the void. The method of gate operation was changed to provide for a more uniform flow distribution, thereby reducing the danger of scouring. Over the following eight years the Corp of Engineers continued to improve the system, during which time the river flooded again in 1974, 1975, and 1979. Each time the river flooded the Corps struggled to save the control structure, and each time modification of the design and construction were made. By 1981, engineers concluded that the structure had been seriously and permanently damaged by the flooding, and would not be strong enough to maintain the desired 30 percent flow, preventing the Mississippi River from changing its course. It was obvious that the force of the river was underestimated when designing the structure, since it nearly failed with the first flood waters to test it. The Low Sill structure was only effective in controlling the prescribed amount of water during normal flows. More would have to be done to hold back the mighty river during flood conditions.

Construction began on a second control structure in 1981. The Auxiliary structure was completed in 1986 and, like the Low Sil structure, was connected by a second inflow channel. The idea behind the Auxiliary structure is to have dual control of the water flow. During emergencies like the 1973 flood, both structures could be opened to allow more water to pass from the Mississippi into the Atchafalaya. While the Auxiliary structure was still under construction, building began on a 192-megawatt power plant to be located just above the overbank structure. Since there is normally a 22-foot drop from the Mississippi River to the Atchafalaya River, a hydroelectric plant could utilize the energy of this water. The 12-story, 25,000 ton plant was constructed on the river in New Orleans. It was then towed 208 miles up the river and placed on its foundation. It was the largest "vessel" ever towed up the Mississippi River. To pass under a bridge at Baton Rouge, water was allowed into the massive hull to sink it to a level that would clear the bridge. The ballast was then pumped out, once beyond the bridge.

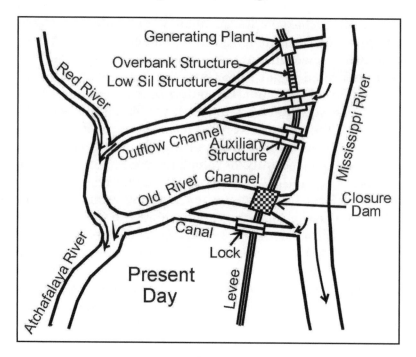

The big question now is—will it hold? There are varied opinions. Based upon the water flow during the great flood of 1927, the
U.S. Army Corp of Engineers claims that the structures, along with
the spillways, should be able to handle the amount of water that
flowed that year. I visited the Waterways Experimental Station in
Vicksburg, Mississippi, where there were large models of the structures. Tests were constantly performed on the models. When I
asked an engineer if the structures were capable of withstanding
similar pressures to that of the 1927 flood, he answered, "We hope
so." That answer had a lower confidence level than I am accustomed
to hearing from that agency. Ask that question of most rivermen
along the lower Mississippi and Atchafalaya rivers and the answer
is usually something like, "If that river decides to change course,
there's nothing we can do about it".

Some geologists suggest that the unstable ground beneath the
structures could cause their failure, plus there is always the threat
of the New Madrid fault shaking up the area once again, just as it
did in 1811. Having seen the models and visited the structures, I
have my own opinion. I think that the massive structures could
hold, but wonder about the surrounding levees. After all, those levees are just a composite of earth with a concrete cap in some sec-

tions. Visualize the flood levels of 1973 and the amount of pressure on the levees, and it isn't difficult to picture them giving in. The estimated water flow during the flood of 1927 was three million cubic feet per second. Whether that estimate from over 75 years ago was accurate has been questioned, but that is the magic number that the MCR says the system can handle. If that number is correct, can not the 1927 quantity be exceeded?

We already know that the river rises higher with less water than it did a century ago, due to the levee system. The single factor that gives me some assurance that the system may hold is the spillway systems, located far from the structures. A young Corp of Engineers man name Charles Ellet said that the river must be let go, and that it cannot be held back. He said that in the 1800s, but his advice was not taken until after the 1927 flood. The spillways are emergency outlets that will send river water into valleys, and in some cases to different routes to the sea, much like release valves on a steam boiler. Only time will tell. The MRC printed an excellent booklet that tells stories of the challenges in trying to control the Mississippi River. With their permission, the following poem is reprinted from the booklet that tells the story about Old River and the control structures.

Old River

After the war there was a great test
A natural process the Corps had to arrest
The great Mississippi longed to be free
To seek a shorter, new route to the sea

The Commission knew much was at stake
The river had roamed like a fancy-free snake
Moving its mouth first here and then there
Building new deltas out into the mere

Above Baton Rouge at a place called Old River
The Mississippi gladly gave flows to its neighbor
The Atchafalaya did openly design
The Father of Waters to capture and claim

The Commission carefully, urgently raced
To make sure the main stem stayed in its place
Yearly diversions rose to 30 percent
A disaster portended it had to prevent

Congress agreed the Corps must regulate
Diversions through the beckoning gate
Plans were drawn for channels and structures
Built of concrete and steel to long endure

The Low Sill and Overbank throughout every year
Maintain proper diversions the Corps engineered
Navigation between the Mississippi and Red
Was kept open by a lock in the Old River's bed

1973 Flood

In the '50s and '60s the river seemed beat
The timeless opponent seemed on the retreat
The valley safely passed through 23 years
The stages stayed down, quieting fears

But the burly giant of power and brawn
Was simply keeping its sharp fangs withdrawn
Some were seduced, fell into ennui
Then the river struck hard in '73

It was almost as if it had been gathering strength
The flood control system to ravage and break
The Corps and its allies bravely fought back
As the Father of Waters pressed the attack

Day after day people coped with the stress
Working and hoping to pass the flood crest
Some of the data sent chills down their spines
For the river had changed its capricious flowline

In some places where levees were low and deficient
They were raised and strengthened throughout the event
Yet the levees endured and held fast
Despite a few slides there was no crevasse

The greatest blow the Mississippi delivered
Was at the Low Sill down at Old River
A turbulent fist undermined the guide wall
That fell into the waters to the amazement of all

Scour holes grew beneath and in front
The structure vibrated for the river did want
To sweep it aside as a noisome pariah
And surrender itself to its lover "Chafalaya"

In the midst of the roar and relentless brown spray
Innovation and courage carried the day
A mountain of rock was placed in the holes
An ocean of grout to seal and enfold

Emergency repairs and major rehabilitation
Kept the Low Sill safe and on station
The MRC soon developed the vision
That more control was needed to fulfill its mission

Auxiliary Structure
Once again came forth a grand plan
To keep the Mississippi a servant of man
An additional channel to handle diversions
An Auxiliary Structure to provide regulation

Working in concert with neighbors time-tested
The "Chafalaya's" charms to more fully arrest
Much more control to mount and invoke
Build for the river another strong yoke

Concrete, rocks, and huge tainter gates
Were melded together, put into place
The river to better control and compel
Ceremony and pomp for a new citadel

Lessons Learned: It is not human nature to comprehend a power greater than oneself. We arrogantly believe that we can control nature. I believe that the Corp of Engineers has, or at least should have learned from those voices from the past who understood the power of the river. In the mid-1800s Charles Ellet said the river must be let go, perhaps where it will do the least damage. Engineer James B. Eads, during the same time period, said that man can manipulate the river to utilize its great power, but cannot truly control it. He understood that we can tinker with the river but not change it. Mark Twain said, "The military engineers of the commission have taken upon their shoulders the job of making the Mississippi River over again—a job transcended in size only by the original job of creating it."

Chapter 16

Steamboat Passengers

The steamboats are often chartered for large groups. A charter cruise has no passengers purchasing individual cruises. The charters consist of special-interest groups who have the boat to themselves and plan their own itineraries. They will often bring on their own entertainment and set up their own shore tours, while the boat is in various ports. They also have special programs during the cruises, and we on the boat do our best to accommodate them and their needs.

On one such cruise we had an interesting group that insisted upon having the very best of everything, including arranging for well-known musicians for the evening entertainment and famous authors to give lectures. They even brought their own fine wines and specified what would be on the dinner menu each day. The cruise was a seven-day trip on the lower Mississippi River in that included Easter Sunday. The charter tour company had elaborate plans for Easter, including a special morning worship service. The plan was to have the musicians set up on the bow of the boat, with seating for all 150 passengers. This required special wiring, and chairs had to be brought to the bow from all over the *Boat*, as we had no folding chairs. It was no easy task to set this up, particularly in the rain. Yes, it was raining that morning but the charter tour manager insisted on setting it up and keeping the chairs dry, on the chance that it would stop raining. The musicians were not happy about setting up their equipment under those conditions, and kept them covered up as much as possible.

To further complicate things, the group planned to have a special magic moment during the service. While the sermon was being conducted there would be a cue for the musicians to play, while everyone in the audience would open a tiny box to release a butterfly. They envisioned the perfect words to be spoken by the minister, while beautiful butterflies fluttered off into the sky with back-ground music to complete the desired effect. The butterfly part required some master planning on the part of the tour company. There apparently is a business that can provide butterfly deliver-ies. The tour company purchased two hundred butterfly larvae in advance of the cruise. Each larva was enclosed in a pretty pyramid-shaped box with a bow on it. Timing was crucial, since the larva must change into beautiful butterflies and survive their entombed environment, to be released at the right moment on Easter morn-ing. I peeked into some of the boxes a couple of days before the event to see how they were doing to find that they were indeed metamorphosing, but a bit early. I informed the tour manager that, while I didn't know much about butterflies, I assume they would need some nourishment to survive the wait for their debut performance. I mixed some thick sugar-water soup and carefully placed a dab of it in each box. The butterflies immediately began consuming the brew and became a little livelier, or at least as live-ly as one can be in a two-inch box. I continued to monitor the lit-tle critters and became the keeper of the butterflies. I have done a lot of things in my life, but never expected that I would be responsible for the care, feeding, and general babysitting of two hundred butterflies. When I discovered that two butterflies had died, despite my efforts, I felt somehow responsible. Lisa, the gift shop girl, and I had a memorial service for them and gave them a proper "burial at river."

On Easter morning everything was in place and, amazingly the rain stopped just in time for the services to begin. I joked that it was incredible what money can buy. The weather, however, was far from ideal. It was windy, cold, and the sky was still threatening more rain. We were near our port stop of Helena, Arkansas, but the captain was asked not make a landing until the Sunday service was over. We could have gotten out of the wind in the harbor, but the charter manager wanted the service to be played out while under-way. The deckhands were hurrying to uncover and dry the chairs and equipment. We recommended that the Sunday service be moved inside as we looked at the sky with nervous eyes. They refused since it would ruin the whole ambience of the service to release the butterflies inside the boat. I suggested that the butter-flies might have a better chance of survival in the boat than out in the present elements. By now I had become the guardian and pro-tector of the butterflies, but to no avail. The event would go on as planned. As passengers began taking their seats, the rain began to sputter once again, but most had umbrellas. The problem with umbrellas was the wind, which created a few casualties among them. It was cold, wet, and windy but those folks were determined to continue with their well-planned ceremony.

The sermon began after everyone was given one of the tiny boxes with a butterfly inside. A printed program listed exactly what was going to take place, including the cue for the time of the butterfly release. At the beginning of the song "I'll Fly Away" the passengers began opening the little boxes with their cold, numb fingers. I can only imagine what I, as a butterfly, might think upon being subjected to the choice of cold and wind versus staying in my little warm box with sugar soup. Apparently that was what the butterflies were thinking, since they refused to or could not "fly away" as planned. Common sense tells me that a butterfly might want to dry its wings and stretch a while before its first test flight, particularly since its life up to that time had been lived as a worm. The music continued but not one butterfly voluntarily left the boxes. Some passengers were talking to their butterfly, trying to convince it to come out. Who do those butterflies think they are anyway, not following the plan? It didn't take long for people to take matters into their own hands.

Various methods were used to extract the poor butterflies from their cozy boxes. Some plucked them from the box with their fingers and pitched them into the air. Others held their boxes upside down and shook it until the butterfly gave up its hold. Some even went to the side of the boat and shook the little critters out of the box over the water. One thing among the methods of extraction was consistent. The butterflies did not fly. Panic was setting in among the passengers as butterflies were falling out of the sky and onto the deck. Many were trampled by the chaotic scrambling of those trying to retrieve "their" butterfly. A few passengers began to cry as they watched the massacre. I suppose the only good that came of it was for the fish that received butterfly snacks from all the ones thrown over the side of the boat. The poor butterflies were torn apart, stepped on, cast aside, and drowned in the Mississippi River. I stood there shaking my head in disgust. I might have thought it to be humorous had I not become attached to the little fellers.

When the music stopped the passengers went back to their seats and the program continued, while they tried to ignore the dying and dead around them. That was about the time the rain came hard and suddenly ended the service. The band was trying to save their equipment, the passengers were trying to save their hairdos, but nothing would save those poor butterflies being washed off the deck by the rain. It was a disaster but I have a confession to make. Before the service began I kidnapped one of the boxes with a butterfly in it. I kept it in my room for a couple of days, making certain that it had sufficient nutrition. On a sunny afternoon I went to the upper deck and carefully opened the box. The butterfly was reluctant to leave so I waited patiently. The butterfly began working its wings and drying them out in the sun and when it was ready it fluttered off toward the trees, near where we were docked. Yes, I had saved one butterfly from the horrors of the Easter Sunday Butterfly Disaster.

It is our duty on the boats to see to the needs of the passengers and provide for their entertainment. There have been times when the table is turned and the passengers entertain us. One such time was related to me by Capt. Gabe Chengery, while he was serving as Master on the *Mississippi Queen*. On the first day of a cruise before the boat had left the port, the purser's office received a call from a distressed lady in one of the passenger cabins. The lady explained that she could not get out of her cabin. The concerned purser asked if her door was jammed, knowing that all the locks are on the inside and no one can be locked in. The lady replied that a jammed door was not the problem and went on to explain. She told the purser that there are two doors. One of the doors leads to the bathroom and the other has a sign hanging on the knob that reads "Do Not Disturb".

During my time on the steamboats I have also had some, shall we say, interesting questions and suggestions (I'm being kind). Listed are some of my favorites.

Question: Does this boat make its own electricity?
Answer: No, we have a 600-mile long extension cord plugged in at our last port.

Question: Is there water behind that Island?
Answer: (None, just a bewildered look.)

Question: Where is the dining room? (third day of the cruise)
Answer with question: Where have you been eating?
Response: In the dining room but each time I finally get used to where things are, you turn the boat around.

Question: What powers the steam whistle?
Answer: Steam.

Question: What was the *Delta Queen* before it was a boat?
Answer: A pile of wood and steel.

Question: How deep is the river here?
Answer: All the way up to the boat.

Comment: River towns should cut down those trees to provide a better view of them.
Response: You are right. Cut down those trees so we can see the backs of buildings.

Comment: You should avoid landing at towns that have hills to have to walk.
Response: All towns are on notice. Lower your city to the river level or else.

Comment: What a waste to see all this beautiful land not developed.
Response: It would be a terrible waste to develop it.

Comment: We should have skeet shooting off the stern like cruise ships do.
Response: While traveling in Tennessee people will be shooting back.

Comment: You should have computer classes during the river cruise.
Response: Now that would add a lot to our old-time steamboatin' experience.

Comment: Someone should have better control of the river levels.
Response: The only one who has that kind of power can also walk on the water.

During my years on the steamboats I also acquired a sense of the passenger's character. I suppose one could call my next list passenger profiles. We of the crew appreciate all passengers, and are grateful that they travel with us. However, the job of Riverlorian is very high-profile and is the position that has the most exposure to the people. Given that, we do become familiar with the predictable traits that can be categorized, which can become entertaining or at times frustrating.

Ex-Navy men top the list of those who tax my patience regarding terminology on the river. They insist upon using words and asking questions that are related to ocean-going vessels. I explain river terminology on the first day out during my chat, but that doesn't stop them from asking how many knots we are going. I tell them that knots is something that I tie into a rope, but I can tell them how many miles per hour we are traveling (we use statute miles on the rivers). They will ask questions about celestial navigation. I explain that for me the stars just twinkle and look pretty and we do not use the constellations or stars for guidance on the river. By now these fellows are aware that there are differences between ocean and river navigation but that doesn't stop them from taking exception to the way we do things. They have a good sense of direction and are very insistent that the boat is going the wrong direction to reach our destination. I try to explain that we don't have north, south, east, and west on the rivers. We only have two directions, that being upriver and downriver. Since the river winds around in all directions to get from point A to point B, we could be going any direction. They don't accept that and continue to want to know our heading. During pilothouse tours they will interrupt to tell everyone how it was done in the Navy. I often get cornered and must listen to their Navy stories, but sometimes they are very interesting. I remember one hard-line Navy veteran who demanded to have a conference with our captain. He was certain that he could give him some tips on navigation, as he could see many things that were being done wrong. I warned the captain that this gentleman was looking for him and what his intentions were. The captain did his best to avoid an encounter, but one day I witnessed his capture and the captain pretending to appreciate all the advice he was being given. What would we have done without this ex-sailor?

Engineers are the most curious about the workings of the boat. They want to know every detail of the engine room, structure, paddlewheel ratios, etc. They are relentless in their pursuit of knowledge and of questioning the efficiency of the operations. One engineer made drawings to show our engineer how he would re-design the engine room. I was doing a river chat about historic Vicksburg, Mississippi, and at the end of the chat I asked if there are any questions (expecting questions about Vicksburg). A gentleman who I had already identified as a retired engineer raised his hand. He asked, "What are the pounds per square inch of pressure in the hydraulic lines that operate the cylinders which lower the smoke stacks?" I explained that I really never had a need to know that, but that he should ask the chief engineer. I found out later that he had already asked the captain, one of the pilots, and even the hotel manager the same question. None knew the answer but had also suggested that he asked the chief engineer, which he never did. Often an engineer, even after getting his question answered by a qualified individual, will question the answer and disagree with it. After all, the chief has only been working in that engine room for 40 years. What could he know?

River and steamboat buffs can be very challenging and can be separated into two categories. One would be those who have traveled the steamboats so often that they think they have nothing more to learn and do not attend our programs. The others are those who also think they know everything there is to know and want to share that knowledge with everyone around them, including the Riverlorian. It is those of the first category who ask the most questions. The answers to those questions have usually already been provided in the talks that they did not attend, so I must repeat many things often. These folks are on the boat primarily to sit on the deck and watch the river go by, which is fine. In fact, sitting on the deck and watching the river go by is one of the things I do best.

The second category can often be bothersome. They will stand by anytime I am away from my station to answer questions, and sometimes interrupt a conversation I am having to provide their input about a question that was asked. They want everyone to know how much they know and just love to show me how much they know, which means that I must politely listen to long accounts of information that I already know. They forget that I am being paid to provide information and have already heard all their stories. I must admit, however, that on occasion I do pick up a good story or some new information from these folks. Sometimes though I stand there wondering how someone could make such a short story so long and look for an opportunity to get away. Trouble comes when two or more river/steamboat buffs get together and compete for attention or adamantly want to prove they are right in an argument. The difference of opinion of the tiniest detail can cause hostilities that would lead to a dueling match if they were armed. They sometimes find a more peaceful means of settling the dispute. They bring the Riverlorian into the issue. I try to avoid such confrontations because one may be wrong and one may be right, or they both may be wrong. In any case, I will make an enemy with my answer to their question. Ah, you gotta love 'em!

There are those who like to play "Stump the Riverlorian". Yes, these are usually highly educated people who will ask questions that they know the answer to. They like to test me and will often have questions that have nothing to do with American rivers and steamboating. They are also the ones who enjoy telling me of their world travels. I remember a veteran guest speaker who came aboard who was familiar with the burdens of listening to boring stories. On introduction night he ended by saying straight out, "Just remember folks that I am here to tell you stories, and not to hear yours. I have already heard them all." I admired his directness, but it did him little good. You cannot escape those who want you to know about their trip to the South of France or their cruise on an ocean liner. When someone would asks me questions about the Nile, Rhine, Danube, or Yanzee Rivers (that they know the answer to), I simply say that I haven't traveled every American River yet, so why go that far. That answer does not help me escape their answering the question for me in great detail. Oh well, maybe I will go on the Nile River some time. I really don't mind being stumped by a legitimate question because I will go to great lengths to find the answer. The result of that research will not only satisfy their question but I will have learned one more thing in the process. So I say, "Go ahead, make my day."

Most people want to travel the rivers aboard a genuine steamboat to travel back in time. The steamboats are time machines in the sense that they allow us to experience river travel of the 1800s. Some apparently ride the boats for a different reason. Their first shock is to find no television in their stateroom. No TV? After the initial shock, withdrawal symptoms begin to appear. They then begin to get hungry for the latest news and ask when the daily newspaper will be delivered. I explain that our newspaper delivery boy hasn't swum out to the boat yet today. No newspaper? How can they get away from it all without knowing what's going on in the world? For yuppies everything must be well structured, precise, and on time. When we announce a schedule change due to low water, they panic. The yuppies also must have the best toys. They bring lap-top computers, fancy cell phones that take pictures, and GPS systems that are better than we have in the pilothouse. They may bring thousand-dollar motion-compensating night-vision binoculars, but seldom use them. The yuppies like to party late and sleep in. Even though they want everything to function on schedule, they are late for most events.

These folks often bore easily and begin to wonder what it is that people see in sitting on the deck watching the river. They think the deck is for getting a cell phone signal outside the boat, or maybe catch some sun (while being covered with sunscreen, hat, sunglasses, and a Newsweek magazine). The yuppies do ask questions, though. They want to know when all meals are being served, when the boat lands at a port, and where can they buy batteries for their toys. I think they have it easy. If it was up to me the steamboats would be even more authentic, complete with chamber pots instead of toilets. There would be no hot showers and we would dip our drinking water from the river. The closest thing to air- conditioning would be an open window. Now that would be steamboatin'!

Some passengers like to share their knowledge and usually do have some knowledge of what they are talking about. There are others who are know-it-alls and are capable of impressing others with their bull. I have seen people who have the amazing ability to take charge of any conversation and seem to know everything about everything. I have heard these folks talking with great authority on subjects they know nothing about. How do I know? Because I know the truth about the subject. Once one of these posted himself on the bow deck and proceeded to describe everything to anyone who would listen. He commanded attention and got it. I was listening in on one of his speeches as he described the workings of a passing towboat. First he called it a tugboat. Then he told of the 12-foot draft of the vessel. He explained how the boats have a jet drive. He said the lead barges have thrusters to help them turn. He spoke of the tonnage each barge carries, totaling about 50 tons. The rhetoric went on and on as I listened with a smile on my face, allowing him to enjoy his temporary glory, even though he had made up all that he said. He didn't notice me in my ball cap and sun glasses. This type of thing happens often but this time I decided to do something about it, without confronting him.

The next morning during my Riverlorian chat it just happened that I decided to talk about towboats. I explained the difference between a tugboat and a towboat and that we would see no tugboats on the river. I also brought up the nine-foot draft of the vessels and explained how they steer from the stern, since the only method of steering was with the rudders near the propellers. I also mentioned that each barge carried an equivalent of 58 semi-truck loads, which is 1,500 tons. OK, I know that it was not a nice thing for me to do, but it is my job to be informative and I was just doing my job. Can I help it if it that particular subject happened to have come up the morning after this man made his speech?

As long as I am on a roll here, I might as well mention one more passenger profile. That would be the ones who are never happy, regardless of the best efforts of the crew. They start the cruise out by not liking their stateroom for some reason and demanding another, while hoping for a free upgrade. The stateroom they get, if available, will also be poorly lit, have a bug in it, or be improperly serviced by the housekeeping staff. If the schedule gets changed in any way, they will complain that they are not getting what they paid for. I remember one cruise that, due to high water, we could not get under the Wheeling, West Virginia, bridge on the Ohio River and had to bus passengers from our planned embarkation point of Pittsburgh, Pennsylvania. After getting on the boat a passenger came to me whining about missing some of the river between the two cities. That is a valid point, but beyond our control to do anything about it. In fact, it cost the company a great deal to bus the passengers to the boat. Still not satisfied, he asked how many miles the trip would have been from Pittsburgh to our destination of Louisville, Kentucky. I gave him that information. He then asked how many miles it would have been from Pittsburgh to Wheeling, and I provided that figure.

I discovered later that he went back to his room and did some math. He figured the percentage of river miles that he was being cheated out of, and then went to the purser's office to demand a refund of that amount. He was offered a full refund of his money if he would like to get off the boat before it departed Wheeling, which he chose not to do, but continued to complain about it all the way to Louisville. Another passenger was very unhappy because her cabin was located next to an outside walkway where the porters put the trash cans, and the noise was irritating. Hers was a valid complaint, but unfortunately the boat was full and there were no rooms available to move her. The porters were notified to be as quiet as possible, but she continued to be upset. One evening in protest, she went out to the trash cans (a crew area only), gathered up trash and taped the stuff on the outside of her door with a sign that read "trash alley". Her timing was excellent because it just happened that the entertainment staff was having a door decorating contest throughout the boat and they gave her first prize.

I suppose that is enough roasting of passengers. It is all in fun and I have shared these insights with passengers and had them laughing at themselves. I am not perfect and make fun of myself also, including within chapters of this book. The bottom line is that they are all unique individuals and keep life interesting for us. We do love um!

Chapter 17

The Ghost of Mary Greene

Mary Becker was born in 1869 and she was a young debutante of only twenty-two when she met and was courted by a man named Gordon C. Greene. Her family was opposed to the match since he was a riverman; they felt she could do much better within the circle of their high society. Love prevailed, and Mary married Gordon. She left her comfortable surroundings and went to the river with her husband. They became very successful, eventually owning an entire fleet of steamboats. Greene Line steamers began when Gordon and Mary purchased the *H.K. Bedford*. They went on to own 27 steamboats over time. Mary did not sit home waiting for Gordon to come home from the river, but rode with him and worked on the boats in various capacities. She spent a great deal of time in the pilothouse with her husband. In fact, she spent so much time there that in 1896 she earned her pilot's license, becoming one of the first female steamboat pilots. Little did her family know that when Mary met Gordon met that she would spend the next fifty-nine years of her life on the rivers.

Following is an interview with Mary Greene published in the Wheeling Daily Intelligencer on February 3, 1896. She was piloting the *H.K. Bedford* at the time:

> When asked how she became a pilot she said, "Well, it was very easy you see, I spend a good bit of time in the pilothouse with the captain—my husband, you know—and it is only natural that I should get to know the river. Of course, he took a great deal of pains to show me everything and often let me try my hand at managing the boat. In the course of the years of our married life I have seen a great deal of the river, and it seems very natural that I should learn something of it. It requires only a good memory to know the channel and as for learning to ring the bells, and

how to handle the boat, that is comparatively easy". Do you keep a home? "You see, we have never gone to housekeeping yet. This boat has been my home ever since the captain and I was married, and I nearly always stand watch with him. Five years as a 'striker' ought to qualify almost anyone for a pilot, even if they had a less able and willing instructor than I had." But do you like the river? Is your floating home as pleasant as one on the bank would be?" asked the reporter. "Oh yes. I like the river ever so much. The captain has to be with his boat nearly all the time, and if we were keeping house we would be practically separated. Then I have very nice rooms here, and when I want to get away from the passengers I can retire to them. There is a constant change of scene, which is very agreeable, and then one is always meeting so many people that one knows. A great deal of my time is spent in the pilot house though, and altogether, I think it very nice to live on a boat."

Do you intend to stand a regular watch on the boat? "No indeed; I didn't get my license for that. We have a pilot and Mr. Greene stands one watch, so there is no necessity for my doing anything of the kind. I wanted my license because I felt that I was entitled to it. Then I can help the captain when he is on watch, or take the wheel for awhile for amusement if I like. If we should be left without a pilot for a time I could take a turn in the pilothouse until we could get someone else. That is all the piloting I expect to do." Are we to infer from you entering the ranks of pilots that you look with favor on the new woman idea? "Several of my friends have asked me that since I got my license," she said, laughing. "I always tell them that I don't bother much about such stuff. I am contented to be just what I am, a woman, in the good old fashioned way. I don't think there is anything unwomanly or advanced in my being able to steer a boat, and I am contented to let the captain do the voting for the family." The captain has a far higher opinion of his wife's abilities than she has herself. In response to a query as to whether he was not a little proud of his new pilot, he straightened himself up, and said in a way that was eloquent of his earnest sincerity; "You bet I am." When the H.K. Bedford left the harbor Friday afternoon, Mrs. Greene was in the pilothouse, and her husband stood on the roof watching her clever manipulation of the big pilot wheel. As it spun around and the Bedford rounded out into the stream, he looked as well satisfied as if he owned the whole river.

Gordon C. Greene died in 1927, leaving Mary and her two sons, Chris and Tom, to run the steamboat operations. They had sold off some of the steamboats due to a drop- off in business. Tom Greene was a man of vision, and in 1946 heard about a steamboat for sale in California. It was a passenger steamboat owned by the U.S. Navy, and been used to ferry troops around the Bay area during WWII. In 1946 the Navy placed the boat on auction block. Tom went to California to see the vessel, and even though it was in rough condition and painted battleship gray, he saw her potential. The boat that the Navy called the *YFB-56* at one time traveled the Sacramento River in all her elegance as the *Delta Queen*. Tom bid on the boat with the notion of having the finest steamboat on the western rivers. He was the only bidder and purchased the vessel for a mere $46,000. The boat was then towed down the Pacific Ocean, through the Panama Canal, and across the Gulf of Mexico to the Mississippi River. From there the *Delta Queen* went up the Mississippi and Ohio River under her own power to be refurbished in Pittsburgh, Pennsylvania.

When Mary Greene saw the *Delta Queen* it was love at first sight. Even before her restoration, Mary was captured by the charm of the 285-foot steamboat. When the work was completed everyone knew that the *Delta Queen* would be the Grande Dame of the waterways. Capt. Mary Greene moved aboard the *Delta Queen* and began piloting, along with her son, Capt. Tom Greene. From the time the *Delta Queen* was put back into service in 1947 until her death Ma Greene, as she was widely known, spent her time piloting, serving as master, and working in the purser's office, dining room, housekeeping, and in just about any other capacity that would serve the needs of her passengers. She did everything except for one job. She was never a bartender because there was no bar on the *Delta Queen*. Mary was a fierce backer of temperance, and forbade the sale of liquor on the boat. Mary lived on the *Delta Queen* and died on the *Delta Queen* at the age of 80, in 1949. Tom Greene continued to operate the boat until his death just one year later at the age of 46. Tom's widow Letha, took ownership and operated the only boat left of the Greene Line Steamers and the only overnight steamboat still operating in America- the legendary *Delta Queen*.

After her death, many convincing stories have emerged providing evidence that Mary Greene's spirit is still aboard the *Delta Queen*. As a member of the crew of the boat I never had definite encounter with her but, would welcome it if she was there. Captain Mary Greene was once described as "five feet of femininity, as refreshing as the river breeze, and as modern as the moment." The diminutive queen of inland waters, now enshrined in the National Maritime Hall of Fame, wasn't shy and retiring. She could sometimes be quite feisty. Her feisty nature prevailed, and she gained

Photo by Author

The Delta Queen

widespread fame when she beat her husband in a 1903 steamboat race from Pittsburgh to Cincinnati. She also piloted their new boat *Greeneland*, to the 1904 World's Fair in St. Louis, despite proessing that she didn't share many of the "new woman ideas." Her feistiness, sense of humor, and dedication to the *Delta Queen* and her passengers prevails to this day in the accounts of her ghostly appearances and events. I prefer to refer to her as a spirit, rather than a ghost. I believe it is more respectful, and as a crewman on the boat I don't want to take any chances of getting on her bad side. The closest that I came to a possible encounter was when I was in the aft cabin lounge telling some passengers about Mary Greene. We were standing next to a glass door cabinet that displayed the Greene family photographs. The cabinet has a rather stiff door catch that does not open easily. I had mentioned that Mary did not allow drinking on the *Delta Queen*, but there were rumors that she had kept a little stash in her cabin. As soon as I said that, one of the cabinet doors opened slowly for no apparent reason. I carefully closed the door and changed the subject. Not that I am completely convinced of her presence, but after that little event I decided to take no chances.

Letha Greene was having a hard time making a go of the steamboat business, but was dedicated to keeping the *Delta Queen* on the rivers. It was by then the only overnight passenger boat still in operation. Letha sold the boat to a group that had marketing skills and would offer a better financial future for the boat. One of the changes the new owners made was to install a bar for additional revenue. They refurbished the observation lounge on the Texas deck and converted it to the Texas Lounge. On the first cruise with the Texas Lounge in operation, the bartender was preparing the first cocktail. At exactly that time there was a sudden crash on the starboard side. The *Delta Queen* was jolted so hard that the glassware and bottles of liquor came crashing down. A towboat had accidentally run into the side of the *Delta Queen*. There wasn't much damage to the boat, but the new Texas Lounge was in shambles. Some people who knew the story of Mary Greene's temperance attitude joked that she must have caused the accident. The joking stopped and turned to shock as the towboat backed away from the *Delta Queen*. There on the pilothouse of the towboat a the sign with the name of the vessel. It was the *Mary B*. Mary Greene's maiden name was Mary Becker. Was this a coincidence, or was Mary Greene protesting the addition of the bar? If so, she apparently finally accepted it because the bar was repaired and restocked with no future damage.

There have been other incidents of less catastrophic proportions that have occurred in the Texas Lounge. The *Delta Queen* is an old boat and it is inevitable that the ceilings may leak from time to time. When people comment on those leaks, I often tell them that when you are on a boat, don't worry about water coming in from above. But if it is coming in through the floor it could be a bit more serious. During one heavy storm I witnessed something that had been told to me earlier. The entire boat remains dry; accept for the bar in the Texas Lounge. The water seems leak into the bar, no matter how many repairs have been made to the ceiling.

There have been many sightings of Mary by both passengers and crew. On one cruise we had landed at Madison, Indiana, during the night. The following morning a lady passenger came to me with an interesting story. She had trouble sleeping that night and had gone for a walk around the deck at 3 am. She noticed that the deckhands were on shore tying off the boat at the Madison landing and she decided to walk up to the Texas deck bow and watch. From the inside of the boat she could see someone sitting in one of the rocking chairs on the boat. She described the woman as short and heavy, with a bun hairstyle. The passenger decided to join the woman to watch the boat's landing procedures. As she walked out the port side door she was shocked to see nobody in the rocking chair. She approached the chair, noticing that heavy dew was on all the furniture. She touched the seat of the rocking chair and found it was also wet with dew. By then she was quite shaken about the disappearing lady who could sit on a chair without causing the seat to dry. She slept no more that night and came to me with her story the next morning. I could offer no precise answer to this mystery, but did tell her about Mary Greene and advised her that Madison, Indiana, was one of her favorite places during her later years. Mary would sometimes drive to and from Madison to get on and off the vessel. The boat had not been to Madison for quite some time, and I could only suppose that Mary was very happy to be visiting Madison again. Sitting on the deck watching the landing would have likely been something she would do upon seeing her favorite river stop again. Well, that's only a theory that I shared without acknowledging an absolute belief that her spirit is on the boat.

A guest pianist encountered the apparition. For three consecutive nights, from the corner of her eye, she saw a woman in a 1930s dress drift by. Whenever she looked up, the woman had always disappeared. After the third sighting, the lady thought perhaps the woman was sleepwalking or ill, so she reported the incidents to the cruise director. He pointed out a portrait of Capt. Mary Greene, whereupon the pianist exclaimed, "That's her!" The cruise director responded, "She died in 1949."

The most compelling and believable story happened in 1982. For six weeks each winter the *Delta Queen* is taken out of service and enters lay-up at home port. During lay-up the boat is cleaned, repaired, and refurbished. Each night after the workers go home, one man is left on the boat to serve as watchman. The watchman sleeps on the boat, but must be ready to respond to emergencies or intruders. During this lay-up the watchman was a first mate name Mike. One night Mike was sleeping until a whisper in his ear awoke him with a start. Mike could not ascertain what the whisperer said, but he jumped up to find no one in the cabin. He sat down and wondered if he had been dreaming, but had a strange feeling that he was not alone on the boat. At about the time he convinced himself that it had only been a dream, he heard the sound of a door closing somewhere down the hall. He was supposed to be the only person on the boat, so he went out of the cabin and down the hall, calling out to whoever might be on the vessel. He got no answer and found no one. Next a noise came from the deck below; that is the crew area on the same level as the boiler room. By then Mike was nervous as he proceeded down to the next level. He stopped calling out and tried to move quietly so he would not divulge his location. Another noise that sounded like something being dragged came from behind the boiler-room door. He decided to call out a warning, but got no reply. Mike flung open the door. Nobody was in the boiler room, but what he found startled him.

The boilers draw water from the river through an intake pipe in the hull. The intake pipe had a broken connection, causing river water to flow into the boat at a high rate. When Mike saw this problem he forgot all about any intruder and took immediate action to stop the flow. If he did not act fast, the boat would be swamped and sink. After making repairs and pumping the water out, his mind went back to the whisper and the noises that had led him to find the broken intake pipe. No one was on board the *Delta Queen* but Mike. That young man is now Captain Mike, the master of the *Delta Queen*. To this day he is convinced that it was Mary Greene who whispered in his ear and led him to the boiler room. Had he not found the damaged pipe, the *Delta Queen* would almost certainly have sunk that night. There is no question that if the spirit of Mary Greene is on the *Delta Queen*, she would have done what she could to see that her beloved boat did not sink.

Over the years several documentary films have been made about the ghost of Mary Greene. Some have reported strange happenings on the boat, but nothing with solid evidence has been discovered. Passengers and crew members continue to relate unexplained phenomena regarding Capt. Mary. One thing is constant among the crew members and the many repeat passengers. No one fears the ghost of Mary Greene. I, even being objective about her presence, am as convinced as everyone that if she is on the *Delta Queen*, she is a benevolent spirit. She may be there, still looking after the needs of her passengers and keeping an eye on her boat. I have never known of anyone who chose to leave the boat for fear of the ghost, even when sightings or

Hay Collection Photo
Mary Greene

anomalies occur. I would personally love to meet the lady, and will never bring up that story about her stash again.

Chapter 18

River Royalty

There have been many great people who have been responsible for exploring, improving and romanticizing American rivers. This chapter will feature the accomplishments of a group that I call River Royalty. Focus is on those who came after the Native Americans and great French explorers. There are too many men and women to include all of them in one chapter, so following are my favorites.

I have chosen **Capt. William Clark** for several reasons. He was co-commander with Capt. Meriwether Lewis on the Lewis and Clark Expedition. The men of the expedition called themselves the "Corp of Discovery", and it was the greatest river journey in history. Captain Lewis was also very important to that successful mission but could not have accomplished it without the skills and leadership of Captain Clark. I also have a special interest in Captain Clark since I was chosen to portray him during the bicentennial events celebrating the expedition. Much has been written about that expedition, so there is no need to duplicate the enormous amount of information, but Capt. Clark certainly belongs on the list of river royalty.

William Clark was born on a plantation in Virginia in 1770. While growing up he spent a great deal of time in the forest. He was a born explorer and developed great skills. When he was fourteen, his family moved to Kentucky and purchased a farm near Louisville. At age nineteen he followed his older brother's footsteps and joined the Army. His brother, George Rogers Clark, had made quite a name for himself as a general. William had become an Indian fighter, but little did he know that one day he would be grateful to many Indian tribes and become their friend and representative. During his time in the Army he became a captain and met a young lieutenant named Meriwether Lewis, who served in his command. He and Lewis became good friends, and Clark knew that Lewis had the potential to be a great man. Captain Clark eventually retired from the Army and settled in present-day Clarksville, Indiana, located across Indiana the river from Louisville, Kentucky. Lewis remained in the Army and became a captain. He was also appointed personal secretary to President Thomas Jefferson, who hand-picked Lewis and groomed him to lead a special mission that he had wanted to pursue for many years. Jefferson had an eye to the west and wanted to explore that unknown territory beyond the Mississippi River. He had visions of American expansion from sea to sea, and wanted to find the elusive Northwest Passage that so many had tried to find. He also wanted the expedition to be a scientific one and document plant and animal life. Another goal was to create a peaceful co-existence with the Indians. The only known route west was up the Missouri River.

Author as Capt. William Clark

Clark had heard about the plans for the expedition and the Louisiana Purchase. He had also kept in touch with Lewis. One day he received a letter from Lewis explaining that he had been commissioned to proceed with planning the trip across the continent. Lewis asked Clark to join him in co-commanding the expedition. This river trip actually began in Pittsburgh where Lewis had a keelboat built. He joined Clark in Louisville, where he was recruiting men. It would be a difficult journey that would require young, strong men. They continued down the Ohio River to the Mississippi, then up to St. Louis where they wintered across from the Missouri River. During this long winter Lewis and Clark made many more preparations, including disciplining the men. This was a military expedition, in fact the first non-combat mission for the U.S. Army. During the long journey up the Missouri River, across the Rocky Mountains, and down the Snake and Columbia Rivers, it was Captain Clark who held things together. His skills on the river, including his amazing mapping abilities, along with his leadership proved invaluable to the success of the mission. Clark had charted the rivers from St. Louis to the Pacific Ocean with a hand compass and guesswork measuring. He estimated the journey at 4,133 miles, which was later discovered to be within 40 miles of being accurate. He had an uncanny feel for the river and could pick the right one to travel at questionable forks. It was Captain Clark who could rally the troops when things became the most difficult. Everyone on the expedition was important to its success, but Capt. William Clark stands out as the true riverman and leader without whom, the mission may have failed.

The Lewis and Clark expedition was the most difficult and important river journey in American history. It was a river trip that helped change America forever and lead to it becoming a nation from sea to shining sea. Some years after the expedition William Clark wrote the following words about that great river trip:

"Time and circumstances separated the members of our expedition, but we all shared vivid memories of our trip across the continent. Memories of an awesome new world to the west. Of adventure, trial, and danger. Of drudgery and fatigue. Of boredom and excitement. Of sickness and sundry aches and pains. Of eating horses, dogs, and roots. Of numbing cold, pelting rain, and baking sun. Of deadly rattlers, bellowing buffalo herds, and yowling wolves. Of ferocious grizzlies and pesky mosquitoes and gnats. Of endless days on foot, horse, and boat. Of our fallen comrade Floyd. Of encounters with strange Indian bands. Of spectacular mountains, surging rivers, and the shores of the western ocean."

In 1833 the steamboat *Carrollton* was headed up Mississippi River to St. Louis. On board was 13-year-old **James Buchanan Eads**. James spent most of his time in the engine room, fascinated with every detail of the powerful machine. Not far from the St. Louis landing, a chimney flue collapsed and the boat caught fire. Caught between the flames and the water, James took his chances with the river. Struggling to swim to shore, he swallowed mouthfuls of thick, brown Mississippi water. James made it safely to shore and spent the rest of his life in a struggle to understand and control the Mississippi. He came to know it better than anyone. As an engineer he built master works for the river that will alter the country's history.

When Eads arrived in St. Louis it was a river town ripe for development. The Eads family had lost all but the clothes on their backs to the river, so James went to work at a dry-goods store. At only 16 years old he was known as a man of, "towering ambition". He had a way of seeing inside something and figuring out how things worked. In his time off James built a miniature steam engine and dreamed of one day working on a steamboat. He learned to play chess and could play the game in his head without a board. His employer was so impressed by the young boy's talent that he allowed James to use his personal library. Here, Eads began his self-education as an engineer. When James was seventeen he signed on as a clerk of a steamboat. He had been on the boat less than a year when it hit a snag, sending it, and its cargo of lead, to the bottom of the river. This was not uncommon as hundreds of boats had been lost to the river. Their cargoes were considered lost, but James was convinced there might be a way to reclaim them. He walked into the office of a large St. Louis boat-builder. There he presented a plan for a double-hulled riverboat, open in the middle and equipped with hoisting gear strong enough to retrieve the many riches that remained in the bottom to the Mississippi River.

To find the lost cargo, a diver would need to descend to the bottom of the river. Eads designed a diving bell consisting of an open-ended barrel, attached to a pump and hose for air. Finding no one brave enough to dive for him, he got in the barrel himself. He could not see the river so much as feel it. He found the bed of the river a moving mass and so unstable that his feet penetrated through it until he could feel the sand rushing past his hands, driven by a powerful current. He also walked on the bottom of the Missouri and the Ohio rivers, all the way to the Gulf of the Mississippi and because he would try to figure out how the current worked, and how it affected the bottom. He came to know the entire river. Salvaging turned out to be as profitable as it was dangerous. James was soon known as "Captain" Eads, in command of his own crew and salvage boat. He was 22, and ready to take his place in the world. Then in the spring of 1849, disaster struck St. Louis. The steamer *White Cloud* caught fire at the city wharf. Flames soon engulfed the downtown and twenty-three steamboats. What was a devastating loss for St. Louis proved to be a windfall for James Eads. He hired additional crew and sped up plans for a new salvage boat to help bring up the sunken cargo. By the 1850s, Eads had developed his salvage boats that he could raise entire steamboats, earning upwards of $4,000 on individual salvage jobs.

The Civil War also propelled James Eads into action. Missouri was a border state — Eads was strong for the Union. He realized early on that if Federal forces lost control of the Mississippi, the Confederacy might prevail. He lobbied for a river navy to defend it. When the government invited bids for the construction of river gunboats with iron plating, Eads made an extraordinary proposal. He would build seven, "ironclads" and have them ready within sixty-five days. He won the contract. Now the course of the war would depend on his ability to deliver. This would be a major undertaking that would require boat builders, iron and steel workers, ordnance suppliers, finan-

Library of Congress Photo
James B. Eads

ciers, and management personnel, all pulling as a team together. The first gunboats were launched in October 1861. They were unlike anything ever seen before on the river. The fleet steamed south to attack the confederacy at Fort Henry and Fort Donelson. The assault was successful beyond expectations. These were the first important Union victories of the war and made a hero of the commander, General Ulysses S. Grant. Eads still actually owned the gunboats, but had loaned them to Grant. These victories not only helped establish Grant's reputation, but also served to develop a relationship between Eads and the general that would prove very important later.

St. Louis was on the western side of the river, which was the wrong side for the railways, so it didn't have a strong connection to eastern railways. St. Louis was tied to the weaker western railway lines. Chicago investors had already bridged the Mississippi upriver at Rock Island, IL. Now they were driving deep into markets that St. Louis needed. James Eads turned all his attention to the construction of a railroad bridge at St. Louis and by the spring of 1867 had developed a revolutionary design. 500-foot arched spans - the

longest ever conceived - were to be made of the new metallic com-
pound, steel. This would be the first attempt in the world to build a
large structure out of steel.

Support would come from four massive piers grounded on
bedrock, as deep as a hundred feet below the river bed. No one
worked at such a depth before. In recent years many bridges had collapsed under the weight of railroad trains. The east pier would be
sunk to its extraordinary depth using a pneumatic caisson, a structure similar in principle to Eads' diving bell. The caisson, an iron
and wood structure similar to an upside down shoe box, was floated
into place in the river, and was held there with pilings driven down
into the sand. Then Eads' plan was to build the masonry courses of
the piers atop those. This would allow the masons to work on the
surface, out in the open air. As each new course of masonry was laid,
the caisson would be forced down toward the riverbed. The caisson
would hit the sand bottom and workers would go down into the caisson and then excavate the sand. As they did so, the caisson would
sink further down toward bedrock.   By February 1870, four masonry foundations emerged from the river bed, but it had yet to be
shown that arches made of steel could stride them.

Each day the huge arches inched toward one another. Then,
just as the spans were ready to close, steamboat owners claimed
that the arches of the bridge were too low. They demanded that
construction be stopped and the bridge torn down. The U.S. Army
Corps of Engineers held jurisdiction over river improvements. The
Chief of the Corps of Engineers, Andrew Humphreys, informed
Eads that if his bridge remained, he must build a canal around it
so that tall vessels could pass around the bridge. Eads was outraged and called on a man who owed him a favor-President
Ulysses S. Grant. Eads explained how his bridge had come under
attack. He reminded him that the Secretary of War had approved
the design and Grant overruled Humphreys. On July 4, 1874, the
Illinois and St. Louis Bridge opened with a gigantic celebration.
An estimated 300,000 people turned out to watch a parade that
stretched for fourteen miles. Eads' bridge started an engineering
revolution, bringing in the age of steel bridges and the skyscrap-
ers that followed. Techniques developed by Eads were used on
many other structures, the Brooklyn Bridge among them. While
other bridges have been built, then fallen down or replaced, the
Eads Bridge is still carrying trains and cars across the
Mississippi River.

As the Mississippi River approaches the Gulf of Mexico, some

100 river miles below New Orleans, it spreads and gradually slows, depositing its huge load of sediment. In the years following the Civil War, as ships increased both in number and size, sandbars often blocked the mouth of the river, threatening its future as an international waterway. One could go down to the mouth of the Mississippi River at any given time, and find fifty or sixty ships waiting for enough water to get over the sandbar. The entire Mississippi River basin relied on the Gulf for access to the rest of the world. Chief Engineer Humphreys was under great pressure to solve the problem. He recommended to Congress that a canal be built from below New Orleans to an arm of the gulf, bypassing the natural channels. James Eads was sure the plan would fail, being a violation of the natural order of things.

Eads' approach to the problem was to work with the river. He proposed building jetties, which are wall-like structures within the river, extending and narrowing the channel out into the gulf. The narrower opening created by the jetties would speed the current, causing it to scour out the sandbars and carry the sediment out to the gulf. Humphreys, still angry from his encounter with Eads over the St. Louis Bridge, staked his reputation on the failure of this plan. He argued that the jetties would merely cause sandbars to be formed farther out in the channel. Eads then made the government an offer they could not refuse. He would build the jetties at his own expense and his own risk, and the government would only pay for them if they worked. His plan for the operation was fairly simple. The trunks of willow trees were bound into mattress-like structures, placed between guide pilings, and sunk with layers of stone. When they reached the surface, they were capped with concrete. Sediment deposited by the river would build up against the structures, making the jetties impermeable.

Within a year Eads' gamble was paying off. With much of the mattressing in place, the channel was already deeper. Humphreys, now his bitter enemy, falsified water depth records to show that his plan was not working, but Eads knew better and fought back with an ingenious plan He called in a favor from an old friend named Captain Gager, who operated a deep-water steamship named the *Hudson*. Eads asked Gager to bring the *Hudson* through the channel." The *Hudson* was an ocean going vessel with a draft of fourteen feet, seven inches. If the channel were any shallower, the ship would run aground. Captain Gager ordered full speed ahead. All work stopped as the men watched the ship approach the two-mile stretch of jetties. One of Eads' men observed that as long as the

Hudson carried that "white bone in her teeth" (the wave that her bow pushed ahead), there was enough depth for the ship to pass. Tension rose as the ship raced between the jetties. Everyone knew there was little room for error. Then the *Hudson* nosed past the head of the jetties, and a cheer rose up all around. Because of Eads' jetties, New Orleans would grow from the ninth-largest port in the United States to the second largest, after New York. Just before James Eads died at age 66, his last words were, "I cannot die. I have not finished my work." In an era held captive by geography, Eads helped open the country with his innovative technologies. His work inspired a new generation of engineers and entrepreneurs. In the early 20th Century, when deans of American schools of engineering were asked to name the greatest engineers of all time, in the top five, along with Leonardo da Vinci and Thomas Edison, was James Buchanan Eads-the young boy who had swum from a sinking steamboat and built a bridge where he came to shore.

Like Eads, **Henry Miller Shreve** was a self-taught engineer. His contributions to the river and river travel were not on such a grand or large scale as Eads, but certainly

Corps of Engineers Photo
Henry Shreve

important. Shreve greatly improved on the Fulton steamboat design with his own steamboat, the *Washington*, which had greater power for the fast currents of the western rivers. He also placed the engine on the main deck instead of in the hull, which allowed for a much shallower draft for the minimal water depths. He built multiple decks on a wide-enough beam to support them. His design was copied and is still used today. The first steamboat was the *New Orleans*. She was under-powered and inefficient, but she made her way down the Mississippi River to New Orleans first, where the owners established a monopoly. It was Henry Shreve who broke the unfair monopoly by ignoring it, securing government cargo contracts, and fighting it out in court, opening the river for future vessels.

Shreve was also active in making the rivers more navigable. One method was to make cut-offs at difficult bends of the rivers. By cutting a relatively narrow ditch across a bend that was deeper than the channel, he could cause the river to change its course and scour out a new channel around an obstructed or difficult area. He and his crew did this often and effectively shortening the Mississippi River. Even though this work was praised and did save many vessels, and probably many lives, it wasn't discovered for many years that this method would create different problems in the river, as discussed in chapter 15 of this book.

Snags were the terror of the rivers. The rate of steamboats sinking to the bottom of the rivers after hitting snags was astounding. Enter Henry Shreve. In 1829 he designed and built the *Helipolis*, a specially designed steamboat that would help rid the rivers of those awful snags. She had a composite hull (catamaran-style), with lifting machinery connected to the engine. A heavy snag beam joined the two hulls at the bow. In going into action, the snag boat was run full-tilt at the projecting snag in such a manner as to catch it on the snag beam and force it up out of the water. This powerful blow was often enough either to break off the snag or to loosen it from the riverbed. Then the snag was brought under the snag beam, raised by the winch and cut up. The heavy portions such as the stump and roots were either dropped into a deep pool or carried ashore. In 1833 Shreve tackled a series of log jams on the Red River that choked it for a distance of 160 miles. Shreve eventually opened up the Red River for navigation and a new port was founded—Shreveport, Louisiana.

One cannot compile a list of River Royalty without including **Samuel Clemens**. Clemens made no direct impact on the rivers. He was not an engineer, nor did he do anything to improve naviga-

Library of Congress Photo
Samuel Clemens

tion. He was a riverboat pilot, but not for all that long. There has been so much written by and about Sam that this writing will do little more that recognize him for his accomplishment regarding the river. He put the Mississippi River on the world map and sparked the imagination of everyone who has read his work, particularly *Life on the Mississippi* and of course *The Adventures of Huckleberry Finn*. Without Mark Twain, people today would probably view that river only as moving muddy water. He inspired us with his clever stories of beauty, power, adventure, and mystery that the Father of Waters and, indeed, all rivers provide. He is the most quotable writer in history. Following are a few of his quotes that show his pride in being a river pilot.

"I love the profession far better than any I have Mark Twain   Library of Congress   followed since, and I took a measureless pride in it. The reason is plain; a pilot, in those days, was the only unfettered and entirely independent human being that lived in the earth."

"Your true pilot cares nothing about anything on earth but the river, and his pride   in his occupation surpasses the pride of kings."

"In truth, every man and woman and child has a master, and worries and frets in servitude; but in the day I write of, the Mississippi pilot had none"

While it is true that Sam Clemens took the name Mark Twain because it meant two fathoms of deep water on a lead-line, Sam was not the first to use the name. **Capt. Isaiah Sellers** of St. Louis was a well-known Mississippi River pilot. Owners of new, expensive steamboats wanted Captain Sellers. His reputation for piloting excellence was known all along the rivers. He was also what was called a fast pilot. He knew the rivers so well that he could proceed at full speed in areas where other had to slow down or stop for the night. He was the first known pilot to officially log one million miles. Captain Sellers developed the whistle signal system for steamboats to help avoid collisions between vessels. Those simple passing signals saved many boats and lives. Captain Sellers also believed in communicating with other pilots, and posted river changes and hazards at ports. He also wrote journals, which provided detailed accounts of new hazards and other important navigational information. He was so well respected that virtually all river town newspapers published his journals whenever he submitted them. Other pilots made certain to check on Captain Seller's reports before heading out.

For a short time, Captain Sellers had a young cub working under him in the pilothouse, training to be a pilot. This young man was training with the very best and was fascinated by his skillful piloting and writing abilities. The cub also admired the way in which the captain signed his journals—Capt. Isaiah Sellers, Mark Twain. He signed off this way because mark twain was a water depth that was good news to hear and meant safe navigation, and he felt it an appropriate way to wish other mariners a safe journey. The cub pilot was so inspired by the Captains writing that he begin writing too. His name was Samuel Clemens. A few years later Sam wrote a satirical account of a misfit steamboat crew traveling from St. Louis to New Orleans, a description which had great similarity to Captain Sellers and his crew. The captain was so outraged by Clemens' poking fun at him that he never wrote for the public again. It was not until Captain Sellers died that Sam Clemens took the pen name Mark Twain. Years later Twain was asked about the incident and he responded, "There was no malice in my rubbish, but it did laugh at the Captain. It seems that nothing I ever wrote as the truth is believed, and nothing I wrote in jest is doubted."

It is interesting to note that of the River Royalty mentioned, all are buried in the same place with the exception of Mark Twain. William Clark, Henry Shreve, James Eads, and Isaiah Sellers were all laid to rest at the Bellefontaine Cemetery, on a hill overlooking the Mississippi River at St. Louis. Other notable rivermen are also buried at Bellefontaine. **Manuel Lisa** was early trader with the Indians on the Missouri River, and traveled over 26,000 miles on flatboats and keelboats. He was good friends with the Indians and was called the "Great White Chief" by them. Lisa was responsible for keeping the Indians from joining the British in the War of 1812. He also provided useful information and supplies for the Lewis and Clark expedition. Lisa was the first of the rivermen to be buried on the hill in 1820, the site being his boyhood home.

Solomon Smith, the great showman on the showboats, along with being a doctor, lawyer, printer, gambler, steamboat pilot and about anything else he chose to be, is also buried there. Smith's name appears often and in many capacities in river history. He had his stone inscribed before his death. It reads: "All the world's a stage and all the men and women merely players......Exit Sol." As I walked through Bellefontaine, with its view of the Mississippi River, I sensed that this was an appropriate gathering place for these men who contributed so much and left their mark on American rivers

Eternal Review *Photo by Author*

Chapter 19

Top Ten River Towns

Each of us may have our own reasons why we prefer one town over another. There are many great places along America's rivers, and would require an entire book to discuss them all. I have chosen my ten favorite river towns, based on my experiences and preferences. I like cities and towns that have a pleasant riverfront. These places have not forgotten their river heritage, and have enough pride in that heritage to keep their riverfronts attractive, convenient, and functional. As a boatman, I prefer towns that have access to fuel and supplies. Historic places are also on my list of favorites, and towns that retain their identity are appreciated. These are places that have not yet been taken over by the strips of familiar franchises, but keep them out on the highway away from downtown. Friendly towns with people who welcome and even embrace travelers are enjoyed. Generally, I prefer small towns. It seems that the older I get, the larger some small towns seem to be. Smaller communities are usually friendlier and much easier to access than larger cities. One can tie off his boat along the bank and walk into a small town without too much concern. It is interesting that given my preference for small towns, the number one on my list of top ten river towns is the sixteenth largest city in the United States. Read on to find out why.

#1...Louisville, Kentucky

Louisville (pronounced Lawvle), at mile 663 on the Ohio River, has a metropolitan population of nearly one million. To me Louisville means the entire Louisville area, which includes the Indiana side of the river. The folks there like to call it the "sunny side of Louisville". To start with, downtown Louisville is absolutely beautiful from the river. Traveling past Louisville at night on the river is the kind of scene postcards are made of. One can also see the 120-foot ball bat leaning against the Louisville Slugger Museum. The riverfront at

Louisville is equally beautiful, efficient, and easily accessible. A riverfront park is almost always busy with festivals and activities. A good sense of humor by officials is apparent, when one reads the no-parking signs along the wharf. It says "Cars will be launched". There are several river excursion boats operating on both sides of the river. Best known is the legendary *Belle of Louisville*. The *Belle* is a genuine steamboat and the oldest one still in operation, built in 1914. Each year, the *Belle of Louisville* and the *Delta Queen* have a race during Kentucky Derby week. The twelve-mile race is intense and attracts thousands. The steamboat that wins the annual race receives the "gilded antlers" to mount on the pilothouse, which she proudly carries until the next race. The gold-painted elk antlers are a symbol of speed, a tradition that began with steamboat races in the 1800s.

On the other side of the river are Jeffersonville and Clarksville, Indiana, and not far is New Albany, Indiana. The Indiana side has a lot of activity, including many eating establishments, lodging, and convenient places to dock a boat. Jeffersonville is the home of the largest inland boat-building company in the U.S. Many famous steamboats were built there, including the *J.M. White* and the *Mississippi Queen*. The Falls of the Ohio was a navigation nightmare opposite Louisville before a lock and dam was built there. The 38-foot-lift McAlpine Locks and canal bypass the falls, which is dammed. At Clarksville there is a beautiful state park at the site of the falls, and one can walk along the rapids finding fossils embedded in the rocks. Rare for a big city, Louisville appreciates its river heritage and it shows. My hat goes off to Louisville.

Photo by Author

Downtown Louisville, Kentucky

#2...Clifton, Tennessee

I have only been to Clifton once, but that was enough to cause me to fall in love with this tiny town of only twelve hundred people at mile 158 on the Tennessee River. Our *Steamboat* was on a Tramping Tour. This is a cruise that lets passengers know where they will board the boat and where the trip will end, but are not told where the boat will be stopping along the way. These trips afford a chance to stop at places not normally on our schedule. I recalled passing by Clifton on our way to or from Chattanooga, and the company decided to make a stop there on a tramping cruise in 2003. The townspeople were obviously excited about the news of the impending visit by the *Steamboat*. Upon our approach to the landing, many turned out to greet us. The mayor and some southern belles in period costume stood by the landing to welcome our passengers and crew. Clifton had also arranged for something very unique—lunch. This was not just for the boat's officers. Lunch was on the town for the entire crew and all passengers of the *Steamboat*, which included 350 people. And it wasn't just lunch, either. It was a barbecue, complete with a delightful bluegrass band for entertainment. It seemed like everyone in Clifton was there to see to the needs and entertainment of their guests. The Girl Scouts were even on hand to provide any assistance for our elderly passengers. I was so taken by this that I gave the girls a private tour of our pilothouse.

Clifton may not have much appeal for tourism, and that is fine with me. Traffic, gaudy signs, and golden arches haven't spoiled it. I don't know if the town specially spruced up for our visit, but I prefer to think that it is always as clean and litter-free as we found it. Quaint homes and friendly people were everywhere. We have a policy of no visitors on the boat unless accompanied by a passenger. A visitor's pass will be issued in that case. But our passengers were so fond of the people of Clifton that they took it upon themselves to walk the streets and bring people back who otherwise could not get aboard the boat. The mate ran out of passes, gave up on the policy, and let those wonderful people visit the *Steamboat*. It was the least we could do for their generosity. As I walked the street along the river, I was invited on a porch for coffee and conversation. The sidewalk was rather rough but there was a sign that explained that the walkway has historical significance so it will not be replaced. Way to go Clifton! I hope they never re-pave their little paradise on the river. I will go back!

#3...Madison, Indiana

I have to admit that Madison, Indiana, is a bit touristy, but with its beauty and location, nestled in a picturesque valley surrounded by 500-foot tree-studded hills, there is no escaping that. In spite of the weekend crowds with their loud motorcycles and road-hogging RVs, it still ranks among the nicest river towns, particularly during the week. One hundred, thirty-three blocks are on the National List of Historic Places. The riverfront is park-like and features a floating restaurant, with plenty of docks. It is an easy walk into town, where all needed supplies can be found. If one is into antiques, there are plenty of places to browse. Located at mile 558 on the Ohio River, it also offers a beautiful view of the high bluffs on the Kentucky side. Each year Madison hosts a thrilling Regatta, with racing boats from across the nation competing at over 200 miles per hour for the Governor's cup. Some river towns have nearly died away, while others like Madison continue to thrive. Madison is a favorite stop of steamboat passengers and crew. Hoosier hospitality still prevails in the good people of Madison. It is indeed a fine place to stop over or stay a while.

#4...Marietta, Ohio

Marietta is much like Madison in its charm and historical significance. It is located at mile 172 on the Ohio River at its confluence with the Muskingum River. The boat landing is so close that if one steps off a boat, he or she is downtown. Marietta is the oldest settlement north of the Ohio River. The Ohio River Museum, which includes a full- size replica of a flatboat, has much to offer for history buffs. The *Becky Thatcher* showboat is moored on the Muskingum. The Lafayette Hotel is a historic landmark that is located just across the street from the landing. Since the *Delta Queen* is also considered a hotel, it is said that this is the only time one historic hotel is visited by another. It is an easy and enjoyable walk around town. Marietta was a major port in the early days of steamboating, and the town's pride in that shows today. The riverfront is always busy with people enjoying the river. I always enjoy watching the people watch the *Steamboat* as we depart. They are happy that steamboats still land there, and show it with their enthusiasm and friendliness. Marietta is one of the jewels of the Ohio River.

#5...LaCrosse, Wisconsin

LaCrosse is located at mile 695 on the upper Mississippi River. It was a large river port in the 1800s with as many as two hundred steamboats landing each month. There is a 600-foot bluff at LaCrosse called "Grandad Bluff". The view of the city and the river from the top of this bluff is spectacular, and it is worth walking the steep trail to the top. LaCrosse shows the same pride as many of the upper Mississippi River communities, as indicated by its clean streets and well-kept buildings. The riverfront is a beautiful park with a well-designed landing to accommodate large and small craft. A walk around the park will take one downtown, past sculptures, and to a nice river museum. Landing the steamboats at LaCrosse is always a pleasure, as we are greeted by many local people, including a local band for entertainment. The charming steamboat *Julia Belle Swain* is located at LaCrosse and offers day and dinner cruises. There are marinas and many pleasure boats in the area. LaCrosse captured me with its charm.

#6...Natchez, Mississippi

Natchez sits about two hundred feet above the lower Mississippi River at mile 364. It is the oldest settlement on the Mississippi River, dating back to 1716. The boat landing is called "Under the Hill", and at one time it was a rough and tough river port, complete with brothels, bars, and swindlers. The oldest tavern in Mississippi is still operating, conveniently located at the landing. When cotton was king, Natchez became the home of the wealthy plantation owners who built grand antebellum mansions, many of which have been preserved and are well worth seeing. For boaters there is neither marina nor fuel at Natchez, but one can land along the foot of Silver Street. Natchez is a busy tourist spot, but handles it very well. While walking the streets of Natchez, one can easily visualize fancy carriages and ladies in hoop skirts. On our steamboat journeys on the Lower Mississippi, we never pass by Natchez without stopping.

#7...Bluffton, Indiana

Not many people have heard of Bluffton. It is a small town in northeastern Indiana where the tiny headwaters of the Wabash River flow through it at mile 66. The people of Bluffton recognize their river heritage and have done much to make the river as much a part of the community as their courthouse. Bluffton created the River Greenway, a series of parks and adjacent roadway that follows the river. As is at many headwaters, the river there can be very shallow and rocky or become a mighty torrent after heavy rains. Bluffton has several easy access points for canoeists. While canoeing through Bluffton, I was greeted by wonderful people who offered their generosity to me. I was so taken by the beauty and the people of Bluffton that when writing the Wabash River Guide book, I called it the "Star City of the Wabash".

#8...Paducah, Kentucky

Paducah is strategically located on the Ohio River at mile 934 and mile 0 of the Tennessee River whose mouth is at Paducah. Only twelve miles upriver is the mouth of the Cumberland River, flowing into the Ohio. Forty-five miles downriver is the confluence of the Ohio and lower Mississippi rivers. Four major rivers within fifty-seven miles have been a major factor in making Paducah an important port and maritime center. It is rightfully called "River City". Many towns have flood walls, as does Paducah. The difference there are the beautiful paintings on the inside of the wall. Each section is masterfully painted with scenes depicting Paducah's past and present. When we land the steamboats there, the Red Coats appear. These are volunteers who show up in red coats or shirts to greet passengers and offer any assistance to them or the crew. The landing at Paducah is busy and very close to downtown. There are many shops, a great river museum, and many other things to see and do there. I often judge a town by the friendliness of its people, and remember a time when I walked from my boat a fair distance to a small store for supplies. The owner asked his wife to watch the counter so that he could load my supplies into his car and take me back to the landing. Now that's what I call good people in a great town!

#9...Burlington, Iowa

Burlington is a city of about 27,000 people, located at mile 401 on the upper Mississippi River. It is larger than some of the towns discussed here, but has the convenience and friendliness of a smaller town. One of the outstanding features at Burlington is the boat landing. There is a wonderful Welcome Center right at the landing, complete with friendly volunteers, coffee, historical information, maps, and a computer for visitors to check their email on. Every river town should have a Welcome Center like this. It is an easy walk into a city that has about anything one might need. Burlington is known for Snake Alley, which is listed in Ripley's

Believe it or Not as the "Crookedest Street in the World". It was designed as an experimental street in 1894. I walked the 275- foot-long street, that ascends 58-feet, and can verify that it really is crooked and steep. The Heritage Hills Historic District consists of twenty-nine blocks of Victorian homes and is truly beautiful. Nice people, clean city, and easy access make Burlington my kind town.

#10...Chattanooga, Tennessee

Chattanooga is located on one of the most beautiful sections of river in the country. Located at mile 464 on the Tennessee River, Chattanooga has revitalized their riverfront with matching beauty. Completed in 2005, the river park, docks, and landing facilities are second to none. Access to the city is easy, there are plenty of marinas, and it has been my experience that the people are friendly and have great pride in their city. There are incredible fresh water and salt water aquariums near the riverfront. All along the river there are nice walkways and things to do and see. The steamboat landing is beautiful and efficient. Congratulations go to Chattanooga for recognizing their river heritage and making their riverfront a wonderful asset to the city. I hope other cities will follow their example.

Honorable Mention

Terre Haute, Indiana, is the largest city on the Wabash River at mile 300, and where I grew up. During the past thirty years, the city has made great progress with water quality, riverfront improvements, and the creation of more river-related activities.

Dubuque, Iowa, on the upper Mississippi River, has completed a multi-million dollar project of riverfront improvement. This includes the new National River Museum, a beautiful new landing for passenger boats, and other great things to keep its river heritage alive.

Nachitoches, Louisiana, is located on the Cane River, which really isn't a river, but an old Red River channel that closed off. Nachitoches is about as pretty a town as one will find, with the Cane River meandering through the park-like downtown.

Red Wing, Minnesota, is a busy river port for mostly recreational boats. Like LaCrosse it has a park-like riverfront and easy access to the well-kept city. Many marinas are at Red Wing, which explains the large number of big cruisers and houseboats. The area surrounding Red Wing has some of the most outstanding scenery on the Mississippi River.

Hannibal, Missouri, is a tourist town on the upper Mississippi River, with its claim to fame being the home of Mark Twain. Even with embellishments of Mr. Clemens, it is still very quaint. It has a nice landing and easy access to town. Twain's Hannibal is a must stop if traveling by boat or car.

St. Charles, Missouri, is a lovely and historic community along the Missouri River. The fine folks of St. Charles have kept their heritage intact and provide visitors with a user-friendly riverfront along Big Muddy. (Yes, Big Muddy is the Missouri River).

Defiance, Ohio, is located on the Maumee River in northwestern Ohio. Besides my admiration of its rebellious-sounding name, the town is very pretty and has maintained the Maumee as part of its charm. Nice parks and an amazing Gothic-style library are situated at the fork of the Auglaize River. My canoe trip to Lake Erie was highlighted by my stop at Defiance.

A town need not be particularly beautiful to leave a good impression with me. It doesn't need to have historical significance. It is people who make the difference, and I have fond memories of towns that have people who treated me kindly. Even if a community does not have the funds to offer a fancy dock or riverfront park, it is all right with me. A town may be suffering from economic decay and not be as clean as we would appreciate, but the people we meet can make the difference. Towns like West Point, Kentucky, and Wellsburg, West Virginia, have people who treated some stranger with respect and kindness, so I am left with warm thoughts of those places. The nice fellow in a pickup truck who gave me a ride back to the boat with full cans of gas will forever leave me feeling good about New Harmony, Indiana. A little kindness goes a long way.

*Author's note: I did go back to Clifton, Tennessee by car. The town was just as clean and the people were just as nice to a stranger.

Chapter 20

Canoeing Misadventures

Even though I use a variety of powerboats, I still enjoy floating down a river in a canoe. It is the closest one can get to being at one with the river. Whether it is a silent drift on a meandering river or shooting rapids in a rocky stream, the canoe provides the means to let the power of water propel one into beauty and adventure. I had heard that the Hiwasee River in Tennessee was a nice float with mild rapids. Since I needed to get away for a few days, it seemed like a good place to go. I loaded my canoe and gear and found a small motel near Lake Hiwasee, where I would put in just below the dam. This made a convenient place to leave my vehicle. Soon after arriving, I put in and discovered that what I had heard was true. It was indeed a beautiful river in the foothills of the Smokey Mountains.

Since I had pushed off late in the afternoon, I did not intend to go very far the first night before making camp. The current was fairly swift and the river was narrow and winding. Then it suddenly widened and split around a gravel-bar island. After pulling up to the island to do some fossil hunting, I began assessing it as a possible campsite. I enjoy camping on islands with water rushing on either side. Islands also provide more security from human intrusion than do riverbank camps. There was no significant high ground and the river appeared to be on a slow rise, but I decided to make camp there anyway. Taking care to prepare for rising waters, I secured the beached canoe with a line tied to an auger, then drove a stick in at the water's edge to keep an eye on any changes in the level. That night I sat by the campfire enjoying the beauty and sounds of this wonderful place, oblivious to what was happening upstream.

The Hiwasee flows from the mountains into a lake, then through the control dam and back into the river again. There had been some rain in the mountains and in preparation for that, more water than usual was let through the lake. I turned in that night with an uneasy feeling. I checked the stick again, but the level appeared to be rising at a slow enough rate that it would not be a problem by morning. Still, I planned to check it about every two hours during the night. Three hours after falling asleep I got out my flashlight and aimed the beam in the direction of the stick, noticing that the river was noisier than it had been. The stick was nowhere in sight. I jumped out of the tent to find the river rising very rapidly, carrying a lot of debris. At that rate I knew that it would not be long before my camp would be swept away. My canoe was now floating and I was glad that I had tied it off. Breaking camp quickly, I loaded the canoe in the dark and pushed off to find higher ground. Canoeing down a swift river at night in the company of floating logs is not my idea of a relaxing float, and was certainly not something I had expected to do.

My plan was to get off the island and reach the shore, then get out of the river until daylight. From what I could see (which was little), the closer bank on the inside bend was too steep. I needed to get to the opposite bank, which appeared to have easier access. The problem was that the outside bend was where the current was the strongest. As soon as I got into that bend, I knew I was in trouble. I did not have the strength to reach the bank, and the canoe had spun broadside to the current. I fought to straighten out, and was just beginning to get control when the worst thing that could be imagined happened. I was swept into a logjam. The canoe hit the first log broadside and flipped over, drawing the boat and myself under the tangled logs. By the time I realized what had happened, I found myself pinned underwater against a submerged tree limb. To make matters worse, the bottom of the canoe was pushing against me with the open side facing the current. The powerful force of the water held me tight between the canoe and the tree. I was struggling in the dark, raging, cold water; not even knowing which way was up. My mind was racing between getting out of this mess and thinking, "This is it."

I'm not certain what happened next. Either the canoe shifted or I twisted my body into a different position. In any event, my body was stuck sideways and suddenly I was facing toward the front. The front of my torso is not as thick as sideways, so when I got into that position there was enough room to get out and I was set free. My daughter later claimed that my guardian angel was with me, and I couldn't deny that. My life jacket lifted me to the surface and

I was able to fill my lungs with wonderful fresh air. I was still in the logjam and not out of trouble yet. I hung on for quite some time recovering my strength. It wasn't until then that I noticed that I had never let go of my paddle. I needed to work my way to shore and get out of the cold water. Even though I didn't feel cold yet, I knew that it was dangerously cold and would not take long for hypothermia to take hold. I slowly began to work my way to shore, then was able to climb onto a tree limb that was still attached to a downed tree on shore. This happened to be the tree limb that had held me under the water. I continued to slowly work my way up the tree trunk until I was finally able to plant my feet on dry ground. I made it! I was alive!

The moonless night was pitch black, but warm. After a short time I was still wet but warmed up and assessing my situation. I could see no canoe or gear and was not about to chance going back after it, even if I had seen it. I remembered going under a bridge a few miles upstream from my campsite, so that seemed the logical place to go. Hiking along the river's edge had its own hazards. I stumbled and fell often on the rocks and undergrowth. During one fall I hit my eye on the stub of a broken limb. I remember seeing a white flash, then feeling warm blood coming from the injury. My paddle was helpful in keeping me from several falls. As I came to a wide spot in the river, I could see that my former campsite was now completely under water.

About two more hours passed and the sun was beginning to rise when I finally made it to the bridge. The sunlight felt good as I began the walk back to the motel. A nice fellow name Bob pulled over to offer me a ride in his truck, which I graciously accepted. My life jacket and paddle gave him a clue that I was a canoeist who might need a ride. When I climbed into the truck he could tell by my eye and torn clothing that I was not having a great time. We arrived at the motel and I went straight to the room to get my damp clothes off. I was hungry and most of all exhausted, so I took a wonderful hot shower and went to bed. It was 7 am when I lay down, thinking of taking a short nap. I slept until 3 pm, after which I spent a good deal of time reflecting on my mishap and feeling grateful to be alive. The canoe and gear were probably gone, but I would get to see my family again. Ironically, before leaving for this trip my wife jokingly said, "Have fun and don't lose your canoe". I called her to let her know that I did exactly that.

Bob had given me his phone number and said I was welcome to call him if I wanted to try to recover the canoe. It was getting late in the day and I wasn't ready to go back there just yet, but I called and he agreed to go back to the river the next morning and check it out. He said he knew where the logjam was and could get pretty close to it with his truck. We planned to meet in the morning. By 7 pm it dawned on me that I had not eaten since the day before, so I bought a box of fried chicken and relaxed in front of the TV for the rest of the evening. Bob showed up right on time the next morning. He was well equipped with ropes, life jackets, hand winch, and other useful gear. He knew that stretch of river and with amazing accuracy. He drove across a field, through a wooded area, and even crossed a creek to arrive within a few hundred feet of the logjam.

I looked down the steep bank at the swollen river and the logjam, which had even more debris piled against it. I realized again how lucky I was to have survived and that I could have still been down there below the logs in the cold water. The only thing visible was a yellow nylon rope that was snagged on a tree limb. I recognized the rope and was hoping that my canoe was still attached to the other end of it. If it was, we might be able to grab hold and simply pull it out from under the logjam. Bob was an incredible fellow of about fifty years old, and in great physical condition. He was ready to jump in then and there to fetch the canoe, but I convinced him that it was not worth the risk. If we couldn't get it safely, we would leave it. I had had enough adventure for a while. The alternative was to work my way down the tree limb and attach a line to the yellow rope, then try to pull or winch the canoe out. I attached a lifeline to my waste in case I slipped, and then carefully inched along the tree limb. The closer I got to the logjam, the more frightening my thoughts became of that night. I was able to reach the yellow rope and upon tugging it, found that it was indeed attached to something. I attempted to pull on it but it wouldn't budge. After tying the line from shore to the rope, I made my way back to the bank. First we tried pulling by hand with no luck. Then attached a hand winch to a tree and then hooked the line to it. We cranked until the tension on the line was very tight, but there was still no movement. We decided that one of several things could happen. The canoe could eventually come loose, the line could break, or the canoe would be pulled apart. Any of those things would leave me no worse than I was so we kept cranking. Suddenly there was a snap and the line went limp. I said, "Well that's it", assuming the line broke at the canoe. Bob started cranking the winch to bring in the cable, but then said that it was still hooked to something. Then the blue bow of the canoe surfaced between some floating logs. We pulled it as close to shore as possible, and then were able to dump it over to make it light enough to drag up the steep bank. Most of my gear was still onboard and tied down.

We hauled the canoe and gear to the truck and were on our way. I bought my new friend lunch and we celebrated our successful mission. Later I headed out for my eight-hour drive home from the shortest and most dangerous canoe trip of my life. I was thankful to be alive and would have gone home satisfied with that, but thanks to a river rat name Bob, I was returning with my favorite canoe.

Lessons Learned: My enjoyment of the island overpowered my common sense. I was reading the river and it was giving me the warning signs, but I chose to take the risk and camp in a place that I knew was susceptible to flooding. A wiser choice would have been to go on to higher ground. Even though breaking camp and putting in at night was my only choice, I should have paddled toward the inside bend, where the current wasn't as strong. My choice of the outside bend was because that is usually higher ground, but reaching the closest shore would have been safer. My course should have been toward the closer and milder side. I have learned from past experience that the paddle is a very important piece of equipment. That statement may sound obvious, but it can serve other purposes in addition to steering a canoe. The paddle can become a pry bar, a crutch, a life-saving grabbing device, or a weapon. In hind-site, I should have waited until daylight to hike back to the bridge. The walk in the dark was very dangerous and there was no reason to hurry out of there. I was warm, unhurt, and should have waited until morning. I received more cuts and bruises from the walk than I did from the logjam. Sometimes our instincts can be of great benefit to us, particularly those instincts that develop from experience. Then there are those times when instincts, like grabbing for safety that isn't there, blindly heading for high ground, or immediately fleeing a place of fearful experience, is not as reliable as thought and logic. The best that we can hope for is the selective use of both these qualities. I believe that instinct is our alarm system, but that logic is our salvation.

Another canoe trip that I had been thinking of making for quite some time would take me from the Wabash River to Lake Erie. This would be a trip that no one has done, so far as I know. The main reason for that is because few people realize that there is a waterway connection between them. In the mid-1800s there had been a navigable connection via the Wabash-Erie Canal, which connected the

Maumee and St. Mary's rivers to the Little River at Fort Wayne, Indiana. The Maumee flows to Lake Erie and the Little River flows to the Wabash. Since the closing and filling in of the canal that connected the two rivers, it has been assumed that the waterway connection was severed. During my research of the Wabash River headwaters years before, I found what appeared on maps to be a connection. Beaver Creek flows into the Wabash in the state of Ohio, from Grande Lake. On the other side of Grande Lake is a feeder canal. This canal was built to supply water to the St. Mary's River and Miami-Erie Canal. St. Mary's River flows north to Ft. Wayne, where it is joined by the St. Joseph River and becomes the Maumee River. The Maumee then flows to Toledo and Lake Erie. I decided to drive as much as I could along the route to scout it. While scouting the trip I found several challenges, mostly in the form of dams to portage, but the journey still seemed feasible. There was a waterway connection and I wanted to navigate it.

As with other journeys, this required much planning and good timing. Water levels were important, even with a canoe, since parts of Beaver Creek dry up during low water and many bridges are too low in high water. The trip of nearly 300 miles would not be easy and would take around two weeks. In April of 2002

Photo by Author
Wabash River near Bluffton

all conditions looked favorable. The spring rise was mild and good weather was forecast for at least a week. The logical place to begin was Bluffton Indiana. I have a friend in Bluffton who agreed to keep my truck and pick me up at the end of the journey. Much of the trip is upstream and I would have to navigate four rivers, a canal, and a lake, so I took a small outboard motor for the upstream portions. I met my friend at Bluffton and put-in as planned. Just above Bluffton the river is shallow and rocky in places. I started out using my motor for this section, destroying my prop within six miles. I put on my spare prop, aware that it had to last much longer. I had to be more careful. There are no dams on the Wabash from Bluffton to the mouth of Beaver Creek, so at least there would be no portaging in that section.

The next morning I awoke to the sound of rain spattering on my tent. I thought, "so much for the weather forecast". Rain or not, I had to move on and by midday had reached Beaver Creek, which is actually a ditch that was dug from Grande Lake as an

Photo by Author
Beaver Creek

overflow into the Wabash River. Some sources call Grande Lake and Beaver Creek the source of the Wabash River. This is not possible, since the artificial lake was built as a reservoir for the Miami-Erie Canal in 1835 and the Wabash was formed thousands of years ago. As my motor pushed the canoe up the creek, the rain continued. I reached the overflow dam and set up

camp, hoping the rain would end during the night and that the winds might subside before crossing the seven-mile-wide lake. The following morning the rain stopped for a while, but the wind was fairly strong from the southwest. I decided to skirt the lake instead of crossing the open choppy waters. This made a greater distance, but was far safer in a canoe. I was glad to have the motor.

After making my way across the lake, I portaged the dam to the feeder canal. Portaging at dams is very difficult with a 109-pound canoe, a 70-pound motor, fuel, and supplies. It took several trips to manage this at each dam, and I wondered if I might be getting too old for this stuff. The rain returned before I could get across the lake. I got to the feeder canal and carried my canoe and gear into it. The canal was choked with water lilies, so I could not use the motor. I had to paddle, push, and pull the canoe for a couple of miles. The canal leads to the St. Mary's River then downstream. Once on the St. Mary's, I removed the motor and stowed it in the bow of the canoe. It continued to rain sporadically, and the St. Mary's River was rising.

On my second night on the St. Mary's, I made camp in an unusual place. It was an abandoned silo with a good roof, located on high ground and reasonably dry inside. I was interrupted a few times by visits of some nocturnal critters, but for the most part we co-existed in peace. Compared to the previous night of rain and mud, this habitat was a luxury. The river was still rising, but not at an alarming rate. Just to be safe I had dragged to canoe to the silo. The next morning I found a swollen river with swift waters, and a lot of

Photo by Author

Feeder Canal

debris floating down it. Knowing that there were low bridges ahead, and that the river was rising at nearly flash- flood rates, I decided to end the trip. I would float to the next bridge and call my friend to pick me up. I did not want to cancel the trip, but understood how dangerous small rivers can be during flash flooding and wanted no part of it. The rain finally stopped, but that didn't mean that the river would stop rising.

The current was even faster than it appeared as I made my way to a take-out point. Having scouted the river, I knew that the upcoming bridge was low, so I planned to take out well above it. The bridge is just below a tight bend in the river. As the canoe rounded the bend, I was unable to paddle it to shore in time. The current swept me toward the bridge. There were only a few inches of clearance under the bridge, and not enough clearance to allow the canoe to pass beneath. As the canoe hit the bridge broadside, I grabbed the railing on the iron bridge and quickly pulled myself up. I expected the canoe to be drawn under the bridge, but it caved in against it, held by the current. I was able to lie down on the bridge and reach it. I did not have the strength to move the canoe, but was able to retrieve my waterproof pack and outboard motor. Then a large floating tree rammed the canoe, taking it under the bridge. I watched what was left of the canoe and gear come up the other side and tumble down the river. I had my cell phone in the waterproof pack, so after some recovery time I called my friend in Bluffton to come and get me (technology has its place). During the three-hour wait for my ride, the river began to overflow the bridge and spill over its banks. My well-planned two-week trip ended on the fifth day. At this writing I still plan to make that trip. I will put in where I left off and make it to Lake Erie, come hell or high water, (OK, maybe not high water).

Lessons learned: Never rely completely on weather forecasts. I should have not gotten back onto the river that morning at the silo. It was a remote location and not near any roads, but walking out of there without the canoe would have been much safer. I could have stashed the canoe and other gear to retrieve later. While canoe and gear can be replaced, life cannot.

The next misadventure is one that I should not even admit to. I did several things that went against my better judgment. In fact, it makes me wonder why my favorite quote is, "I don't make the same mistake twice; I'm too busy making new ones." In fairness to myself, I will say that even though I was aware of some things that could go wrong, it was my first experience with a kayak, so that could account for some accuracy in the quote.

It all started one day when I was driving some back roads in western Indiana, not far from my home on the Wabash River. I had often crossed a small tributary to the Wabash called Raccoon Creek. It is normally a mild, rock-bottomed stream but that day it was different. The creek was roaring with water, even though there had been no significant rainfall. There is a large earth dam upstream from the bridge, and I assumed that excess water must have been let out in preparation for the winter pool, which results in a lower lake level. I was fascinated by the water and thought about canoeing the rapids. Then I thought about making a little trip of it by putting in at this spot and canoeing down to the confluence of the Wabash, which would take me back home. I couldn't be certain just how long this amount of water would be released through the dam gates, so I drove to the dam to ask. The Corp of Engineers' office is the place to find out and upon locating someone there I was told that it would be at the current flow rate for three more days. I went back to the bridge and watched the water for a while. From my previous experiences with rapids, I decided that I should not try to canoe these waters, but began to consider kayaking them. I had never used a kayak before, but I had witnessed their amazing maneuverability. I have even seen them paddled back upstream in the eddies, then turn around to shoot rapids again. It seemed a kayak would be the right boat for these waters, and I had a friend who owned one. The creek was calling my name and the water would be back to normal in a few days.

My friend Mark said that if a seasoned riverman like me couldn't handle a little kayak, no one could. He confidently provided the vessel and accessories for my expedition. The kayak looked very small, but it had a fairly wide beam which, while making it a less maneuverable, would also cause it to be more stable. The kayak also had a skirt to fit around the cockpit and the paddler's waist to keep water from coming in. My first thought was that I did not want to be strapped into a little plastic bowl upside down. I wanted to be able to bail out if the going got rough. My quickly formed plan was to have my son take me to the bridge to drop me off. I would then paddle the thirty miles down Raccoon Creek to the Wabash River. Once reaching the Wabash I would camp overnight, then paddle downriver to my home the next day, which is another thirty miles.

The next morning we drove to the creek. Upon our arrival the first thing I discovered was that there is not much room for storage in the little kayak. I am accustomed to pitching about anything I need easily into a canoe, then tying it down in case of an upset. Very little could be shoved into the hull of the kayak and still allow me to have any legroom. The solution would be to bungee my packs and camping gear on top of the kayak, both in front of the cockpit and behind it. Finally ready to go, we slid the heavy kayak into the water, which sat much deeper in the water than I had expected. With Darin's assistance I got into the kayak as it precariously rolled back and forth in the swift water. Once I was finally in, the distance between the water and the cockpit opening was only a few inches. The vessel was definitely top-heavy with the gear on top, but there was no place else to stow it. Upon getting sense of the instability of the vessel, I decided to put the life jacket on before pushing off.

Darin waved goodbye as I was swept away in the current. I started to turn and wave but the kayak began to roll. I quickly turned forward and regained the critical balance I would apparently need to keep the thing upright. It was beautiful weather with foliage beginning to turn. After a few miles I got used to the boat and began practicing some close-quarter maneuvers in the event quick action was needed. I made two miles, then five miles before the call of nature came. I needed to relieve myself, which meant that I would have to pull the kayak over, extract myself, and then re-enter with no help. I swung the boat around upstream and headed for a shoreline eddy, very pleased with myself as the boat skidded along the bank to a stop directly under a low-hanging limb. I attached a line from the kayak to a root, lifted myself out of the cockpit with the overhead limb, stretched one leg toward the bank, and made it to shore with a little hop. After taking care of business I went back on the limb and carefully lowered myself into the cockpit, which was much easier than trying to step into the kayak from shore. I set off again.

The current was even faster than at the bridge and I was having a good time. I passed under a beautiful covered bridge and was very pleased with my little journey so far. Then things begin to happen that put a damper on my joy. Upon rounding a bend I could see nothing but green to the water's edge. A tree had recently fallen, but was held up by other trees across the stream. Long limbs still full of leaves were dangling down to and into the water like a giant green curtain. I immediately paddled hard to the left bank into an eddy and held my position. I had choices to make. I could take out and portage around the obstruction, or get the kayak straight and push through the limbs, which appeared limber with the force of the water thrashing them about. I should have gotten out of the boat and walked the bank to see beyond the brush, but that would have meant getting out and back into the kayak. I decided to give it a try and slip through the weakest-looking limbs. I made sure everything was tied down and thought I checked my waterproof packs. The water was moving very fast and was very noisy. I took a deep breath and paddled upstream in the eddy as far as I could so that I could get turned around in time to head straight into the limbs. I did not want to go into that curtain broadside and roll the kayak over.

When it was time to turn around I shot out into the current and paddled hard on the right side to spin the boat about. I did that very well; in fact I did it too well. The kayak swung around and kept on swinging. I tried to stabilize by back-paddling, but it was no use. I was being swept into those trees broadside. I lay forward to keep a low profile and avoid having my body catch any limbs still hoping to push through. My efforts were futile as the kayak hung for a few seconds on the limbs, then tipped to the left. As soon as it tipped far enough for the water to start pouring into the cockpit, the kayak rolled over. I bailed out and the current pulled me through the brush. Then things got worse. Only about fifty feet below the curtain of limbs was a blowdown. This is a tree that has fallen across the river with roots still attached. The tree had come to rest in the creek near the surface, with about half of the trunk in the creek. Water was being drawn under the trunk and was rolling over the top of it. I knew I was in trouble, particularly since I had already experienced the dangers of getting drawn under a logjam. My only thought was getting myself over that log, not drawn under it. I didn't know how much brush might be under there to capture and hold me. As I hit the tree trunk my wind was nearly knocked out, but I already had one leg up. The current pinned me against the trunk and was trying to pull me down, but I continued to hold on and wiggle my way over the top. With my strength nearly gone I finally succeeded and slithered over the log like a snake.

I was so grateful to be free of the obstruction that I had no concern about the kayak and gear. I was focused on getting to shore. As soon as I slipped over the trunk I swam hard to the left bank and climbed up, exhausted. As I lay there recuperating, I began to wonder about the rest of the stuff. I sat up and looked back at the would-be tomb and saw that the kayak had hung up on the blowdown. It was swamped with the current keeping it pinned against the trunk as it had me, with the open cockpit facing upstream. I really wanted to retrieve the vessel but had already made up my mind that I would not get back into those raging waters. After studying the situation awhile, I noticed that the fallen tree extended from bank to bank and came out of the water near the left bank. If I could straddle it and carefully work my way out to the kayak, I might be able to free it. After all, I would already be on top of the trunk so the worst that could happen would to be swept off into the stream below it. As I made my plan I watched some of my gear from the kayak float down past me. I hoped to catch up with it after completing my mission.

After walking along the left bank to the tree, I carefully got past some large limbs and sat down, straddling the trunk with my legs in the water. The water felt much colder than it had during my first time in. Fortunately, there were no more limbs sticking up between me and the kayak, giving me a clear path to it. Keeping my legs tight against the two-foot diameter trunk, I leaned forward on my hands, and then slid forward a few inches at a time. By the time I got near the kayak, the water was rolling over the trunk and up to my belt. When I reached the swamped kayak I tried in vain to pull it over the log, but it was much too heavy with the water in it. I managed to shift it around, causing more things to float out of the cockpit, including my wallet, which I snatched before it sank. I had to bail some water out of the kayak in order to get it over the half-submerged trunk. My cooler was still held down by bungee cords on the top of the kayak so I pulled the cords sideways enough to open the cooler and found the only thing with which to bail. I pulled out a can of soda, took a few swallows, and then ripped the top off the can. Now I had a bailing bucket. The kayak had to be repositioned to stop water from re-filling it, which I was finally able to do with difficulty. As I reached into the cockpit for each can full I had to hold on with the other hand and both legs to stay on the log. I bailed and bailed and bailed for at least thirty minutes, to get enough water out to move the kayak. When I thought I could shove the it over the trunk, I tied the line from the kayak to myself determined that it would not go down the steam without me. With all my strength, I gave a mighty pull and dragged the boat over the trunk and into the swift water below. It was a great thrust that pulled it over, so great that I was pulled back into the water with the kayak. I quickly swam ashore again, this time with the kayak in tow.

I reached the same place along the left bank again, and then pulled the kayak to me. The top-heavy loads had shifted a great deal, and as I pulled the boat rolled over, hanging upside down. Something below the surface had caught hold of the cargo. I had to go back in the water again to set it free. The stream bottom was mud—deep mud. It was pulling me down while the rush of water was trying to pull me downstream. When I reached the kayak I flipped it back over and shifted the load back to near center. As I walked the kayak toward the bank, I suddenly sank into deep mud to my knees. I kept my grip on the kayak, but it tipped sideways and filled with water again. There I was, stuck in the mud holding onto the swamped boat. I struggled to free myself and to keep the kayak from getting away. Nonetheless, it did break away but the line was still attached around my waist. I wondered if I had survived the blowdown just to starve to death stuck in the mud. With great effort I finally pulled my feet from the mud, minus my shoes, which I didn't need as much as I needed to get the boat and myself to shore. Upon reaching the bank again I repeated the process of pulling the kayak toward me. It was full of water, but at least it had remained upright.

Photo by Author

Swamped kayak and loose gear

Again I had to recuperate and plan my next move. As far as I could see down the stream there were no obstacles. Barefoot, I carefully walked around the next bend to check it out. I took what was left of my gear out of the kayak, emptied it of water, and found my waterlogged cell phone in the process. Some of my waterproof packs had kept the contents dry, and some did not. I changed into dry clothes and repacked the gear and kayak. I was hesitant to move on, but really had no choice. I hoped there would be no more obstacles like this to deal with, and also decided that any more obstructions would be dealt with by portaging around them. I put in, again with great difficulty, as the little plastic boat tried to tip, and set off down the rapid stream.

Only an hour or so later I came to a serious logjam that appeared to choke the entire stream. The pileup was so thick that it effectively dammed the stream, and the rapid current was eroding the bank and cutting a new channel along the right bank. I could have risked taking the chute of the new channel, but decided not to. Having had enough swift water excitement, I swung around and landed along the right bank, well above the chute. The bank was very steep and would be difficult to portage, so I walked along the bank with a line attached to the boat. This allowed the boat to slip through the chute without me in it. If it tipped over, at least I would be on shore with the attached line. That plan went very smoothly and I re-entered the kayak below the natural dam. I was already behind my schedule, and had to portage around two more logjams. Both were accomplished with great difficulty, but no serious incidents. By then it was getting late in the day, and my mission then turned to finding a place to camp. With the high water, there had been no sandbars on which to camp. That is when the storm hit.

The storm came in from the west so fast that it caught me by surprise. I had no place to go, as the high muddy banks could not be ascended. When I spotted a tree near the bank in some slack water I turned about and headed for it. I know that trees are not the best things to hug during a storm, but it was either that or continue in such hard rain and wind that I could not see a safe distance ahead of me. One thing that I really wanted to do was to be able to see any more obstacles as far ahead as possible. I stayed in the kayak holding on to a tree limb until the storm passed and became a gentle rain. I needed to relieve myself again, but was not going to try to exit the kayak along the muddy riverbank. I would also have enjoyed stretching my legs after such a long confinement in the kayak. It would be dark soon and I needed a place to camp.

Finally, some luck came my way in the form of a large sandbar with high ground on an inside bend of the stream. I celebrated the arrival by drinking as much water as I wanted without worrying about disposing of it from my body. It was very hot and humid and had it not been for the swarms of mosquitoes, I would have not used my tent. After setting it up I found that my sleeping bag was drenched. The waterproof bag had gotten torn. Then I found a worse problem. I could sleep in the hot, wet tent and endure the discomforts of insects, but my coffee was ruined and my pot was missing.

Those press-and-seal bags do not seal very well, and all I had were lumps of coffee dough. This was not a good thing. I did still had my thermos, but that was only because I make my coffee the night before so that I can reach for it when I wake. I know this is pathetic, but I really need my coffee meditation in the morning. Then I can go all day without it. It was difficult to get a fire started with wet wood, but I finally sacrificed an article of dry clothing as a starter and got a warm fire going. With the fire I was able to somewhat dry out the sleeping bag, but it was still very damp. Now for the coffee issue! I had coffee dough, but no filters, nor a pot to perk it in. I did have a small cooking pot for boiling water, a thermos, and a spare sock.

Photo by Author

Camp along Raccoon Creek

As the water came to a boil I filled the sock with the wet coffee grounds and dipped it into the water. In just a few minutes I had black water. I continued to swirl the sock around in the pot to make certain that I got all the coffee juice I could get. I then poured the brew into the thermos and felt relieved that I would survive the next morning. I slept pretty well that night, considering that I had to lie nude on top of a damp sleeping bag. Another storm rolled through during the night, but I was on high ground and felt comfortable about my location, and had no problems.

Morning came and I woke to sunshine and the strongest coffee I had ever tasted. It was delicious! I wasn't sure how far I was from the confluence with the Wabash River, but I was anxious to get on it. I know the Wabash and was ready to get off this unpredictable logjam-ridden stream. After breaking camp and putting the site back the way I found it, I moved on and all went pretty smoothly on my two-hour journey to the Wabash. I celebrated the arrival at the big river, but the curse that was apparently put on this trip was not over yet. It had become extremely hot with a strong south wind. I still had thirty miles to go and intended to get home that day. One of the items that survived the blowdown was a large umbrella. I had brought it along in case I found a nice beach on which to lounge and shade myself, while peacefully reading a book. I never found that peace and the book was one of my contributions to Raccoon Creek. I opened the umbrella to shade myself, since I had lost my hat, sun screen and sunglasses. I had a difficult time trying to bungee the umbrella handle down to provide shade, so I attempted to hold it by running the stem through my shirt and between my legs while I paddled. Each time I finally got it positioned, the wind caught it and sailed the

kayak upriver as I paddled downriver. I gave up on this device
and suffered the sun.

Paddling against the wind was difficult, even with the low-pro-
file container I was in. I was getting exhausted and had to drink a
great deal of water, which meant more stops that I would have preferred not to have to make. I was getting better at extracting myself
from the vessel, but entry was still a challenge. I was about twenty
miles from home when I heard something that sounded like an airplane coming down the river. It was a fellow I know named Jack,
who is often seen on the river with his airboat, a flat-bottomed boat
with a large propeller on the stern that is most commonly used in
southern swamps and bayous. Jack pulled up and we chatted for a
while. He asked if I would like to ride in his boat, since he was going
my way. I gratefully accepted his offer, more than ready to end my
journey. Finally some good luck! We unloaded the kayak and stowed
the gear on the little airboat, then put the kayak across the beam.
At first we considered towing the kayak, but decided it would probably swamp. Once the airboat is on plane it would run at about thirty miles per hour. I would be home within the hour. Or so I thought.
Jack pushed the boat to high idle, then half throttle, then full throttle, but we were barely moving. Something was wrong. An airboat
must get on plane to move. That means most of the hull must be on
top of the water and not in it, or the resistance against the hull is
too great. The additional weight of the kayak, the gear, and me was
too much for the little airboat. We shifted some weight around, but
to no avail. The airboat was making no better time than the kayak
did, and using up a lot of his limited fuel. We had to remove the
kayak, reload my gear, and set me off to get home the hard way. I
thanked him for his efforts and watched as Jack's little airboat
popped up on plane and sped down the river.

I pressed on in the wind and the heat. By late afternoon I landed at my home. To me it was as much of an oasis as one would experience after the drudgery of crossing a desert on foot. I pulled up to
my dock, made the last exit that I will ever make from a kayak,
headed straight for the shower, and slept through the evening and
all night. The plastic enclosure that I had been confined to would be
unloaded the next morning and returned to Mark.

Lessons Learned: Kayaks are different than canoes and are
great for handling rapids. A test run before I left would have shown
me that there was not enough space to properly stow the gear.
There are those more skillful than I who have no problems entering and exiting this type of vessel and who take long journeys in

them. I suppose a larger kayak would have been better for the amount of gear that was needed for an overnight journey. I should never have entered a section of river that I could not see. Even if the low-hanging limbs had not upset the kayak, I would still have been in trouble making contact with the half-submerged tree. I took a chance and was fortunate to survive by getting over the trunk. The correct thing to do would have been to get out and look beyond the obstruction, which is what I did upon approaching other such obstacles for the rest of the trip. Small creeks are dangerous at flood stage. I knew that, but it wasn't flooding. It was simply filling with water that was being released through a dam at a high rate. Why did I think that was any different? It is no different. I believe that clear thinking is what I lacked the day I decided to take the trip. A stream can appear clear from a bridge, but just around the bend it may have deadly traps. Portaging can be difficult, but paddling into the unknown can be deadly.

*Note from Author,

I would like to mention that the three stories told in this chapter were not my only canoe/kayak trips. I have made hundreds of other trips that went very smooth. I even canoed the rapids of the Colorado River from West Water Canyon to Moab, Utah, with no serious problems. I have paddled the entire five hundred miles of the Wabash and over four hundred miles of the White River, making good decisions and having safe journeys. I wanted to share these stories because they are interesting and provide lessons. Two things are most apparent in these stories. Even experienced canoeists can make little mistakes that are potentially disastrous. High water on little streams is dangerous, particularly with the presence of log-jams and low bridges.

Chapter 21

Grand Excursion 2004

The year 1854 saw the completion of the laying of railroad track from Chicago to Rock Island, Illinois. This was of great importance, since it meant that passengers could travel by rail all the way to the Mississippi River, from where they could board a steamboat bound for St. Paul, Minnesota, or to many destinations downriver.

Completion of this track was considered of national importance. No less a dignitary than President Millard Fillmore led the excursion of many notable persons, all of whom traveled from Chicago to Rock Island by rail. There they boarded palatial steamboats and headed upriver to St. Paul. There were a huge number of steamboats in the flotilla and boat owners were thrilled to have the railroad come to the river, providing additional passengers and freight for their business. That is, they were happy about it until the railroads begin to build bridges across the river, taking business from them and creating navigational hazards.

Many cities along the upper Mississippi River began planning a re-enactment of that excursion about ten years before the 150th anniversary of the event. It was a huge undertaking to organize and implement. From the Quad Cities to the Twin Cities the river portion of the excursion required the commitment of many cities, thousands of people, and boats. They needed many passenger boats to carry people who wanted to participate in all or part of the flotilla. The vessels officially participating in the event were the *Mississippi Queen, Delta Queen, Julia Belle Swain, Spirit of Peoria, Celebration Belle, Anson Northrup*, and *Harriet Bishop*. Private boats were also invited to join the flotilla.

I was disappointed to discover that I would be on vacation from my duties as Riverlorian on the *Mississippi Queen* during the Grand Excursion. I had known of the event for several years and looked forward to taking part in it, aboard one of the steamboats. The excursion would officially begin in late June and end on July 4th in St. Paul. I was scheduled to get on the *Mississippi Queen* on July 4th. I did make other plans for my time off in June, including a visit to one of the Lewis & Clark re-enactment camps in Booneville, Missouri, and a white-water rafting trip in Colorado. I also had a high school class reunion later in the month, but I still would have loved to have been part of the Grand Excursion.

With the excursion only a few weeks away, I received a voice mail message from the Great River Steamboat Company of LaCrosse, Wisconsin, which owns a beautiful little steamboat named the *Julia Belle Swain*. The message asked if I might be available to serve as Riverlorian on their boat for the Grand Excursion. After calling back and agreeing to serve as their speaker, I began to alter my other plans. I would still go rafting on the upper Arkansas River in Colorado, and would still visit some historic river sites on the way back, but would not be able to make it to my 40-year class reunion. Oh well! Maybe I'll see my classmates for the 50th. I know where my priorities are. I would not be able to board the boat at the beginning of the excursion at the Quad Cities (Bettendorf and Davenport on the Iowa side of the river and Rock Island and Moline on the Illinois side), but would catch up with it at Dubuque, Iowa, then stay with it to the Twin Cities (St. Paul and Minneapolis). This worked out great because I was scheduled to get on the *Mississippi Queen* at St. Paul. I would get off one boat and right on the other the same day, for my 30-day regular rotation. Little did I know that this would be the wackiest six days of steamboating that I have ever been on.

After arriving home from my journey out west, I spent two hours there before renting a car and heading for Dubuque. I was looking forward to the Grand Excursion and to riding the *Julia Belle Swain*, since she was to be one of only three real steamboats in the flotilla. The *Delta Queen* and *Mississippi Queen* actually began their cruises in St. Louis, with passengers taking an eleven-day cruise to St. Paul. One difference for me would be riding on a boat that is an excursion boat, with no overnight cabins. This would mean being transported to hotels each night, then being returned to the boat each morning for the next leg of the journey. Another challenge was the high water. The upper Mississippi valley had been experiencing a lot of rain, so the river was rising higher each day. This might pose a problem for the big steamboats that may not be able to get under some of the low bridges. I kept in close touch with the *Mississippi Queen* to see how she was doing. I really wanted her to participate in the flotilla, particularly since she was my ride back down the river.

While en route to Dubuque I called again to find that the *Mississippi Queen* could not get under the bridge at Hannibal, Missouri. She would wait there, hoping the river would fall enough to provide clearance. The smaller *Delta Queen* had barely gotten under the same bridge and was proceeding toward the Quad Cities. When I rented the car, the attendant had given me an address in Dubuque as a drop-off. The Great River Steamboat Company had given me the name of the hotel where they had reserved a room for me, so everything appeared to be well organized. I say appeared to be, but little did I know that upon my arrival at Dubuque, I would begin the least organized few days in my life.

My first challenge was finding the rental car drop-off. The street name was Collision Drive, an interesting street name for a car rental address. Thinking it may be the airport address, I went to the airport but there was no rental office for the company I had rented from and no one knew of any office for that company. In fact, no one had even heard of the street name. I drove into town and got

Photo by Author

Julia Belle Swain Steamboat

tangled up in a huge traffic jam of visitors to the Grand Excursion. There was so much traffic that parking facilities were set up in fields far from downtown and people were being shuttled to the various events. I stopped at a convenience store to get directions to Collision Drive. I got the same bewildered look and response, "What drive?" Than a mail carrier walked in and I felt saved. Surely a postal employee could help. He knew of no such address, but the numbers told him that it was well on the west side of the city. He did know of an auto body shop called Collision Center and suggested that they might rent cars there. I had rented the car from a well-known national company and thought that it was a slim chance, but had to try something. I called the company on my cell phone and all they could do was repeat the address with no information about how to find it. There was no listing for the company in the local phone directory.

I also called the hotel to confirm my reservation, after seeing how many thousands of people were in Dubuque. They had no record of my having a room, and no rooms available. I then called the boat company office to see what had gone wrong. The girl said they had changed hotels but forgot to tell me. With the postman's directions I set out through the hectic traffic and found my way to the west side, then to a street he had named that might take me north toward the body shop. I finally found the body shop but there were no signs indicating a car rental agency. I pulled in anyway to see if anyone there could help and upon turning into the parking lot I discovered a very small portable building on the lot with a sign saying "Rental car returns." Yes, they were expecting me and I was one hour late, but was forgiven. I asked the attendant how I might get transportation to the hotel; he kindly offered to give me a ride. Things were getting better. Upon delivery to the hotel I was delighted to find that they had reserved a beautiful suite for me. I had planned to spend the evening at the riverfront, watching the other boats and visiting my friends on the *Delta Queen,* but by then I was tired and did not want to join the thousands of spectators, moreover I was several miles from downtown with no car.

I did not feel like leaving the comfort of my suite so I went to the vending machine to get my dinner of nacho chips and packaged blueberry pie. While there I met a crew member from the *Julia Belle Swain.* Her name was Judy and she was the cruise director. Judy told me that the crew would leave for the boat at 4:30am and I would have to be in the lobby at that time to ride with them. I said, "Excuse me, but did you say 4:30am?" she confirmed that time so I ate my vending machine meal and went to bed.

The next morning I arrived in the lobby on time and found myself alone. By 5:15 the rest of the crew had sauntered in. The crew was in two shifts so I was with the morning crew. I chose to do this since mornings were the part of the journeys that would take passengers from one city to the next, instead of short dinner cruises. Judy looked nervous and could be seen flashing by as if looking for something, then she was on the hotel house phone. Someone on the night crew had gone to bed with the van key and no one knew who had it, so each one was being awakened to find the key. After it was located we proceeded to the van that had a rental trailer hooked on it for our baggage. The key to the trailer was supposed to be on the dash of the van but it was missing too. Not wanting to try to locate that key we decided to pile the luggage in the van with all ten of us. We were now quite late for the boat and the young man driving the van was trying to make up lost time. I was beginning to feel grateful for all the travel bags under, next to, and between us for added cushioning in the event of a crash.

During the ride the crew was talking about the events of the day before at Quincy, Illinois. Since there are so many passenger boats in the flotilla, some of the towns had to provide additional temporary docking to accommodate them. At Savannah, the *Julia Belle Swain* was tied off to a barge anchored with spuds. Spuds are large vertical pipes that are lowered into the riverbed, provided a stable mooring platform. The *Julia Belle Swain* had been temporarily grounded at the docking, due to the now falling river stage, but successfully freed herself, then re-tied to the barge to complete loading of supplies. A local towboat had been dispatched by someone to assist getting the *JBS* from her grounding. The towboat pilot apparently thought the steamboat was still stuck, so he came alongside, had the deckhand hook-up to the *JBS* and began pulling her backward. The problem was the *JBS* was still attached to the barge. The frantic yells from the crew went unnoticed as the barge shifted, causing one of the spuds to bend over and break some of the smokestack support wires. At the same time the *JBS* swung sideways and the paddlewheel crashed into the nearby pier, breaking some of the boards. As the *JBS* pulled away from the landing, the towboat took off to catch the barge that was now drifting down the river. Having had enough of the port of Quincy, the *JBS* headed on up the river leaving the chaos behind. That was the story told by the crew. I did hear different versions of the story from people on other boats. One of those stories, and the one most likely, was that the pilot was needing assistance and had given the go-ahead to the towboat pilot to pull, but had forgotten to have the deck hands untie the *JBS* from the spud barge.

We finally got to the Dubuque riverfront and found our next challenge. The *JBS* was gone! It could not have left without us, since the entire crew was stuffed in the van with me. Knowing that the night crew must have left it nearby, we began to drive along the floodwall, looking for her smokestacks. When we finally saw her stacks just above the 16-foot floodwall, the driver pulled off the road and onto a sandy field toward the wall. We got within 100 feet of the wall when the van became stuck in the soft sand. The watchman was standing on top of the floodwall, paying out a ladder. He said that the only way we would get on the boat is over the floodwall. We unloaded our baggage and began to climb the aluminum ladder. At the same time the watchman was sending a rope down to pull the luggage up and over the wall. Even though we were late, we were not as late as others They were waiting for a fuel truck to arrive, not having enough to make the next stop at Prairie du Chien, Wisconsin. They were also very low on food and were expecting a truck delivery of 74 boxes, which would have to be hauled over the wall.

The first thing we noticed was thousands of mayflies all over the boat. They were so thick that the deck was slippery to walk on. Mayflies emerge from hatching in the riverbed, take to the air, mate, and then die in a day or so. They were dying all over the boat. The crew was sweeping and hosing the decks, in a failed attempt to be rid of them by the time we took passengers aboard, if indeed we ever got to the public landing to pick them up.

The fuel truck finally arrived and began pumping fuel through a line that went from the truck, over the wall, along a catwalk, and onto the boat. I had been exploring the boat and planned to help the crew load supplies when and if the truck arrived. As time went on the crew began going to the sun deck of the boat to look over the floodwall for the truck. Then a towboat came by and pulled alongside the *JBS*. No one paid much attention to the towboat until a deckhand on the boat called out, "Does anyone want all these boxes or do we take them back?" The crew was delighted to find that the delivery had been sent by towboat so they would not have to carry the boxes over the wall. I was thinking that this, the missing boat, and the lost keys were probably just little glitches in communications and that the rest of the cruise would be better organized. I was wrong!

We finally had the boat ready with fuel and supplies. The decks were fairly clean of mayflies and we pulled away, heading upriver to pick up the passengers who had been waiting for two hours to board. It was a hot, humid morning and I felt bad for those folks, but they were amazingly cheerful and excited about their steamboat journey. After all passengers were on board I saw a huge difference in the crew. Now they were in their element. I was impressed by how well they all did their jobs and saw to the needs of the passengers.

In fairness to the crew I should mention that overnight trips are not what they are accustomed to. They normally operate out of LaCrosse on short day and evening excursions, so this was a new experience for most of them. Once the boat was underway with a complement of passengers, they were very well organized and pro-

Photo by Author

Lee Havlick

fessional. We eventually caught up with some of the other flotilla boats and had a very pleasant cruise to Prairie du Chien. Considering the limited working space in the kitchen, the food was excellent. On a small boat like the *JBS* the crew must be multi-functional and they did a fine job. One gentleman name Lee Havlik was exceptionally versatile. Lee was officially the assistant engineer. He was constantly monitoring the steam pressure (he called it the steam-o-meter) and oiling the cylinders. Lee could also be found in the dining area entertaining passengers with corny jokes, playing the banjo, harmonica, or guitar. The passengers loved Lee, who could do just about anything

on the boat; however, I will say that he might have added to their steamboating experience by not singing to them.

That afternoon we arrived at Prairie du Chien one hour late. As we passed under the bridge and island the *JBS* turned right into the harbor, where huge crowds of Grand Excursion sightseers were on hand to greet the boat. The captain did the steamboat version of a fly-by. He ran the boat close to the long dock full of people at full speed, blowing the whistle, while everyone waved and cheered from the boat and shore. He then did something that I had never seen a steamboat do. After passing the onlookers he turned the boat around to land. That is not particularly unusual, but he maintained full speed with full right rudder. The little steamboat dug into the water hard and listed so much on the port sided that water actually came over the freeboard and onto the deck. Most passengers were holding onto something but didn't know enough to be concerned. I will admit that leaning a narrow beamed, flat-bottomed, top-heavy boat, with a three-foot draft over that far made me a little nervous. I was relieved when the *JBS* straightened out and came in for a landing at the dock.

Since we were late arriving, it was necessary for the crew to hustle the passengers off, clean the boat, and then get the new passengers on as quickly as possible for a dinner cruise. The debarking passengers had buses waiting to take them back to Dubuque. The crew worked quickly and efficiently. I tried to stay out of their way and could only do that by continually moving around the boat. I was tired and decided not to join the evening crew for the dinner and moonlight cruises. All I wanted was a shower and a soft bed. The day crew finally got finished with their duties and it was not until I saw them leaving that I realized that I must catch up with them or be marooned on the boat until midnight. I caught up with them and rode in their van to a motel. It was not until then that I found out that it hadn't been necessary for me to go with the regular crew at 4:30am that day, but could have ridden with the entertainers and pilots at 6:00am. I would remember that the next day.

The next morning we arrived at the boat for the 7am departure from Prairie du Chien to LaCrosse. My duties on the boat were to do a Riverlorian chat during a meal, mingle with passengers, answer questions, and make announcements of interesting sights along the way. When the passengers boarded I saw a lady who looked familiar and after she spoke to me I found that she recognized me. She was an author whom I had met before. She boarded the boat with a large supply of her books and had arranged to have them sold in the onboard gift shop. We chatted for a while and she mentioned that she too would like to make some announcements about things she was familiar with. That was fine with me and I told her that I would be happy to assist in any way I could.

As soon as the boat was underway, she went into action. She was on a mission to sell books and tell everyone everything she knew. She made announcement after announcement on the public address system about anything that came to mind. When I make announcements I usually only will talk about something people can see. This lady was going into long detail about the most insignificant things. It didn't take long for comments to surface from passengers that they wished she would shut up so they could enjoy watching the river. She went on and on and on. I believe that most passengers, crew, and I adapted to blocking her out. She must have enjoyed hearing herself talk because she was the only one listening. I continued to answer questions and did my talk, but did not want to put those poor people through any more announcements. She did hint that she would enjoy taking part in my scheduled talk but that is where I drew the line and did my thing solo. Other than the annoying author, the trip to LaCrosse went very well and the weather was perfect. We arrived with happy passengers, as the crew again began to prepare for the evening cruises. The hotel was within walking distance of the boat landing, so I did not have to endure another van ride.

LaCrosse had a huge River Fest at the same time as the Grand Excursion, so the riverfront was very busy with venders and rides. I took a pleasant walk through the festival that evening and enjoyed the laser light show. LaCrosse is a beautiful city with a park-like riverfront second to none. The next day would be a little different. The *JBS* would deadhead to Lake City, Minnesota. That meant that there would be no passengers. It also meant that I could get to sleep in the next morning, and I did. The boat would need only the navigation and engineering staff to take the boat to Lake City, so the rest of us would take the van and meet them there.

That sounds simple enough, but it didn't turn out quite that way. I received a call from the *JBS* office with a message that the crew van would leave much earlier and that they would be picking me up at 10:15am (instead of 1:30pm). I was actually surprised that they remembered to call me. The reason for the change was that the boat was near Wabasha, Minnesota and needed to take on fuel. We needed to hurry to Wabasha to get on the boat before it headed for the busy port of Lake City.

One of the problems we encountered was getting the van to and from the boat during the Grand Excursion, through the crowds and traffic. It made some sense to get on at Wabasha where the flotilla was not having activities that day. I hurried to pack and waited at the hotel entrance for the ride. An anticipated fifteen minute wait turned into forty-five minutes. When the van finally arrived and loaded me and my bags, the girl driving sped out of the parking lot and turned a sharp corner, forgetting about the trailer attached to the van. I don't know how that trailer hitch held after jumping the tall curbs, but she was in a hurry to catch the boat and would not waste time stopping to check it.

As we pulled onto a very hilly and curvy two-lane highway, I again felt endangered by the ride. The brakes were bad on the old van, so it shuddered violently during downhill attempts to slow-down or stop. I hung on to my backpack for crash protection, having left my large bag and computer case onboard the boat. During the ride, one of the crew mentioned that a large rat had been spotted in the bar of the boat. It was discussed briefly and quite casually as though it happened often. The mate said that he would put Vinny on the mission of killing the rat, since there was not much else he could do right. The others agreed the Vinny was the right choice for this search-and-destroy mission. We finally reached Wabasha to discover crowds, traffic, and many blocked-off streets. After several attempts to get the van to the river, the driver flagged down a policeman patrolling in a golf cart. He escorted us to the riverfront, opening the barricades along the way.

We discovered two things upon arriving at the riverfront. First, there were indeed activities and other riverboats at Wabasha, and that the *Julia Belle Swain* was nowhere to be found. Once again, we could not find our boat. There is no flood wall at Wabasha so it was easy to see that the *JBS* was either late or had left without us, since we were one hour late getting there. I was surprised to find that they have no cell phone on the boat because Judy, the cruise director, had to call the office in LaCrosse. Someone in the office told her that the *JBS* had just come through a lock a few miles down the river and would arrive soon to fuel and pick us up. I was relieved that she had not left without us, so that we would not have to make another frantic race to the next town in that van. It was very hot at Wabasha with no breeze.

There are a few small trees along the riverfront, but the little shade they provided was taken. While waiting, I decided to seek shade elsewhere and watch for the boat. Finally I found a little shady spot away from the crowd. It was a good decision to find a comfortable spot because the few minutes that we expected to wait for the *JBS* turned into two hours. The lock we had been told that she was just leaving was actually the second lock down the river, resulting in the boat having yet another lock to pass through before approaching Wabasha. She finally came around the bend and I hurried back to the landing to get aboard.

Passenger vessels always notify a town that they are arriving to insure that a landing spot is provided, particularly for the well-organized Grand Excursion. However, the officials in Wabasha had no idea that the *Julia Belle Swain* was to arrive there. Security had been set up for the arrival of another boat in the flotilla, so they were upset to see the *JBS* coming in, unannounced, along with a tanker truck to fuel us. The landing barge was roped off and the officials would not allow us to go to the boat. We had no official badges, credentials, or anything else to prove we belonged to the boat. All crew members were supposed to have a badge but no one did. It was not until the pilot came off the boat and vouched for us that we were allowed to pass. The fuel truck then hooked up and the crew began making ready for our passenger pick-up at Lake City.

I was having coffee and thankful that I was back on the boat again when a young deckhand sheepishly said in passing, "Oh, sorry about your baggage." When I asked what he meant by that, he told me that my bag had got a little wet when he used a fire hose to get rid of mayflies. I went to my bag to find it completely soaked. Not only was it wet, but so was my laptop computer bag. My first concern was the computer. The outer pockets of the bag and papers in it were very wet, but fortunately the computer itself was still dry. I then unzipped the bag with my clothes and some printed material, which was soaked nearly all the way through. I can't imagine how anyone could hold a fire hose on a large travel bag without recognizing what it was. Shirts, pants, underwear, socks, and many other things were wet and I had no way to dry them. This was not a good start for the day.

After finally getting underway to Lake City, Minnesota, the pilot pushed the boat's engines hard at their maximum rpm. The *JBS* is a fast boat and we were making good time. With no passengers aboard, some of the crew was relaxing. I had taken some of my wet clothes from the bag and hung them on equipment around the main deck, but after donating two shirts to the river, via the wind, I put them back. Lake City is located on the western shore of Lake Pepin. They have little mooring space for big boats so they also had a spud barge along the bank. The *Delta Queen* steamboat was on one side of the barge and we landed on the other side. After landing only thirty minutes late, the passengers for the evening cruise began boarding. I made a brief visit to see friends on the *Delta Queen* but wanted to make sure I got back on the *JBS* before she left. I just knew that they would not notice me missing. Poor Judy, the cruise director, was in a constant state of anxiety about everything. She was doing her best, but the lack of organization and communication was getting to her. One time I advised her to just stop and breathe to calm down. It didn't help much. This was only her fifth day on the job.

The dinner cruise went very well and, as usual, the crew work flawlessly seeing to the needs of the passengers. Upon arrival back at Lake City, there were more people ready to board for a moonlight cruise. I would have been happy to stay for that cruise and just roll up in a blanket to spend the night on the boat when it docked. I would have had no terrifying van ride or the frenzy of getting a room key. I would just curl up on a lounge and be perfectly happy, except that the boat had no shower. Given that, I skipped the moonlight cruise and rode with the day crew to the motel, only to learn that there had been a last-minute change in plans. We would not be staying in the motel in Lake City. We would drive to Red Wing, Minnesota, to spend the night, and then drive back to Lake City in the morning for our cruise to Red Wing. I am not sure why the change was made, but I suspect that the owner was getting over-budget and changed the reservations to a cheaper hotel. Most of the crew shared rooms, but I was provided a private room. On the way to Red Wing, Judy told the four of the crew members that the air conditioning was not working in the room reserved for them. They were not happy about it, and I don't blame them. After all, they were four to a room and they worked hard all day, so I gave them my room and took theirs. It wasn't that bad and the motel manger provided me with a fan.

We were told that we must be in the motel lobby by 4:30am the next morning for all crew. That morning we were all there except one. The fellow who told us to be there at that time, and who was to drive the van, was not there on time. He finally showed up at 5:15am to discover that the van key was missing again, so they went through the routine of waking up the night crew to locate it. After another exciting van ride back to Lake City we arrived late, but the crew had the boat ready in time for the passengers. Judy had apparently had enough and quit without notice. I think she made a good decision, for her sake.

This leg of the Grand Excursion took passengers to Red Wing. The cruise was great and it was fun being part of the flotilla with the other paddlewheelers and pleasure craft. Upon our arrival, I had expected them to dock the boat at the downtown landing that I had been to many times on other boats. The *Delta Queen* was in that spot so we went on to a small boat harbor, just north of the city. The *Celebration Belle* and the *Spirit of Peoria* had arrived ahead of us and were landed along the shore, next to a road. Our spot was between the two boats. A towboat was there to assist us in making the tight landing. The towboat came along the starboard side, hooked up to one of our kevels and began to turn the *JBS* around toward the landing. There was a problem! The freeboard of the towboat was lower than that of the *JBS*. This caused the towboat's deck to slide under the *JBS* deck and become wedged. It also put a lot of pressure against the hull of the *JBS*. This was not a good thing, so they unhooked and backed off, leaving the *JBS* to drift in the harbor toward the small boat docks (filled with boats).

Quick action had to be taken. The pilot of the towboat headed back for another hookup while the mate hung boards over the side of the *JBS* for the tow to push against. At the same time the pilot of the *JBS* asked all passengers to move to the starboard side of the boat. The passengers and crew responded, causing the boat to list on the starboard side, which allowed the freeboard of the two boats to match. Everyone stayed in position while the towboat hooked up and carefully maneuvered the *JBS* into her landing. It was a tense few moments, but everything turned out fine and the passengers were pleased with the excitement, and their part in helping. Upon landing and debarkation of the passengers, I waited for the crew to finish with their duties and catch a ride to a motel. They had a lot to do, and had the usual confusion. After waiting so long and enduring the trauma of stuffing our baggage and people in the bus (they forgot to bring the trailer), I was anxious to get past another frightening van ride and to a hotel. What I didn't know was that they had changed motels once again. The one we were staying at was only about three blocks away. Had I known that, I would have walked to the motel two hours earlier. The motel had no restaurant and was not near any place to eat. The young crew had decided to take the van to find a pizza and beer place. I was invited but wanted no more van rides than necessary. I had another vending machine meal and relaxed.

The next morning I chose to walk to the boat. The trailer had arrived to put the baggage into, so I still had to get to the parking lot early and put my things into the trailer. I was hoping that they would not lose the trailer again before getting my things to our next and final destination of St. Paul. I arrived at the boat at 5am, just in time to see something very encouraging. The *Mississippi Queen* was passing the harbor, on her way to St. Paul. At least I now knew that I would have a ride back down the river. I longed to get aboard a boat with a well-organized staff and no land travel each night. The *Mississippi Queen* is an overnight passenger boat, so passengers and crew have accommodations. At 6am I saw the *Delta Queen* go by. With the *Mississippi Queen* now having caught up, the flotilla parade in St. Paul would be complete. That was the part of the journey that I was most looking forward to.

With all passengers aboard, the *Julia Belle Swain* departed Red Wing on time. The plan was to join the flotilla by 3pm, just outside of St. Paul. We had a great cruise and made our rendezvous ahead of schedule. Seeing all the paddlewheelers and other boats gathering for the parade was a beautiful sight. The Grand Excursion officials organized the parade with the smallest boats to start the parade, followed by the larger boats. The last boat in the parade would be the *Mississippi Queen*, being the biggest boat of the flotilla. The *JBS* was second in line, following a much smaller sternwheeler owned by the Audubon Society. The river was to be closed to all other traffic. Much radio communication was required to get the boats lined up before the approach to the city. Hundreds of pleasure craft were escorting the flotilla boats. Each flotilla vessel was also escorted by two official Grand Excursion cruisers. It was an exciting time.

At a pre-determined point all pleasure craft were to drop off fromthe flotilla, since the river would be closed to them a few miles up the river. That was when things got crazy. The people in the boats were de-termined to get past the large boats and ahead of the flotilla. There were cruisers, cigarette boats, and ski boats zigzagging all over the river. The river was being churned up so bad by their wake that pontoon boats

Photo by Author

Flotilla

were nearly capsizing. Some of the fast boats were passing us and the official boats at 50 and 60 mph. The officials in the escort boats were trying to make people slow down by screaming on their bullhorn and waving a slow-down motion. It was useless, as the idiots driving those boats ignored them, or waved back, or flipped them off. The official boats had an official Grand Excursion flag but were not the law and boaters knew that they did not have to obey them. They got too close to the big boats, cut across the bow of other boats, and ran much to fast for the amount of traffic on the river. You might expect this kind of thing from one or two morons, but there were dozens of them creating a dangerous situation for everyone. It was not until they saw the flashing blue light of a patrol boat coming down the river toward them that they slowed down or turned back. I felt ashamed of their behavior on behalf of all sensible river-boaters.

We passed the *Delta Queen* and *Mississippi Queen* that were pulled over to allow smaller vessels to get in their places in line. Once all vessels were in their correct position the Grand Excursion parade finally began. That is when a sudden thunderstorm hit. It came down hard for a while but then settled into a steady rain. However, the rain did not dampen the spirits of those attending the event. Thousands of people lined the shores and bridges. The hearty people of St. Paul warmed my heart by enduring the weather to watch the flotilla that day. At one location, a huge seating stand faced the river, full of well-wishers. A voice on a loud speaker announced the boat, and they even had a radio broadcast from the pilothouse of each boat so that the captain could share his thoughts, while passing by. Rain or not, it was a great parade that ended at a bridge with a large banner that read "Welcome to St. Paul...We've waited 150 years for this". That message was sincere since the original Grand Excursion in 1854 arrived one day early and nobody was there to greet President Fillmore and the original flotilla. The only ones along the riverfront were swindlers and thieves, so St. Paul has always wanted a chance to redeem itself. They did so in grand fashion. I was captured by the charm of the city and her people.

Now that we had made it to St. Paul, the pilot took the *JBS* to a landing across the river from downtown. They had two more evening cruises, then several day cruises beginning the following morning. As usual I chose not to take the night cruises but did have a plan for the next morning. I would board the *JBS* a 10am for a harbor cruise and during that cruise would be dropped off at the *Mississippi Queen*. I had to go on duty on the *MQ* that day so it would be convenient to pull alongside, and I would simply go from boat to boat. But before all that could happen, we would have the typical challenge of getting from the *JBS* to our lodging. By then I did not expect it to be easy, particularly given our past difficulties and the thousands of visitors at St. Paul. My expectations were correct.

The night crew came aboard after landing and preparations commenced for the next cruise. I waited inside toward the bow of the boat, watching for the day crew to leave. I just knew that they would suddenly exit without thinking about me, so I stayed on watch. Just as I expected, they began to leave the gangway without me. It was still raining so I assumed we would go directly to the van and leave. I was wrong. The van was there, but where were the keys? After finally locating them, we piled our bags into the trailer and got into the van and waited for our driver. It was getting very uncomfortable with a dozen wet people, so some of us chose to stand in the rain. The young crewman finally showed up, saying that we could not cross the bridge to get to the hotel. The road had been closed for the Grand Excursion. He could drive us to the bridge but we must walk up many steps and across the bridge, then down some steps, then three blocks to the hotel, in the rain, carrying our bags. As we attempted to leave the dock area we were stopped by a rent-a-cop who said we could not leave. The only road out of the landing area was closed and it was now full of pedestrians. The frustrated young crewman driving the van called back to his boss in the rear of the van, "Hey, Eric, is it ok if we run people over?" Eric said "Hell, why not!" The driver then said to the rent-a-cop, "My boss said it was ok to run people over, so get out of the way." He started moving the van forward and the irate lady had no choice but to move. He proceeded slowly through the crowd. I was happy that people moved and were not run over.

After finally getting through the crowd we entered a parking lot with many buses and noticed that one of the buses had a sign reading "downtown". Eric jumped out of the van and had a conference with the bus driver. He came back with good news. We could take the bus to the hotel. We quickly gathered our things and boarded the bus. The driver said that he had a schedule to keep so when we got to the hotel, we would have only three minutes to get off and retrieve our bags from the baggage compartment. This was a much better plan than the long walk in the rain. Upon arrival, I tried to confirm the schedule for tomorrow, but without Judy there seemed to be nobody in charge. I had the 10am schedule so I decided to forget the hassle of catching the van in the morning and just take a taxi. After a restful night, I woke up at 7am and looked out the hotel window just in time to see the *Julia Belle Swain* heading down the river. At first I thought she may be going to a fueling dock, but then I saw people on the boat. Many people. The last I had heard was that the 10am cruise was the first one for the day. I thought about what to do and made a decision.

There was no way that I was going to try to get to the *JBS* on the chance that she might be where I could get to her, much less be able to drop me off on the *Mississippi Queen* on time. I had to be aboard the *MQ* by noon. The *Mississippi Queen* was only a few blocks away, so I decided to walk to the boat and forget about even trying to do any cruises that morning on the *Julia Belle Swain*. I found out later that I had made a good decision since the *JBS* had changed its schedule and did not arrive back in St. Paul until 2pm.

The Grand Excursion was a great event to take part in, and the *Julia Belle Swain* is a wonderful little steamboat. Most of the crew was green, and so it is understandable why there might have been some organizational problems, particularly for a multi-day special event. As I mentioned earlier, while the boat was underway the entire crew was magnificent. It was the land part of the journey that was difficult and at times humorous. I admit that I wasn't

Photo by Author
The *JBS* off on another adventure

pleased about my bags being soaked with a fire hose, or the aggravation of getting to and from hotels, or the lack of organization. For me it was the spectators who made it great and worth the hassles. Hundreds and sometimes thousands of people lined the shores to watch the flotilla as we passed by the towns. They waved and we waved back. I knew that most of those wonderful people would love to have been on the boat. At one point during the parade, I noticed that most of our passengers had become tired of waving and had stopped. I got on the microphone and reminded them that many of those people had traveled great distances, waited for many hours, and endured the rain to wave to us. Those people and the cities were celebrating their river heritage and we were making history that day. I asked them to switch arms if needed but keep on waving back. It was the least we could do in return for their honoring. They began waving again. I hope they don't wait another 150 years to celebrate this event again. I suppose that a 200-year celebration will be appropriate. If so, I will be back at the age of 107. Well, maybe I won't be back, so I am grateful to have been a part of this event. It is now part of me.

Chapter 22

Potpourri

This chapter is a mixture of short stories that do not have enough content to make a chapter but make up for it in interest or humor. This is fitting for my nature because as Riverlorian I include personal stories that relate to the main subject of my talk. Something in the talk will remind me of an experience or story, then that may lead to another story. Following are six true stories from my days on the river.

Dover Fisherman

I was on a steamboat trip to Nashville, Tennessee, when we made a scheduled stop at the tiny town of Dover, Tennessee. The landing at Dover is somewhat precarious, due to the narrowness of the river and a sort of a cape that has formed below the bridge. We landed the boat at the public boat-launching ramp by literally sliding sideways against the bank and tying off to trees, (chokin' a stump). After the passengers left the boat I noticed a man fishing along the shore near the stern of the boat. I took a walk along the shore and approached him. We engaged in conversation about fishing, which of course led to our telling some of our finest fishing lies. He was not doing well that day and alluded to the possibility that the big steamboat sitting there was scaring off the fish. After a brief chat I left him to his fishing and went back to the boat. A couple of times during that morning I yelled to him from the deck, asking if he was doing any better yet. The response was always negative. At noon the boat was set to leave Dover. The passengers were accounted for and the deckhands unhooked the lines. I was back on the starboard deck as the boat began to back out, and saw that the fisherman was finally catching something. He was up on his feet and his pole was bent. The man was struggling with what seemed to be a mighty big fish. He looked very excited and I hoped to see what he caught before the boat got much further away. Then I realized something that had not occurred to the fisherman yet. What he had hooked and was attempting to land was our 285-foot steamboat. He did not have heavy enough line to bring that catch in. The last I saw of him, he was standing there with a bewildered look on his face and a broken line hanging from his pole. I was sure that he would have the best story about the one that got away while hanging out with the boys in the tavern that night.

John Deere in the River

While cruising the rivers on the steamboats, I often make announcements on the public address system when I see interesting sights along the way. I try to make certain that what I announce is correct, so I look very carefully. Sometimes it is difficult to be accurate with the distances we are from those points of interest and still allow time for people to go outside to see it. I always hate it when I announce an eagle sighting only to discover that it is actually a buzzard. One day we were cruising up the lower Mississippi River during a period of high water. The river was over the bank but the levee was keeping the water from flooding adjacent roads and homes. I was doing my usual scanning ahead with binoculars and spotted something that was very unusual. I waited until we got a little closer to make certain that what I thought I saw was true. Yes, it was true! A large John Deere tractor was going up the river at a slightly slower speed than we were going. With the steamboat's slow speed we do not overtake many vessels, and I had never known us to overtake an upbound tractor. This was worth announcing!

I grabbed my wireless microphone, flipped the appropriate switches for boat-wide announcements, and headed outside on the deck to do a play-by-play. I had it all figured out by the time I was ready and made the following announcement to the passengers: "Ladies and gentlemen, this is Jerry, your Riverlorian. Just ahead we will be overtaking a northbound John Deere tractor along the starboard side." Announcements will sometimes go unnoticed or gain limited interest, but this one got their attention and people poured out of the cabins onto the starboard deck to see it. I explained that since the river was over the banks, automobiles could not reach the wharf boat that the tractor was heading for. It was pulling a trailer but nothing was in it, which led to the theory that the tractor, with its high ground clearance, was actually on a flooded road and was being used to bring supplies and crew to the wharf for the workboats that were tied off to it. The workboats would then make the deliveries to the towboats. There was a towboat pushed into the bank a few hundred yards above the wharf, which supported my theory. When the tractor got to the wharf, the operator handed a box to a man on it.

My play-by-play continued: "That box is probably a hot part that the towboat ahead needs badly and they will transfer the box to the workboat to be taken to the towboat." I was delighted to see the man hand off the box to the pilot of the workboat. The workboat then released from the wharf and sped off toward the towboat, just as I had predicted. Passengers were impressed with my knowledge of what was going on and were wondering what would be so important that they would go through so much trouble to deliver. Well, I explained, "Could be a water pump, or about anything to keep the towboat operational." The workboat reached the towboat at just about the same time we passed alongside, and we could clearly see the workboat pilot hand off the box to a deckhand. The box was large flat in shape, which eliminated the water pump theory. I then said, "Maybe some 'O' rings, or gaskets," A second deckhand walked quickly to the man holding the box and opened it. He reached in and pulled out the first slice of pizza from the box. Yes, it was a pizza delivery. Well, deckhands need fuel too!

Tater Gun

I mentioned in another chapter about steamboat passenger's comments. One that I will refer to was when a man suggested that we have skeet shooting off the back of the boat like the big cruise ships do at sea. This brought up a discussion that offered a river alternative to such an activity. Back home in Indiana many of us have a homemade device that shoots potatoes. Without going into great detail about the construction of a "*tater gun", it is made of

Photo by Author

Tater Gun

PVC plumbing pipe, with a potato stuffed into the barrel, hair spray in the chamber and a gas grill igniter for spark. It is great fun and will propel a well-aimed potato a great distance. I am certain that the wildlife has no objections to it as they benefit from the delivery of potatoes into the woods and the river. The potatoes come out of the tube at a high velocity so we tater gun owners are as careful with it as we would be with any firearm. The device is fun and has no practical use; however, I did discover a use for it one day on the Ohio River.

A friend and I were traveling on the river in his large cruiser. The boat has twin engines with a V-hull and creates a very large wake, which attracts another kind of boater. While cruising along we would often find ourselves in the company of people riding wave-runners. They love a boat like the one we were in because of the huge wake it leaves. They have great fun running behind the boat, zigzagging and jumping the wakes with their highly maneuverable watercraft. I really don't mind if they do that. They are having a good time and as long as they keep a safe distance, there is no problem. But something happens to many people who ride those machines. Those who may be perfectly sensible otherwise seem to lose that part of their character when they mount a wave-runner or jet ski. They cannot be content for very long with staying behind a boat. The first thing they try is to get annoyingly close to the prop wash. Stage two is cutting across the bow dangerously close. Foolhardiness then sets in as they see how close they can come to the boat before steering off.

That evening we were cruising near Evansville, Indiana. The sun was setting on the beautiful river while two young men on wave-runners decided to try stage one. They then went to stage two and didn't take long to start their rascally behavior of buzzing the boat. Having had enough, I flagged them off by waving my hand toward them, indicating that they should steer away and stay away. One of the men responded with some sign language of his own, which was an unkindly message with one finger. Their harassment continued, so I reached for my tater gun. Now, I don't want to hurt anyone, but I have no problem with giving someone a good scare when deserved. I pushed a potato into the barrel at the cut end of the pipe which made a nice tight plug of it, cutting the potato the size and shape of the inside of the barrel. They could see I was doing something but had no clue of what it was. I then opened the back of the chamber and injected the propellant, which was some cheap hair spray. I raised the loaded tater gun up at just about the time that I could see the whites of their eyes. They must have figured out that I had some sort of weapon, since they began to abandon their final approach. I fired a single potato round, making certain that I aimed well ahead of them. It was a glorious shot that left a tracer behind it in the evening light. That potato had made a very tight plug that sounded like a shotgun, and when it hit the water it sent up a geyser like a cannonball might make. Both the two fellows headed off at full speed into the sunset. I don't think they wanted to wait for me to load up another round. Who knows? Maybe those young men learned a lesson that day.

*Disclaimer: Tater guns, often called "spud guns" may be illegal in some states. Neither the author nor the publisher encourages the building or use of this device. We accept no responsibility or liability for damage, injuries or death that result from a reader building or acquiring this type of gun or any other device that propels potatoes.

Missed the Boat

We have all heard the term; "you don't want to miss the boat." We have had passengers on the steamboats that have missed the boat's departure. Some get lost and others just get carried away shopping and forget the time. When it happens, they usually call our home office, who in turn calls the boat, then calls a local contact to make transportation arrangements to the next stop or available place to land. Crew members are expected to always be aboard the boat thirty minutes before departure. When a crew member misses the boat it is taken more seriously and can result in dismissal, unless the reason is a very good one.

We were on the lower Mississippi River we had landed for the day at Baton Rouge, Louisiana. I knew of a swamp boat rental marina located nearby in a maze of bayous, which I had always wanted to explore. Since we would be at the port all day and most of my duties are performed while underway, this provided an opportunity to rent a boat and take photos of alligators. I arranged for the rental in advance and anticipated a great day in the swamps. The day before my planned expedition, I mentioned it in the officer's mess. A fellow officer asked if he could go with me. I hesitated to take someone with me, particularly a city guy like him. But he was persistent and offered to pay half of all expenses. That offer made his plea more interesting, as the airboat was quite expensive to rent, required a hefty damage deposit, and it would be an expensive taxi ride. I agreed to take him, but disclaimed any responsibility for him being eaten by a 'gator. We left the boat early and arrived at the dock. The man at the dock was friendly enough, but I had to convince him that I was a veteran boater and had a good sense of direction. There would be no need for me to stay in the main lake to keep from getting lost, as I could find my way back. He then explained the charges that would be made if he had to come looking for us. No problem!

We set off in the flat-bottomed airboat. I had never operated this type of vessel before and discovered that steering it was somewhat like steering a car on ice. However, it didn't take long to get used to it and before long we were in the bayous looking for alligators. The old boat was pretty beat up but seemed to be running good, although it was very noisy. The engine was directly behind me with a six-foot propeller blasting us forward. I soon learned that airboats do not handle wakes very well. When I pulled back on the throttle while making a sharp turn, our own wake caught up with the boat broadside and rocked the top-heavy vessel terribly. On we went twisting between cypress trees, enjoying the beautiful plant life and wild-life, but no alligators. Then I thought I saw something some distance away on our port side. My attention toward the movement distracted me just long enough to engage in the first serious problem. The boat came to an abrupt stop with a precarious upward angle toward the bow. I had run up onto a cypress knee (stump). The supposedly flat-bottomed boat had a rake on the bow that allowed it to climb the stump. Not good!

My first thought was to back off the stump. But that would not work, since the boat had no reverse. I increase the throttled and turned the rudders hard right, then hard left, hoping to slide off the stump sideways. All that accomplished was to spin the stern around the stump with the bow remaining stuck and serving as a pivot point. It looked like the only way to get the boat off the stump was to get into the swamp and push it off. When I suggested that, my friend Michael turned white and muttered something about alligators. We had seen none yet, unless the movement I had seen was one. My mission on this excursion was to see alligators, but now I had lost my curiosity about that as I slipped into the water, hoping there would be none in the neighborhood. I instructed my heavy friend to go to the stern of the boat while I lifted the bow and pushed. The water was about four feet deep and very nasty with swamp stuff. The boat was stuck hard so I had him jump up and down while I pushed. The harder I lifted, the deeper I sank in the muck. I finally gave a mighty heave, timed just right with Michael's jump, and it slid into the water with a large splash. Actually there were two splashes. The first was made by the boat and the second was when Michael hit the water after falling overboard. He began to panic while trying to swim in the thick vegetation rather that simply standing up. I went to him and helped the big man back into the boat, which was another test of my strength. I was glad to get back onboard myself before becoming the main course for an alligator.

It was time to head back so I turned the ignition. The engine cranked, but wouldn't start. I tried again while adjusting the throttle. There didn't seem to be a manual choke. Not wanting to run the battery down I started the process of elimination. Fuel was spraying into the carburetor when I cranked it so it couldn't be the fuel pump. I checked for spark going to the plugs and found none, and finally traced it down to a bad coil. This was not a good thing! It was time to start paddling, or rather poling through the swamp. I knew which way to go, but also knew that we would not make it back to the dock in time to get on the steamboat before departure time. Michael tried to call the boat to tell them about our dilemma, but could not get a signal on his cell phone. Then we heard a familiar sound in the distance. It was another airboat. As it got closer I could see that two men were in the boat and I waved to flag them down. As they slowly approached we could see that they were natives of the swamp. They had guns. I heard Michael say, "Oh crap, Cajuns" in a low nervous voice. I think he had some idea that Cajuns are bad. I have been around these folks before and met nothing but fine people, and these fellows looked no swampier than us after our time in the water. But they did have big guns. They stopped and after telling them our problem, one of them agreed it was probably a bad coil and offered to tow us back to the dock. But airboats do not tow well and the going was very slow. They didn't have a very long tow line so we were being blasted by their prop wash, but we nonetheless were happy to be rescued.

By the time we got to the landing it was only thirty minutes until the *Steamboat* would depart. There was no way to get there in time. At last the cell phone got a signal and we called the boat. The chief purser answered and transferred the call to the captain. Michael explained our situation and the captain explained that the boat must leave on schedule. He then told us to find a way to get to a launching ramp about thirty miles upstream. If we made it there before the boat did, they would make a quick landing to pick us up.

Otherwise we would have to find our way to the next stop, which was Natchez, Mississippi. Upon inquiring about some sort of transportation, one of the two men who towed us offered to take us to the landing in his pickup truck. We insisted on paying him, and he replied that he insisted upon being paid. I asked if thirty dollars would be enough—one dollar a mile. The man did some quick math and figured that was only fifty cents per mile, since he would have to drive back. We agreed on sixty dollars.

Steamboats are not known for their speed and we were sure we could reach the landing before the boat, but there was still a sense of urgency to get there. When we arrived we began looking downstream for some sign of the boat. One hour passed, then two hours, and we began to wonder if we did indeed miss the boat. Finally we could see her coming around the bend. What a beautiful sight! We waved as she came closer and began to swing the stage to the starboard side to pick us up. The steam whistle blew, and I noticed that there were a lot of people on the outside decks of the boat, particularly toward the bow. The story of our misadventure had already spread through the boat and everyone turned out to welcome us back aboard. We stepped onto the stage as the crowd cheered like we were heroes returning from a mission. We didn't look much like boat officers. In fact, we didn't even smell very good, being covered from head to toe with dried swamp muck. That did not deter many people from photographing us as we embarked. We took a lot of kidding for the rest of the cruise. Michael was quite embarrassed about the whole thing, but I had fun with it. It all turned out all right. We made it back to the boat and I had got to know a couple of interesting Cajuns, but I never did see an alligator. Maybe another time!

Cruisin' the Bayous

After the failed mission of finding alligators, one might think that I would give up on the notion, and I had for a while. Time and circumstances changed all that. During my travels on the steamboats, I had met some passengers from Morgan City, Louisiana. Morgan City is located in the Atchafalaya Basin, a huge area of wetlands, rivers, swamps, and alligators. Those passengers revived my interest in the creatures and gave me the name and address of a man they knew who operated small workboats. He was not in the rental business, but provided service to the barge and offshore oil industry, and might rent a boat to me. I knew that in December 2002 I would have six days off in New Orleans. Six days isn't enough time to go all the way home to Indiana, so I thought that would be a good opportunity to take another try at seeing alligators in the wild. I really didn't want to call on this man and ask to rent a boat if he was not in the business, so I searched the internet for a rental business in the basin. There was none to be found. I could not find a phone listing for the man with the workboats, so when I got off the boat in New Orleans, I rented a pickup truck and headed for Morgan City. If nothing else, I would drive the area and get to know it better. I knew there were several places where one could go on a swamp boat charter, but I did not want the tourist version. I wanted to do it myself, or not at all.

Upon finding the wharf where Jimmy kept his workboats, I asked around and was told that he was expected in soon from a delivery in one of his boats. His fleet was not that impressive. He appeared to have three beat-up aluminum open boats full of parts and nets. When Jimmy arrived I introduced myself and told him of the passengers I met who said he might rent a boat to me. Jimmy knew the people and explained that he didn't have any kind of insurance for such a thing. But he had not exactly said no. I am not a pushy person so I said that was ok, and that I had rented a truck to go exploring the back roads if I couldn't find a boat. He looked at the shiny new Ford truck and asked if that was the truck I rented. He said that was sure a lot nicer ride than that old thing he uses, pointing at an old rusty Dodge. He said, "I'll tell you what. You buy the gas for this old boat over here and I'll use that fancy pickup truck for a few days, and we'll just call it even." I said, "You got a driver's license?" He showed it to me and we had a deal. I unloaded my stuff onto the boat after clearing a reasonable-sized area for it, and off I went in search of alligators.

The old 60-horsepower outboard ran well and I slept in the boat, but not alone. I was in the company of mosquitoes, spiders, and other night critters. It was hot and humid even during the night in December. This kind of boat travel was not exactly of the same style and comfort I had become accustomed to on the steamboats, but at least I had not run up on any stumps. I was having such a great time cruising the bayous that I didn't even care if I saw any 'gators. It was a different world and beautiful. The cypress trees, Spanish moss, glass-like water, and variety of birds were amazing. There were animals that looked like giant rats, which I was hoping were not. Instead, they were nutria, that are such a nuisance that the state of Louisiana offers a bounty on them. I met some great people who were interested in my mission and gave their advice as to where to find alligators. I got into a very nasty storm one afternoon while on the Intracoastal Waterway, which connects with several of the bayous. The wind, rain, and lightning drove me to shore and I took refuge under a pier. The boat was just narrow enough to maneuver between the supports, so I sat out the storm with the protection of the pier above me.

Photo by Author
Author on another mission

On the third day I was cruising easy in the backwaters of Bayou Lafourche when I saw something in the distance that looked like a 'gator. I backed off the throttle and headed toward it very slowly. Yes, it was an alligator lying in the shallows near a shoreline. I hadn't spooked it yet, if indeed this creature of about ten feet could be spooked. I was getting excited as I shut the engine off to sit and watch him for a while. I forgot all about getting the camera out since I was fixed on this magnificent animal. Still no movement! I thought, "This big fellow is a heavy sleeper." He was half in the water with his nostrils, eyes, and back exposed. I moved the boat closer yet, using a paddle. Still no movement! By then I was determined to see this great beast do something— anything! I was within twenty feet of it when I dipped a cup of water and hurled the water toward it to get its attention. Nothing! I noticed then that its eyes appeared sunken and there was some kind of slimy substance around it. Then I knew what was going on. I had been so excited and proceeded with such caution to find a dead alligator. That fact was confirmed when I pushed against its side with an oar and discovered that its soft belly was decomposed, and had been dined upon by other swamp creatures. I could not ascertain what might have killed it or how long it had been dead. Maybe it was just an old 'gator. I guess finding a dead gator was better than finding no gator at all. It was time to head back to Morgan City the next morning. Even though I still never found a live 'gator, I will never forget that wonderland of water in the Atchafalaya Basin. I traded the boat back for the truck, which Jimmy said helped him attract chicks, and went back to New Orleans. Frankly, I am really afraid of alligators and the idea of meeting one face to face is not my idea of a bonding experience, so I really need to just let it go and be satisfied with meeting what some folks in the bayou claim is the only kind of good alligator. A dead one!

Scooter

This story has little to do with rivers but a lot to do with freedom, of which I have a strong sense when on the rivers. I was visiting my daughter in Lexington, Kentucky, where she attended nursing school. We went shopping one evening and ended up at a pet shop in a mall. We both love critters and I came upon an aquarium with some unusual pets for sale—hermit crabs. I had never thought about crabs as loving pets, but the salesperson said they are very affectionate and very low maintenance. There were many little crabs, each inside their shells, but one caught my attention. It was moving much faster than the rest and was climbing over others that got in its way. It appeared to be on a mission, but upon reaching one end of the glass enclosure, it did an about-face to go back. It also had something unique on its shell: a barnacle shaped like a little chimney. How cute is that? I pickup it up and it showed no fear of me, as it walked right up my arm. I was sure it was saying to me, "Please take me away from this crowded place." So I did!

I bought the little hermit crab. I also bought a supply of hermit crab food, a little plastic box to carry it in, and even a book about the care and feeding of hermit crabs. I thought this would be an ideal pet to have with me on the steamboats. He would be quiet (I never heard any barking or chirping from any of them in the aquarium.) According to the booklet they would eat just about anything. No need to paper-train it. Yes, this would be a perfect pet. I named it Scooter for the way he walked, dragging his house shell with him. Hermit crabs adopt an empty shell and never completely leave it until they outgrow it. At that stage they come out and find larger living quarters. He was a friendly little fellow and never showed any aggressive behavior. He was easy to take with me because when I put him in a pocket he would back into his shell and stay there. The first time I had to fly to get on the steamboat, I put him in my pocket and nobody even knew he was there. I did not want to go through the hassle of declaring that I was carrying a hermit crab. I didn't know what the reaction would be, so I just kept it to myself. When I arrived on the boat I found a larger habitat for Scooter. It was a plastic rectangular container. He had room to roam and plenty of food and water.

The first time I brought Scooter into the passenger area of the boat I introduced him to Lisa, who managed the onboard gift shop. After her initial fright, she warmed up to Scooter and it didn't take long for her to start asking me to bring Scooter to the gift shop to keep her company. Most passengers thought he was really quite cute, while a few others were somewhat frightened. I had to be careful about that, and only let people see him who I knew were not "crabaphobic." The little chimney on his shell had a perfect hole in the middle, which made an ideal mount for those little toothpick-size flags. I would put one of those flags in the barnacle and Scooter would proudly march around waving the American flag. He was a big hit! Repeat passengers started asking to see him. Other crew would ask to let him sleep over in their rooms. Even the captain admitted that he had grown fond of Scooter. I could have left Scooter with someone when I went on vacation but chose to take him with me. After all, even a popular hermit crab needs a break, too.

On one such vacation, Scooter and I went to St. Petersburg, Florida, to visit my mother. She also fell for Scooter and welcomed him into her home. One day I decided to take Scooter to the beach. Upon finding the right spot and spreading out a blanket, I let Scooter play in the sand. He was having a great time. He was moving faster than I had ever seen him. I had to be careful that walkers and runners along the shore did not trample him. Scooter went exploring and I followed him into the grassy dunes. He seemed to be searching for something, but I assumed that he was curious about this new world he was in. Needing to go back to the blanket, I reached down for Scooter and he did something strange. He took off as fast as his little legs could take him, almost as though he was running from me. Scooter never ran from me before! I picked him up and he did something else he had never done before. He gave me a little pinch with one of his claws. What is this? He didn't hurt me, but it was strange behavior. I took him back to the blanket and placed him in the plastic carrying box so that I could rest a while without having to watch out for him. As I lay there, he withdrew into his shell and did not come out. More unusual behavior! Then it came to me. I knew what was going on. I had read that hermit crabs are not born in captivity, so any found in pet shops have been captured. When he was loose on the sandy beach and the salt water, he was home.

After witnessing how happy he was at the beach and his reluctance to be brought back to the container, how could I make him live like that again? It just didn't seem right. After all, I have such a strong sense of freedom and value it so highly, who am I to deny this creature his? My first thought was to just let him go right there, but this was not a good place. Too many people! Too many hungry gulls and too much traffic nearby! No, this would not do. I had decided to emancipate Scooter, but not there. I would do some research and find just the right place where a hermit crab would stand a better chance of survival. We went back to my mother's home. It looked to me like there was no suitable place in the St. Petersburg/Tampa area for a hermit like Scooter. There are too many condominiums, people, and traffic. I found an island on a map called Sanibel, about one hundred miles south of St. Petersburg. The next morning Mom and I set off with Scooter for Sanibel Island. Since there was a bridge to the island and much of it is state park, I felt that it might be the right place for Scooter to retire, but I would indeed check it out first.

Upon arrival at the island, we drove around it a few times looking for a place where the road was some distance from the shore. I decided on a remote area on the west side of the island. We walked to the beach and our farewell ceremony began. Scooter seemed anxious to get on with life at his new home, but was still patient with me as I took a final photo of him. As he headed off into the grassy dunes my mother spotted a crane that she was sure was looking at Scooter with a meal in mind. It was rather comical seeing my 82-year-old mother chasing that bird away. Each time it would land, she pursued it until she had determined that it was a safe distance from Scooter. We bid farewell to our little friend as he disappeared into the tall grass. I knew I would miss Scooter, but also knew that it was the right thing to do. Scooter was home. I stood there thinking that if I was a millionaire, I would travel to pet stores around the nation, buy up all the hermit crabs, and set them free.

When I went back to the steamboat the first thing that Lisa asked for was to see Scooter. At first she was upset with me for what I had done, but after explaining the circumstances, she accepted it and was happy for him. I have fond thoughts of Scooter, and am sure that he is still living the good life in his tropical resort.

Lesson Learned: All wild creatures deserve to live where they belong. I will never keep one again.

Photo by Author
Scooter's Farewell Photo

Chapter 23

Wit, Wisdom and Prose

"The river has been the most constant thing in my life. Ever changing but always there, searching for the sea. A place of rest, a place of power, a place of kindred spirits, a place of adventure. Relatively few really get to know the river and become captured by its magic and charm as I have. I am grateful."

Jerry M. Hay

"When you put your hand in a flowing stream, you touch the last that has gone before and the first of what is to come."

Leonardo da Vinci

"I started out thinking of America as highways and state lines. As I got to know it better, I began to think of it as rivers. Rivers run through our history and folklore and link us as people. They nourish and refresh us. We are a nation rich in rivers."

Charles Kuralt

"The song of the river ends not at her banks, but in the hearts of those who love her."

Buffalo Joe

"On the river we are subject to the whims of nature and the err of man."

Jerry M. Hay

"All things are connected, like the blood that runs in your family...The water's murmur is the voice of my father's father. The rivers are our brothers. They quench our thirst, carry our vessels, and feed our children. You must give the rivers the kindness you would give any brother."

Chief Seattle

"We're all like the river, we start as small waters. We gather up strength as we join with another. We grow as we go and we dance, turn and bend. Big waters await us at our journey's end."

Cathy Barton from her song
"Journey Song for Pomp"

"A river seems a magic thing. Magic, moving, living part of earth itself."

Laura Gilpin

"I have never seen a river that I could not love. Moving water has a fascinating vitality. It has power and grace and associations. It has a thousand colors and a thousand shapes, yet it follows a law so definite that the tiniest streamlet is an exact duplicate of a great river."

Roderick Haig-Brown

"No man ever steps in the same river twice, for it's not the same river and he's not the same man."

Heraclitas

"All the water below me came from above. All the clouds gave it to the rivers, who gave it to the seas, who gave it back to the clouds. And so I float on a cloud become water."

David Whyte

"Man can tinker with rivers, but never master them."

Mark Twain

"It was kind of solemn, drifting down the big still river, laying on our backs looking up at the stars, and we didn't even feel like talking loud, and it wasn't often that we laughed, only a little kind of low chuckle. Although it was wonderful to see all that water tumbling down, it would be even more wonderful to see all that water tumbling up."

Mark Twain

"Rivers are magnets for the imagination, for conscious pondering and subconscious dreams, thrills and fears. People stare into the moving water, captivated, as they are when gazing into a fire. What is it that draws and holds us? The rivers' reflections of our lives and experiences are endless. The water calls up our own ambitions of flowing with ease, of navigating the unknown. Streams represent constant rebirth. The waters flow in, forever new, yet forever the same. They complete a journey from beginning to end, and then they embark on the journey again."

Tina Palmer

"The Corp of Engineers have taken upon their shoulders the job of making the Mississippi over again - a job transcended in size by only the original job of Creating it."

Mark Twain

"I know not what streams that I will travel, nor beyond what bridges I'll be lead; But since I know that God is always near me, I'll suffer no loss, nor have any fate to dread."

Jerry M. Hay

**If I was a river...you would find
Children playing in my shallows,
Sunshine shimmering on my surface
And fine, sparkling fish for the taking.**

**If I was a river...you would find
That my channel is well marked,
My depth is dependable,
My water is not clouded
By remnants of old storms and
My banks are securely rooted with
Willows and cottonwood trees.**

**If I was a river...you would find
That my current is strong, but steady...
A safe place for you to drop anchor.**

Ann Wake to Jerry M. Hay

I am the river

I was born long ago, a child of the great melting glaciers that covered the north. As the maternal ice became smaller, I grew larger and longer and stronger. I grew not only from my maker but from my brother streams and rivers flowing from the high country rains, to join me and become one. As I searched for the sea I carried the rich land with me to deposit and create a delta that allowed me to grow even more. As I extended my reach I became restless with my course and flipped back and forth as a great serpent might, building more land with each meandering surge. While building my delta I continued to nurture it as a mother would a child by overflowing my bank with rich alluvial water, bringing renewed nutrients to the soil. My waters were life-giving blood for the land.

Over time others came to depend on me. The plants, fish, birds and animals knew me as their home. I provided for the first humans to discover me by giving them food, mud for their shelters, water for their thirst and cleansing, and even allowed them to ride on my back. These humans took no more than needed and made little difference in my being during their two thousand years with me. Other humans came from across the great sea. I also provided for their needs but they demanded more. They stripped the great forests that kept my banks strong, and then used me to carry the wood to distant places. They cleared and cultivated huge areas near and far from me that caused run-off that not only depleted the soil but dirtied my waters and hindered my flow. While I continued to carry, feed, and quench the thirst of these humans they used me as a disposal. Great cities and large factories located along my shore. I became very ill from the poisons of these places.

The humans were also not satisfied with my natural cycles that had worked so perfectly for millions of years. Levees were built to keep me from overflowing my bank. The soil then became more depleted with each year of cultivation. Sometimes I get angry and burst those levees, creating much more damage than there would have been if I was allowed to gently overflow into my flood plains. Dams were built to try to control me and extend navigation. They do that well but at a cost to wildlife and sometimes lives when I am underestimated. In only two hundred years these humans had taken my forests, altered my course, polluted my waters, killed off many of my animals, and choked me with dams and dikes and levees. The first humans learned to live within my boundaries. Even the wise beaver would thin small trees and never take them all. These humans are indeed the great exploiters of all that I offer them.

My creator made me strong and self healing. In the last half century the humans have discovered that the damage they do to me will hurt them and generations to come. My waters are getting cleaner as the pollution reduces and I flush myself clean. Forests are being replanted and soil conservation is beginning to make a difference. They continue to try to control me but in the end I will have my way and flow where I choose, long after the human efforts fail. These industrious humans will come and go but I will remain and continue my work. I am the river.

Jerry M. Hay

Source Notes

During the writing of chapters that have to do with history and legends, I have often relied upon recall from various sources over the years. Some topics are manuscripts of lectures that I have given. Over thirty years of traveling and researching rivers bring many of the events and people to mind with no direct source to relate to. Following are known sources that have been specifically relied upon for information or confirmation of details.

Books

Appleman, Roy E. 1975. *Journals of Lewis & Clark's Transcontinental Exploration.* St. Louis: Jefferson National Park Publication

Botkin, B.A. 1955. *A Treasury of Mississippi River Folklore.* New York: Crown Publishers.

Berry, John. 1998. *Rising Tide.* New York: Simon & Schuster

Doham, Mary Helen. 1981. *Mr. Roosevelt's Steamboat.* New York: Dodd Mead & Co.

Hartford, John. 1986. *Steamboat in a Cornfield.* New York: Knopf Books

Hunter, Louis C. 1977. *Steamboats on the Western Rivers.* New York: Dover Publications

McPhee, John. 1989. *Control of Nature.* New York: Noonday Press

Salakar, Gene. 1996. *Disaster on the Mississippi.* Annapolis: Naval Institute Press

Twain, Mark. 2000. *Life on the Mississippi.* New York: Dover Publications

Other Publications

Robinson, Michael. 1989. Mississippi River Commission. An American Epic, Vicksburg: U.S. Army Corp of Engineers.

Old River Control. 1993. U.S. New Orleans: Army Corp of Engineers.

Messina, Fred. 1994. Big Mama's Journey to Fate Fought to Years. Vicksburg Evening Post

Additional Sources

Old Courthouse Museum. Vicksburg, Mississippi
Delta Queen Steamboat Company. New Orleans, Louisiana
Steamboat Arabia Museum. Kansas City, Missouri
PBS documentary film. Secrets of a Master Builder

Acknowledgements

Illustrations

As noted, most pictures appearing Beyond The Bridges were taken by the author. Others include those on pages 89, 96, 97, 133, 136, and 204 provided by the U.S. Army Corps of Engineers; on page 94 by Terre Server Imagery; page 131 by Gary Lucy Gallery; pages 153, 155, 201, and 205 by the Library of Congress; pages 157 and 163 by Harper's Weekly; page 160 from the John Hartford Collection; page 196 from the Hay Collection.

Other

I would like to thank my personal editor, Barbara Huffman, for all the time she spent on this work. Not only is she a great editor, but a river historian herself, making her a valuable asset to the accuracy of this book. I also owe a great debt of gratitude to the U.S. Army Corp of Engineers for there valuable assistance during my research and for arranging tours of some of their facilities. They also provided graphics and photos that were very helpful.

The Delta Queen Steamboat Company has provided me with the opportunity to share my knowledge with passengers and also learn a great deal while doing so. They have also been supportive of this work and been the source for much information included. The multitudes of passengers have also encouraged me to publish a book about the things I talk to them about. While on the steamboats I have also had the opportunity to meet with many great authors. They are often invited on the boats as guest lecturers. My attendance at their lectures and conversations with them has been very informative and helpful to this project. Some of those include: John Marszaleck, John Barry, Stephen Ambrose, Gene Salaker, Edwin C. Bearss, Stan Garvey, and Captain Clark Hawley. Thanks to all of them for sharing their knowledge with me.

My many "River Rat" friends all over the country have also been helpful. One of them has been particularly instrumental to the writing of this book. Dennis Meng and I have traveled many rivers together and he has made many of my journeys possible. My friends at American Commercial Barge Line made possible the chapter "Nine Days on a Towboat." I want to thank them for allowing me to ride on their towboat, so that I can share it with others.

Most of all I want to acknowledge a retired riverman named Charlie Pupkies. As a child I sat on Charlie's porch, listening to his river adventures. Charlie planted the seed that caused me to want to become a riverman too. I will forever be grateful to him.